The "Weather Gods" undoubtedly cursed the Gettysburg Campaign, but they have favored scholars of the battle with this groundbreaking new study from Dr. Jon M. Nese and Jeffrey J. Harding. From Napoleon's disastrous campaign in Russia, to Eisenhower's triumph at Normandy, weather has consistently proven crucial to military operations. In this expertly woven narrative, the authors combine firsthand accounts with advanced scientific data to provide students of Gettysburg with the clearest understanding yet of the environmental impact on soldiers in both armies. Their meticulous research underscores the devastating and debilitating effects of oppressive heat, the gruelingly dry and dusty march conditions endured by the soldiers, and the torrential rains that trapped the Army of Northern Virginia along the swollen banks of the Potomac River. Nese and Harding have given historians definitive answers to questions which have endured for more than a century. Perhaps as vital a component to the outcome of the battle as the decisions made by the commanders on the field, the weather during the Gettysburg Campaign is amongst the greatest factors in understanding six of the most fateful weeks in all American history.

—Christina C. Moon, Gettysburg historian and Licensed Battlefield Guide

Dewpoints are one of the most useful yet unappreciated atmospheric measurements (by the general public). And, until now, no one has analyzed the dewpoint data during the American Civil War. There were official weather observers in the 1860s. There was also documentation from the combatants themselves—letters, journals, written by common soldiers and high-ranking officers—collected by Nese and Harding, providing a grander, richer tapestry in weather's tremendous role in the Gettysburg Campaign. In the world of Civil War history, this work is unique. There is nothing like it. A young private in the 4th Alabama Infantry might fathom the brutality that Maine troops serve with a rifle but can't grasp the depth that a sweltering Pennsylvania day can mean to tired troops, and the overall outcome of a tremendous battle. That's the glory of this book—it allows the reader to meteorologically understand what the combatants could not.

—Jen Carfagno (a.k.a. dewpoint diva) and Reynolds Wolf (history buff), The Weather Channel

Combining meticulous research with modern meteorological analysis, The Weather Gods Curse the Gettysburg Campaign *offers groundbreaking insights into the weather's impact on the Gettysburg Campaign. It's a must-read for Civil War enthusiasts and historians alike and fills a critical gap in understanding how natural forces shaped one of the pivotal moments in our history.*

—Mike Seidel, TV meteorologist

Weather profoundly affected military operations throughout the Gettysburg Campaign with rain, searing heat, muddy roads, choking dust, flooded streams and rivers and brutal humidity, yet until now, we have had only an anecdotal record of it. This is the first scientific and deeply researched examination of the weather on a daily basis. A highly original book, The Weather Gods Curse the Gettysburg Campaign *is one that anyone with an interest in Gettysburg will want to read.*

—D. Scott Hartwig, author of I Dread the Thought of the Place

Think you might know what it was like to be a soldier in one of the most pivotal campaigns in world history? Thanks to this groundbreaking work by Jon M. Nese, PhD, and Jeffrey J. Harding we are closer to finding the truth of the actual conditions on the ground for the common soldier in the Gettysburg Campaign in June–July 1863.

—Wayne E. Motts, President Emeritus & Historian Gettysburg Foundation, Licensed Battlefield Guide and coauthor of Pickett's Charge at Gettysburg *(coauthor James A. Hessler)*

PRAISE FOR
THE WEATHER GODS CURSE THE GETTYSBURG CAMPAIGN

History and weather geeks come together and rejoice! Meteorologist Dr. Jon Nese and historian Jeffrey Harding explore the unstudied-but-dominant element that shaped the physical experience of men on the march in America's most famous military campaign: the weather. Nese and Harding use overlooked historic weather data and apply tools used by meteorologists every night on the evening news: dewpoints, the heat index and even retroactive mapping of weather patterns in 1863. Nese and Harding have given us something rare: a book that sheds NEW light on the Gettysburg Campaign and the physical experience of men in a struggle for their lives and nation.

—John J. Hennessy, historian, National Park Service (retired) and author of Return to Bull Run: The Campaign and Battle of Second Manassas

Meteorologist Dr. Jon Nese and Gettysburg Licensed Battlefield Guide Jeff Harding have given us something not just new but thought provoking and, at times, shocking. We have all read pithy accounts of the weather scribbled by soldiers into a pocket diary, but how many of us can divine what a soldier meant by "hot"? In a fast-paced, conversational narrative, the authors not only explain the science of weather in a way we can all understand, but they provide the perfect blend of soldier accounts and analysis needed to take us back 162 years, and all supported by a wealth of photographs and weather charts. In short, they provide us with a "Rosetta Stone," a key to unlock the secrets of the weather during the campaign.

—Robert F. O'Neill, historian and author of Small but Important Riots, The Cavalry Battles of Aldie, Middleburg, and Upperville *and* Chasing Jeb Stuart and John Mosby: The Union Cavalry in Northern Virginia from Second Manassas to Gettysburg

Eight score and two years ago the high tide of the Confederacy crashed like a human tsunami on northern shores at Gettysburg, Pennsylvania. How did the unusually hot and humid weather before and during the battle and the torrential rains that followed feel to desperate, bloodied, and exhausted troops? This authoritative and fully illustrated volume—a collaboration between meteorologist Jon Nese and historian/battlefield guide Jeffrey Harding—provides new detailed weather reconstructions and heart-wrenching, evocative commentaries from the participants. It is a welcome and innovative contribution to Civil War literature.

—James Rodger Fleming, professor emeritus of Science, Technology and Society, Colby College

Authors Nese and Harding undertook an astonishing amount of primary research to reveal a critically understudied but fascinating aspect of the Gettysburg Campaign—how weather variables such as heat, humidity, dewpoint and drenching downpours, among others, impacted both armies. Be certain, however, this book is no dry recitation of meteorological facts. The text crackles with life as the authors explain how the atmosphere was a common enemy for officers and common soldiers as they staggered down dusty, sunbaked roads and across bullet-swept landscapes. Many of us wilt in the blazing sun when we leave our air-conditioned vehicles for a quick jaunt to visit a monument on the battlefield. Well, imagine marching for miles in a wool uniform when the heat index was 117 degrees, as it was during the opening days of the campaign!

The Weather Gods Curse the Gettysburg Campaign *presents a storm of information that truly will change how you think about Gettysburg and give you even more appreciation for the hardy soldiers who fought there. In fact, if you don't read this book, you can't fully understand the momentous Pennsylvania showdown.*

—Dana B. Shoaf, director of interpretation, National Museum of Civil War Medicine

Students of the Gettysburg Campaign generally recognize that weather conditions played a significant role in the outcome of this consequential event. Nonetheless, to date, our understanding of these circumstances lacked a detailed and coherent accounting. To remedy this void, Jeffrey Harding and Jon Nese provide a rendering that fulfills the quest to understand how weather wrought havoc that required unique and imaginative approaches to overcome. The authors offer evidence of their findings and conclusions in graphic detail. Heretofore, the effect weather had prior to, during and following the battle could well be considered the missing dimension of the Gettysburg Campaign. However, these deficiencies are amply overcome given the incisive examination presented in this study.

—*Thomas J. Ryan, author/coauthor of two books,* Spies, Scouts, and Secrets in the Gettysburg Campaign *and* Lee Is Trapped and Must Be Taken: Eleven Fateful Days after Gettysburg, July 4–14, 1863 *(coauthor Richard R. Schaus)*

Since ancient times, weather has always played a major role in military strategy, and the Gettysburg Campaign was no different, it having affected the movements of both armies to and from Pennsylvania in the summer of 1863. Jeff Harding and Jon Nese have composed a much needed and deeply detailed study of the atmospheric conditions that influenced and, at times, delayed the forces that clashed in one of the fiercest battles of the American Civil War.

—*John Heiser, historian, National Park Service (retired)*

David Donald, a noted Civil War historian, said years ago that there is nothing left to say about the Battle of Gettysburg that hasn't been said already. To his point, Gettysburg is one of the most written about battles in all of history and is certainly the most written about battle in the Americas. And yet there is one aspect of the battle and campaign that has never been fully analyzed, the weather. Weather, the lowest common denominator, the one aspect of a battlefield that both armies have in common. One army may have more men, more guns, better training, better morale, better ground, but weather is the same for both. When looking for a description of the weather during the Battle of Gettysburg, one term stands out, hot. *A member of the Twelfth Corps in describing that unit's march to Gettysburg on July 1, 1863, said, "It was a hot day. The sun was hot. The ground was hot. The breezes that fanned our brows were hot, and the men panted like dogs on the chase and sweated and sweltered through clouds of dust." That begs the question, how hot was it? In the past, to answer that question, we referred to the excellent work of the Rev. Dr. Michael Jacobs, who as a professor at Pennsylvania College in Gettysburg, took meteorological readings three times a day during the battle. He recorded temperatures in the 80s with the highest recorded temperature at 87 degrees F on the afternoon of July 3 before Pickett's Charge. But the temperature alone does not tell the full story. What about humidity and heat index? When you figure out what these were then you will know what the soldiers meant by hot. Besides using meteorological data taken from weather stations at the time to determine these factors, and in turn, how hot the weather truly felt to the soldiers, this study also explains what impact the weather had on the men and animals that were exposed to these conditions. No study of this kind has ever been attempted and by better understanding the real weather conditions, we will get a better appreciation of how these men struggled and suffered during the campaign and this important battle in American history.*

—Charles Fennel, Licensed Battlefield Guide, Gettysburg National Military Park

THE WEATHER GODS CURSE *the* GETTYSBURG CAMPAIGN

Jon M. Nese and Jeffrey J. Harding

Foreword by Carol Reardon

Afterword by Gregory Forbes

THE History PRESS

Published by The History Press,
An imprint of Arcadia Publishing
Charleston, SC
www.historypress.com

Front cover art: Watercolor by Garnet W. Jex. *Courtesy of Sharpsburg, Maryland Historical Society*.

First published 2025

Manufactured in the United States

ISBN 9781467158466

Library of Congress Control Number: 2025933731

Notice: The information in this book is true and complete to the best of our knowledge. It is offered without guarantee on the part of the authors or The History Press. The authors and The History Press disclaim all liability in connection with the use of this book.

To my father, who instilled in me from a young age a deep appreciation for history.
Jon M. Nese

To my beautiful wife Teresa, I love you beyond words.
Jeffrey J. Harding

CONTENTS

FOREWORD

At Gettysburg College's Civil War Institute in 2023, a lecture on the topic of weather during the Pennsylvania Campaign of June–July 1863 caught my attention. I felt confident that I already understood the basics. Union soldiers had described in colorful prose the soul-crushing heat that sapped both physical and moral strength on their northward march into Pennsylvania. Licensed Battlefield Guides and Gettysburg National Military Park rangers frequently cite the thrice-daily temperature readings of Professor Michael Jacobs to satisfy visitors' curiosity about the weather. Accounts of the retreat of General Robert E. Lee's defeated Army of Northern Virginia and its pursuit by Major General George G. Meade's victorious Army of the Potomac teem with horrific depictions of rain, mud and fog. But do these familiar elements of the Gettysburg story tell us all we need to know about the impact of weather on the operation of the rival armies in the summer of 1863?

In this enlightening work—a very welcome and detailed expansion of their lecture—Gettysburg Licensed Battlefield Guide Jeff Harding and meteorologist Dr. Jon Nese answer that question with a resounding *no*. In this groundbreaking analysis, they introduce us to the emerging field of forensic meteorology. Using previously unutilized meteorological records from the Naval Observatory and other archival sources, introducing us to an entire battalion of previously unrecognized weather observers and recordkeepers (many reporting directly to the Smithsonian Institution) and sophisticated computer-based modeling, Harding and Nese dig deeply into far more than day-by-day temperature and humidity readings. They apply familiar modern weather concepts such as the Bermuda High and the heat index to describe not just the weather conditions but why they developed and how they affected both the actions of armies and the lives of the individual soldiers who marched in their ranks. They provide essential data compiled from an extended examination of weather trends over decades to demonstrate with precision that late June 1863 was not only uncomfortably hot but also dangerously so in unprecedented ways. Similarly, they use their meteorological data to explain both how and how much the rains that fell after the battle triggered the expansive and localized water rise along the Potomac River that put the safe evacuation of Lee's army at such high risk.

Harding and Nese's work fits squarely at the intersection of two emerging elements of Civil War scholarship. The Battle of Gettysburg can still benefit from a serious application of the methods of environmental history to add to understanding about the ways in which entire armies influenced, and were influenced by, the physical world in which they operated. Daily temperatures and humidity readings only begin to explain the implications of weather's various effects on water supply, the creation of choking dust clouds that enveloped marching columns or the comparative comfort and "breathability" of woolen or homespun uniforms. As Harding and Nese openly wonder, how might the campaign have unfolded differently if the rival generals understood the localized and episodic nature of many weather phenomena or the indicators of an approaching front that might shape plans for long marches or useful delay?

Harding and Nese's work also fits into the study of the human factors in war. The effects of heat, humidity, rain, mud and more also influenced the ability of the individual soldier to carry out his duties. Combatants respond to these environmental challenges personally, and they can do so in ways unique to each individual. Some soldiers, like Private Robert Clark of the 7th Maine, collapsed and died of heatstroke on the march into Pennsylvania; his remains rest today in a small churchyard in Maryland. But why did he die when so many more did not? Many accounts of soldiers in Brigadier General Evander Law's Alabama brigade include complaints about their lack of water on the long march to their July 2 battlefield. Most persevered and made the attack, but at least one regimental colonel fell out, a victim of dehydration (possibly mixed with an aversion to leading from the front). Why does hydration matter, and should it be more prominent in the Gettysburg story than the familiar vignette from the base of the Round Tops on July 2?

Foreword

Harding and Nese present close students of the Gettysburg campaign with a different kind of evidence-based look at how weather works and why it should factor into future analysis of the Civil War's most famous battle. Leadership matters. Decision-making matters. Logistics matter. Individual character matters. And now, weather and its related environmental factors must matter, too.

Carol Reardon
Gettysburg, Pennsylvania

PREFACE

In a quote largely attributed to Mark Twain, the age-old frustration with the weather comes to the fore: "Everybody talks about the weather, but nobody does anything about it." Doing something about the weather may be a will-o'-the-wisp, but doing something about a better understanding of the weather during a pivotal time in American history is another matter. For our purposes, though "everybody" has talked about the weather during the Gettysburg Campaign, at least to some degree, "nobody" seems to have been curious enough to delve into a book-length treatment of the subject.

That said, a few notable historians have addressed various aspects of the weather during the Gettysburg Campaign. In an article in *Weatherwise* magazine in 1960, meteorologist and weather historian David Ludlum offered the first detailed analysis of the weather of the battle and the days following. Drawing primarily from the observations of Professor Michael Jacobs in Gettysburg, plus other weather data known to be extant at the time, Ludlum described the daily pressure, temperature and rainfall patterns during the period.[1] Three decades later, author Thomas Elmore, using numerous soldier quotes and an article written by Jacobs's son in 1885, constructed a largely qualitative meteorological narrative of much of the Gettysburg Campaign for *Gettysburg Magazine*.[2]

In 2007, eminent Civil War historian Robert K. Krick's *Civil War Weather in Virginia* marked a significant stride in providing useful primary source data relevant to the Virginia theater.[3] His coverage of June and July 1863 added to our understanding of the weather facing Lee's and Meade's forces as they maneuvered before and after the Battle of Gettysburg. More recently, Kenneth W. Noe's wide-ranging tome *The Howling Storm* expanded on Krick's work by offering a comprehensive account of weather and climate during the entire Civil War, focusing on how unusual climate conditions may have affected the outcomes of battles and campaigns.[4] Interestingly, both Krick and Noe point to historian Douglas Southall Freeman's 1953 call to fill the void of information on the weather during the Civil War through a "meteorological register of the War Between the States." Freeman stated, "There are a great many days when we know nothing about the weather; we have no report of the temperature; we do not know whether the dust was rising or the mud was covering the men." He then added, "These are factors of the utmost importance and could be employed to inestimable advantage."[5] Thankfully, the aforementioned works have filled significant portions of this void.

Despite these collective efforts, much remained unknown and uncertain regarding Gettysburg's weather in 1863. For example, though Pennsylvania College's Professor Michael Jacobs recorded temperatures three times a day, even during the battle, no one had ever determined what the weather truly *felt* like at the time. For example, what were the humidity and heat index during the battle? And how was this magnified (or not) by the amount of sunshine, clouds, wind and other relevant factors? Almost every day, Licensed Battlefield Guides at Gettysburg field questions on these very subjects. Knowing it was 87 degrees Fahrenheit in the shade at 2:00 p.m. on July 3, 1863 (per Professor Jacobs), one hour prior to Pickett's Charge, is all fine and well.[6] But inquiring minds want to know more. As did we. In a July 2022 *Gettysburg Magazine* article, we began to answer some of these questions by unveiling the first-ever scientifically sound estimates of the heat index during the battle.[7]

What we learned about the weather during the battle served to only deepen our curiosity. Buoyed by a strong interest in our work within the Civil War community and among others as well, we expanded the scope of our research to include not only the period of the battle but the weather during the entire Gettysburg Campaign (June 3–July 14, 1863) as well. Interestingly, while nearly every conceivable aspect of the battle and campaign has been written about and analyzed, with new volumes added to the list annually, *somehow* the weather conditions during the campaign and battle escaped this level of scrutiny. We found much to discover and learn about the subject, and in turn, we also found quite a bit more to tell.

In one example, the heat endured by Union and Confederate soldiers in mid-June 1863, during forced marches of twenty to thirty miles per day, represents a remarkable story in and of itself. However, the typical description of "searing heat" only touches the surface. The suffering experienced by the soldiers was almost indescribable. But describe it they did. We sought to examine and validate their claims with relevant, never-before-used primary source data as well as weather "reanalysis" maps recently developed by the National Oceanic and Atmospheric Administration (NOAA). Beyond this, the weather-related circumstances of July 1–4, 1863, as revealed by additional newly discovered primary sources, represent a quantum leap in our understanding of the weather conditions the soldiers endured during the battle. Moreover, analysis of this new data offers the opportunity for a deeper understanding of how the weather may have affected the battle.

Finally, rain set in after the battle. Not just any rain—the men in blue, gray and butternut detailed "torrents"—the downfall was furious enough to significantly degrade the Confederate army's ability to retreat and the Union army's capability for timely pursuit. The rain transformed a previously tranquil Potomac River into a swollen, swift and furious barrier that threatened the salvation of Lee's retreating forces. Here again, the lack of information and data pertaining to the exact weather-related circumstances and the amount of rainfall that may have fallen at the time have perplexed historians since July 1863. This key aspect of the weather's effect on the Gettysburg Campaign demanded a full and fresh analysis using both the aforementioned previously unused data and the NOAA reconstruction maps.

In the end, perhaps the question was not *why* we decided to conduct a full-blown study on the weather between June 3 and July 14, 1863, but rather, Why not? Ben Franklin may have said it best: "It is better to be weatherwise than otherwise." Certainly, the Union and Confederate armies of the Gettysburg Campaign would have greatly benefitted from being better informed about the weather they were facing. For the most part, they enjoyed no such luxury. But today's historians do. Moreover, those who have analyzed and continue to study this calamitous period in our nation's history stand to benefit greatly from such knowledge. To us, it seems a full understanding of the weather during this period represents a critical piece of the historical "puzzle" that is all things Gettysburg. Kenneth Noe elevated the importance of the weather to that of a "third army"—in essence a third of the historical equation that allows for analysis and interpretation of events and outcomes during the war. We could not agree more. It is our sincere hope that this book offers all those with an interest in the Gettysburg Campaign, military history at large and meteorology as well a deeper understanding of the weather-related circumstances facing the men who shouldered the burden and consequences of the "searing heat and torrents of rain" during the Gettysburg Campaign. In turn, we trust this improved understanding of the weather conditions may lead to a more complete and accurate analysis of the effect of the weather on the campaign and the battle itself.

ACKNOWLEDGEMENTS

Before providing our collective gratitude to those professionals who so graciously supported our efforts, we would first like to offer a few personal notes of thanks.

A personal note from Jeff: My heartfelt thanks to my wife, Teresa, for her never-wavering support during my seven-year "obsession" with all things Gettysburg Campaign weather. Through it all, she embraced my need to dedicate untold hours to producing this work. Without her understanding of my passion for this study, none of this would have been possible.

A personal note from Jon: I owe heartfelt thanks to Gwen, my wife of thirty-one years, who always wholeheartedly supported my academic pursuits. Prior to her passing in 2021, she encouraged me to take on this project, and I am forever grateful. I also extend sincere appreciation to Debbie Donahoo, whose support and patience saw me through the last two years of this project.

We now turn our attention to those who so graciously helped both of us on this nearly decade-long journey. The list forms a virtual parade of experts, and to each we offer our most sincere gratitude.

Carol Reardon leads the aforementioned parade. Carol's historical pursuits represent a landmark contribution to Gettysburg scholarship. Thus our deep appreciation to her for honoring our request to write our foreword. Carol also, very kindly, provided a thorough review of our draft, thereby ensuring the integrity of our manuscript from A to Z. We thank you, Carol, for your overwhelming kindness.

Presenting an afterword as part of a book represents a deviation from most norms. But in this case, we felt such an addition was more than warranted, as our book covers two realms: history and meteorology. Here, Dr. Greg Forbes, former severe weather expert at The Weather Channel, honored our request. Thank you, Greg, for opining on our work and its greater meaning in the sphere of Civil War history.

Regarding the various historical aspects of our work, we extend our heartfelt appreciation to renowned artist Dale Gallon and his wife, Anne, for contributing several original sketches expressly for our book. Thanks also to cartographer and historian extraordinaire John Heiser for his remarkable contributions to this work. Our sincere gratitude to Tim and Vernell Doyle of the Sharpsburg Historical Society for graciously providing the timeless Garnet W. Jex watercolors featured both on the cover of this book and herein. We also offer our appreciation to meteorologist and historian Dr. James Fleming for reviewing our work, providing suggestions and a blurb. Thanks also to Gettysburg Licensed Battlefield Guide Dr. Charles Fennel for sharing a cold winter day with Jeff on the Confederate retreat route through Fairfield and Monterey Pass and for providing a blurb. Our appreciation extends to many colleagues who also graciously agreed to read our manuscript and/or provide blurbs: Licensed Guides Wayne E. Motts and Christina Moon; historians John Hennessy, Robert F. O'Neill, D. Scott Hartwig, John Heiser and Thomas J. Ryan; Dana Shoaf, director of interpretation, National Museum of Civil War Medicine and former editor of *Civil War Times*; meteorologists Bill Syrett, Lee Grenci, Paul Knight and Mike Seidel; and Jen Carfagno and Reynolds Wolf from The Weather Channel. Our special thanks go to Ted Leinbach, great-grandson of Julius Lineback, bandsman in the storied 26th North Carolina Infantry, for allowing us to quote from, and include images of, his ancestor's diary. Thanks also to Jeff's fellow Licensed Battlefield Guide Sue Boardman for her kindness in sharing Private John T. Mark's (147th Pennsylvania) diary with us as well as rare W.H. Tipton images. We also thank retired NPS ranger and Civil War historian Eric Campbell for providing access to a rare drawing created by the famous Civil War artist and bugler Charles Reed, who notably received the Congressional Medal of Honor for his actions at Gettysburg on July 2, 1863.

Our sincere thanks to Ashley Whitehead Luskey and the late Peter Carmichael of Gettysburg College's Civil War Institute for their belief in our work and hosting us for the 2023 CWI. We also thank the Harrisburg chapter of the Civil War Roundtable for the invitation to speak in 2024 and several members' suggestions on directions for our research. We thank Jim

Hessler of the *Battle of Gettysburg* podcast and Matt Callery of the *Addressing Gettysburg* podcast for their collective interest in and support of our work. Micah Connor of the Maryland Center for History and Culture and Paul McCardell at the Baltimore Sun fielded our questions about Baltimore-area data sources.

We thank the following who contributed images and resources from either their private collections or those of the historic groups they represent: Peter Hickok (great-great-grandson of Harrisburg weather observer William O. Hickok), Tim Snyder (including multiple images and troves of information on all things Williamsport and the Potomac River), Steve French, Sandy Izer, Rick Armstrong, Dave Mark, Rick Carlile, Jim Quinlan, Ben Ritter, Chuck LaRocca, Jerry Kleiner, Dan Burrows, Tom Desjardin, Tom Freeman and Professor Christopher Herrick.

Our gratitude also extends to the following individuals and groups for providing rare images and documents from the archival collections of their respective organizations and/or reviewing and contributing their expertise to portions of our work: GNMP staff John Hoptak (a plethora of primary source materials and corresponding expertise); Gregory Goodell and Mike Kwolek (numerous copies of rare images and shared expertise); Ronald Coddington (*Military Images* magazine); Abigail Koontz (Washington County Historical Society); Carolyn Sautter and Karen Drickamer (Special Collections and College Archives, Musselman Library, Gettysburg College); Matt Turi, Caroline Galt and Chris DuBose (UNC Wilson Library); Kay Peterson and Stephanie Kurasz (Smithsonian); Jenny Palter and Joseph Berger (Washington County Free Library); Heather Moran (Maine State Archives); Erin Patterson (Louisiana State Museum); Terry Reimer and Tracey McIntire (National Museum of Civil War Medicine); Mary Mannix (C. Burr Artz Public Library); Adrienne Smith (Gate House Museum); and Joe Bordonaro, Colin Dunn, Kerri Teske, Meg Gers, Michael Miller, Joe DiLullo, Byron Faidley, Mimi Ashcraft, Cheryl Fendrick, Nicole Molyneux, Daniel Leary, Victoria Braidotti, Adrian Vaagenes, Cheryl Custer, Carol Creager, Reverend John Schildt, Shannon Leidig, John and Dennis Frye, Tom Clemens, Tim Sheads, Tom Foley, Dr. Robert Noel, Dr. Karl A. Greene, Dan Welch, Babs Savitt, Walt Evans, Lisa Tassa, Kristin Cooper and Jennifer Roros. We also thank the staffs at the libraries and archives of Georgetown University, Brown University and Columbia University, the Dauphin County Historical Society and the Warren Heritage Society.

In the history realm, a number of colleagues graciously shared their time, documentation, research expertise and resources in support of this work. Here, our thanks go out to historian/publisher Diana Loski and Licensed Battlefield Guides Therese Orr, Jessie Wheedleton, Chuck Burkell and Roy Frampton. We also thank those who supported our efforts with their thoughtful encouragement, including FCCS Gettysburg Leadership Experience program coordinator John Regentin and all Jeff's FCCS colleagues. Thanks also to American Battlefield Trust historian Garry Adleman, actor/filmmaker Bo Brinkman and Kris Webb for their collective interest in, and support of, this work. Finally, Thomas Horn assisted with information about Michael Jacobs.

Turning to the meteorological aspects of our work, we are grateful for the many helpful discussions with other meteorology colleagues at Penn State, including Steve Seman, Ben Reppert and Dr. Kevin Bowley. Penn State undergraduate students Matthew Carlson, Jonah Hurley, Adam Thompson, Rachel Sabo and Dominic Bentley assisted with data analysis, while Penn State graduate student Garett Warner helped with initial computer programming.

Alaina McFarlane, senior hydrologist at the National Weather Service's Middle Atlantic River Forecast Center in State College, Pennsylvania, was instrumental in obtaining and interpreting Potomac River historical data. Senior service hydrologist Jeremy Geiger of the National Weather Service in Baltimore/Washington assisted as well. Mike Bilder also provided invaluable insights and access to numerous press accounts.

Sincere thanks go out to Janet Wall at the National Oceanic and Atmospheric Administration (NOAA) for providing direct access to FORTS, NOAA's historical weather database. Dr. Gilbert Compo, senior research scientist at NOAA, fielded numerous questions about the NOAA reanalysis system. Dr. Dan Vecellio at the University of Nebraska Omaha, Dr. Larry Kenney at Penn State and Dr. Ariane Middel and Dr. Jennifer Vanos at Arizona State University provided insight on the effects of heat and humidity on the human body.

Finally, we offer our sincere gratitude to the entire staff at The History Press, most especially our ever-patient and understanding editor Banks Smither, our tireless and creative publicist Jonny Foster and our world-class editor Abigail Fleming.

Our apologies in advance to any person and/or organization we inadvertently failed to mention. Suffice it to say that myriad and sundry individuals from a plethora of archives, repositories, universities, museums, historical societies and the like offered meaningful assistance in support of our research. To each we offer our ever-lasting appreciation.

INTRODUCTION

Rudyard Kipling likely said it best when he wrote, "If history were taught in the form of stories, it would never be forgotten."[8] To wit, the most successful accounts of the Gettysburg Campaign weave the facts of the battle with compelling stories in a fashion that helps readers remember the history. But to date, the full story of the impact of the weather on the entire Gettysburg Campaign remained untold. No more. Here, for the first time, we present a detailed account of this subject using a combination of previously unused primary source data and a modern weather reanalysis system. Combining the meteorology and the history of the campaign in the form of a story represented a formidable challenge, requiring us to go "inside baseball"[illegible] at times with the relevant aspects of meteorology to establish a solid foundation for what followed. Like anything worth building, be it a structure, a relationship or, in this case, a book—a solid foundation is crucial. Here, we believe the groundwork established in the first few chapters of this book allows for the storytelling that follows. And the stories abound.

For the Gettysburg Campaign novice, most of what is presented here—both the history and the meteorology—will be new. Meanwhile, those knowledgeable of the campaign will find some familiar episodes in this book. But there are some new stories for historians as well. Regardless of whether the reader is a novice or a knowledgeable historian, this book provides the first-ever thorough account of the day-to-day weather during the Gettysburg Campaign. New calculations of variables such as dewpoint and heat index are provided as part of this process. But there is more, much more. In the process of conducting our analysis, we discovered several remarkable, previously overlooked weather-related circumstances—indeed, things we never expected to find.

The aforementioned unused data represents only one part of the multistep assimilation process we used to define the weather affecting the armies between June 3 and July 14, 1863. We also employed a modern reanalysis system from the National Oceanic and Atmospheric Administration (NOAA) that allows us to reconstruct daily maps of dozens of weather variables back into the nineteenth century. Our approach also considered over 1,500 quotes on weather-related aspects of the campaign drawn from over 250 primary source accounts left by soldiers, the press, civilian diarists and others.

It is important to note that this book does not purport to be a new and/or complete account of the history of the Gettysburg Campaign and battle of the same name. That said, we do present select vignettes to demonstrate how certain historic events from the campaign relate to our findings. We do so in three primary ways: through select chapter summaries titled "Situation Reports," through narratives called "When Weather Mattered the Most" and through highlight pieces designated "People, Stories, and Matters to Remember." In each instance, the purpose is to provide context to the weather as we now understand it so that historians can better appreciate the weather's effect on the men who shouldered the burden of living through it. The Battle of Gettysburg represents an astonishing story of heroism, tragedy and sacrifice. So, too, does the Gettysburg Campaign. While many of these stories stemmed from armed conflict, numerous others emanated from forced marches made during episodes of searing heat and torrential rains. And in each case, survival remained uncertain. Indeed, many suffered terribly from these circumstances. In fact, a number died.

This book begins to unfold these stories by presenting a detailed examination of the science that serves as the foundation for the meteorology and analysis that follows. Here readers will learn the important and relevant aspects about temperature, dewpoint, heat index, wet-bulb globe temperature and more. The ensuing chapter provides a robust discussion of our various sources.

The following chapters unfold for the reader, on a day-to-day basis, details of the weather in the form of tables, graphs, weather maps and daily weather summaries (an appendix provides easy access to a generalized daily rundown of the weather affecting the armies). In turn, readers learn of the resultant effect of the weather on the soldiers who served during the campaign. Here, our "When Weather Mattered the Most" narratives examine specific episodes of the campaign when Mother Nature took a major hand in events. Examples include the horrific marches conducted during one of the harshest June heatwaves on record in the mid-Atlantic region; the lengthy forced treks that occurred on the eve of battle in weather that felt hotter than historians have previously understood; and the story of how the heat may have affected soldiers during the battle itself, most notably during Pickett's Charge (Longstreet's Assault). We also unfold for you a revealing first-ever analysis of the rainfall during the retreat and the resultant rise of the Potomac River that trapped the Confederate army for the better part of nine days. Here we reveal significant discoveries related to both the rain and the river.

In addition to these in-depth narratives, we include a variety of "People, Stories and Matters to Remember" features to provide insights into relevant weather-related human-interest aspects of the campaign. For example, you will learn the tragic story of a weather observer who lost his son in the war just miles from his home. In another case, you will find the story of a Medal of Honor recipient who saved a fellow soldier stricken with sunstroke. The focus of these stories also extends to areas such as our photo analysis of the Potomac River at Williamsport in modern times as compared to the status of the river between July 5 and July 14, 1863.

Ultimately, our book provides readers with volumes of primary-source weather data, much of which is presented for the first time. Moreover, this book includes unparalleled accompanying analysis and interpretation of this data to explain in detail the weather conditions experienced by the armies during the Gettysburg Campaign. Finally, you will learn how this new information changes our understanding of the ways in which weather may have influenced various episodes of the campaign and battle. We believe all of this offers a greatly enhanced understanding of the Gettysburg Campaign as viewed through the lens of weather as we now understand it. And in the end, we trust this work will allow you to see, with a clear eye, how *The Weather Gods Cursed the Gettysburg Campaign*.

1

THE SCIENCE

Weather 101

Some are weatherwise, some are otherwise.
—Benjamin Franklin

In large part, this book is an exercise in forensic meteorology—the scientific study of weather, applied to the process of reconstructing the meteorological conditions for a certain time and location. These days, a dense network of government and private weather observers, a quality-controlled national Storm Events database, radar and satellite imagery and computer model simulations form the foundation of any forensic meteorology effort. In the 1860s, official weather observers were few and far between—even fewer in 1863 due to the disruption of the Civil War—and radar and satellite imagery were a century away. Nonetheless, the official observations that are available, blended with soldier and civilian accounts, sound meteorological science and a modern-day reanalysis system form the backbone of our efforts to reconstruct weather conditions during the Gettysburg Campaign.

The details regarding the official weather observers and the weather variables that they measured are presented in chapter 2. Front and center is previously underutilized data from the Naval Observatory in Washington City (as Washington, D.C., was known at the time). This chapter provides the underlying science and background information needed to understand and appreciate the data collected by those observers. We begin with a description of the general flavor of weather in the mid-Atlantic region in June and July—specifically, how the time of year helps dictate the usefulness of the data at our disposal.

Temperature Considerations

In 1863, astronomical summer arrived in the eastern United States in the middle of the Gettysburg Campaign during the evening of June 21. On this so-called summer solstice, the number of hours of daylight reaches its annual maximum and the sun gets as high in the sky as on any day of the year. The angle above the horizon matters because the higher the sun in the sky, the greater the intensity of the sunshine that can potentially reach the surface.

The word *solstice* translates to "sun standing still," referring to the idea that the sun's daily trek across the sky changes slowly from day to day around the first day of summer. In fact, at any given latitude within the footprint of the Gettysburg Campaign, the intensity of sunlight at the ground at midday (assuming no clouds) varies less than 1 percent across the entire period during which the campaign was waged. In addition, the sun climbs so high in the sky around the summer solstice in the mid-Atlantic that, on any given day of the campaign, the intensity of solar radiation in the northernmost part of the theater (e.g. Gettysburg) is nearly the same as the intensity in its southern reaches (e.g. Fredericksburg).[9] Regardless of how you slice it, the proximity of the campaign to the summer solstice, and the relatively small north–south footprint of the theater in which the campaign occurred, provide a useful uniformity in incoming sunlight when reconstructing the meteorology, particularly with temperature.

These first three images, Figures 1–3, show the modern-day average high and low temperatures at many locations in and around the Gettysburg Campaign theater on June 7 (two weeks before the summer solstice), June 21 and July 5 (two weeks after the solstice). Official temperature measurements are taken in the shade, so these values do not account for exposure to direct sunlight. On each day, the north–south difference in the high temperature is generally just a few degrees, largely owing to the high sun angle. In addition, the averages tend to be a degree or two lower in the western part of the theater than farther east, attributable to the higher elevations to the west—Figure 4 shows the elevations of the observing sites. For reference, temperature decreases (on average) about one degree for every three hundred feet of elevation.

Urbanization artificially inflates the modern-day Washington values—overnight lows in June and July average about four degrees higher now than in the late 1800s, while daily high temperatures average about two degrees higher.[10] If this so-called urban heat island effect—which would not

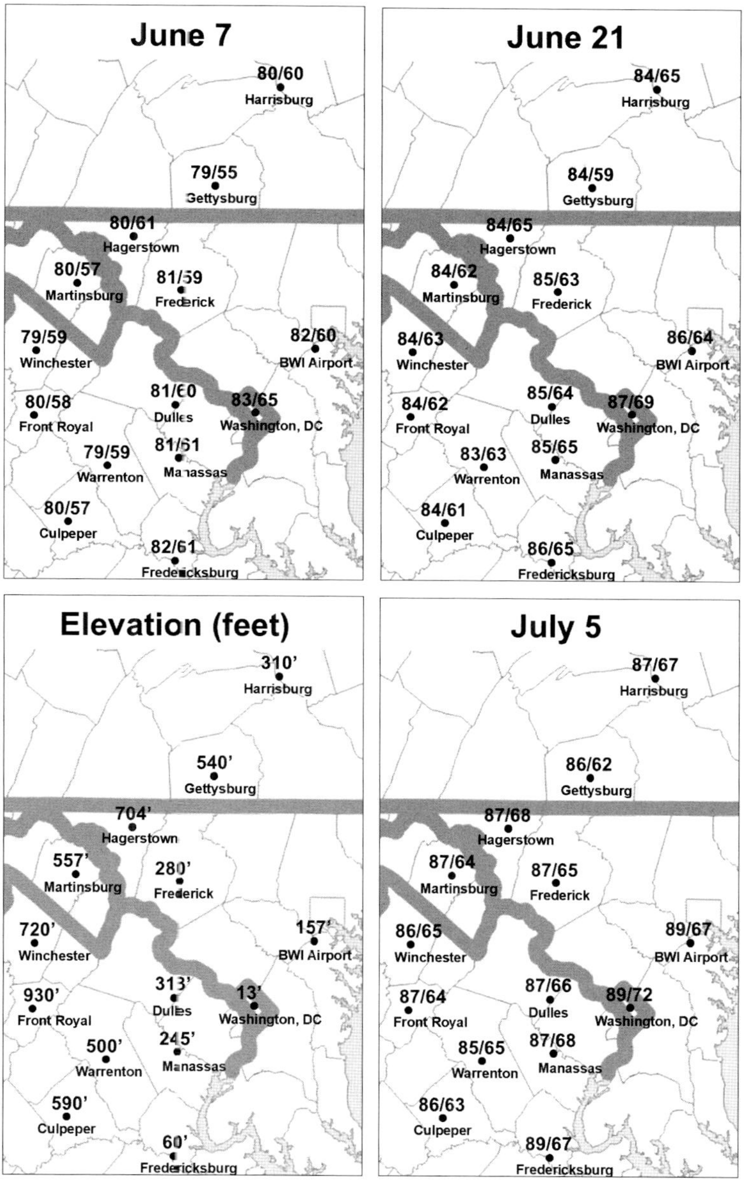

***Clockwise from top left*: Fig. 1** Modern-day average high and low temperatures (in degrees F) on June 7. *NOAA*.

Fig. 2 Modern-day average high and low temperatures (in degrees F) on June 21. *NOAA*.

Fig. 3 Modern-day average high and low temperatures (in degrees F) on July 5. *NOAA*.

Fig. 4 Elevation (in feet) of the observing sites in Figures 1–3. *NOAA*.

have been in play in 1863—is removed, then the difference in average high temperature across the theater on any given day is only about two degrees or so, an important point given that we rely heavily on observations taken at the Naval Observatory in Washington.

Those familiar with the weather in the mid-Atlantic might wonder how these averages translate to day-to-day weather across the theater. After all, weather fronts—the boundaries between warm and cold air that meteorologists talk so much about—commonly visit this part of the country, potentially derailing any analysis that depends on sparse observations. Here's where the time of year of the Gettysburg Campaign comes into play. With the sun so high in the sky in summer, cooler air masses approaching from the north and west are quickly modified, so temperature differences at any given time typically pale in comparison to those in other seasons. And such intrusions occur much less frequently in summer, reducing the number of times when a front might divide the theater and complicate the temperature (or moisture) pattern.

Another tool at our disposal is a relatively new historical "reanalysis" system from the National Oceanic and Atmospheric Administration that assimilates the available observations and then uses standard relationships among meteorological variables to reconstruct, in three dimensions, past weather patterns. This system has demonstrated skill at reconstructing weather events in the late 1800s, but to our knowledge it has never been used to analyze weather during the Civil War. Among other weather features, this system helps us locate fronts that could cause temperature and humidity changes on a day-to-day basis.

PRECIPITATION CONSIDERATIONS

Outside of summer, most precipitation that falls in the mid-latitudes accompanies large, sprawling storm systems and their associated fronts (think "low pressure," marked as *L*s on weather maps). The precipitation shields associated with these storms often cover tens of thousands of square miles and frequently take on characteristic shapes that meteorologists can exploit as they attempt to understand and forecast weather patterns.

The movement and evolution of these storm systems closely follow the jet stream, a corridor of speedy upper-level winds over the mid-latitudes that blows from a general westerly direction. As summer approaches, the jet stream's position shifts northward, and by July it typically resides near the United States border with Canada. This northward repositioning means that the large and predictable shields of precipitation that are common in fall, winter and spring in the mid-Atlantic occur much less frequently there in summer. In their place, as warmer and more humid air gains a firm footing, precipitation becomes much more scattered and "convective"—that is, rain falls mainly in the form of showers and thunderstorms that bubble up largely due to heat and humidity. In essence, rain is often here, there, but not everywhere.

To illustrate this point, Figure 1A (color section) shows a case of widely scattered showers and thunderstorms on a summer evening in July 2023—generally speaking, the reds indicate the heaviest rain, the blue the lightest. Figure 1B (color section) shows the total rainfall for that day. Many areas received next to nothing, while others got about two inches. The takeaway regarding our analysis of rainfall during the Gettysburg Campaign is that with convective precipitation dominant in summer, extrapolating rainfall location and amount from the available observations is much more challenging and uncertain than with temperature. We are mindful of this limitation throughout the book.

A closer look is warranted into air pressure, a weather variable that plays a critical role in our analysis.

AIR PRESSURE

Meteorologists talk a lot about air pressure for good reasons. In the mid-latitudes, weather variations on a day-to-day basis are linked to traveling areas of high and low pressure, represented with *H* and *L* on weather maps. As a first guess, low (or decreasing) pressure correlates with clouds and precipitation, while high (or increasing) pressure favors fair weather. In the mid-latitudes, the highs and lows move in a general west-to-east fashion, steered by upper-level winds that tend to be westerly.

Practically speaking, pressure is the weight of a column of air above a specific point. Because pressure is affected by temperature, pressure measurements are typically "corrected" for temperature differences using standard meteorological tables, and this was commonly done even in the 1860s. The size of this adjustment is modest, however, compared to a second correction that accounts for elevation differences. Pressure decreases with altitude, and so without an elevation correction, lower pressure would always reside at higher altitudes and higher pressure at lower elevations, masking pressure differences related to weather variations. To "level the playing field," meteorologists adjust pressure readings to a standard height, chosen to be sea level, to allow direct comparison of pressure values observed at different elevations. So, when meteorologists show maps of pressure, what's depicted is the corrected sea-level pressure. Once the elevation influence is removed, the remaining pressure differences are related to differences in weather.

Maps of sea-level pressure also allow the wind direction to be estimated. In the Northern Hemisphere, air circulates counterclockwise around low pressure and clockwise around high pressure, with a component directed away from higher toward lower pressure as the atmosphere tries to even out pressure differences. Figure 5, a generic map of pressure, illustrates these flow characteristics. The solid lines are isobars, lines of equal pressure that are commonly drawn to help locate the highs and lows. Notice that east of a center of high pressure (and west of a low), winds tend to blow from a northerly direction, so these are favored regions for winds to bring in colder (and often drier) air. In contrast, west of a center of high pressure (and east of a low), southerly breezes dominate, helping bring warmer (and often moister) air northward.

Figure 5 helps explain why low pressure tends to be associated with cloudy and rainy weather and high pressure with fair skies. Clouds (and precipitation) tend to form where air rises—that's why the rainiest and snowiest places on earth are found in mountainous regions. As air moves inward toward low pressure, it crowds together and the only escape is up. Thus, air rises in the

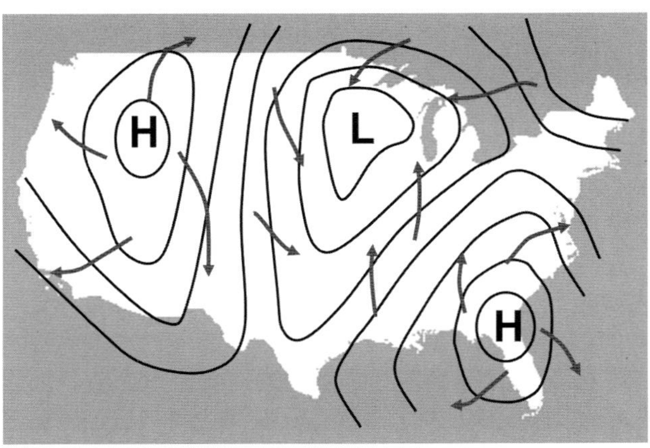

Fig. 5 General circulation of winds around high- and low-pressure systems in the Northern Hemisphere. *Author-generated image.*

vicinity of low pressure, enhancing chances for clouds and precipitation. In contrast, as air near earth's surface moves outward from higher pressure, the air above tends to gently subside. Sinking air is not conducive to clouds, explaining why high pressure favors fair weather.

One other characteristic of Figure 5 bears mentioning. Experience shows that focusing solely on the centers of high and low pressure misses key information. Commonly, areas of lower pressure elongate away from the center of the low. These extended zones of low pressure are called troughs and can be identified by elongations in the isobars. As an example, in Figure 5, a trough extends southward from the low in the northern United States into Texas. Given this close relationship between troughs and low pressure, it's not surprising that air also tends to rise in the vicinity of troughs—they, too, often feature clouds and precipitation.

Troughs come with an important bonus: they help locate fronts. Early meteorologists adopted this terminology from its wartime usage as the meeting ground between opposing armies. In the atmosphere, fronts are boundaries between large air masses of different temperature and moisture characteristics. In the eastern United States in summer, for example, a front might separate somewhat cooler and noticeably drier air that originated in Canada from warmer, muggier air that occupies the Southeast. Fronts are termed *cold* if the cooler, drier air advances, while at warm fronts, the cold air retreats. With that background, here's the key point: fronts are found in troughs, so knowing the pressure pattern also allows placement of the boundaries between air masses, a vital tool for diagnosing weather changes. And the NOAA reconstruction system will help do just that.

Given these characteristics of highs and lows, a simple forecasting tool emerges based on the change in pressure at a point. If pressure decreases at a location over a period of several hours, clouds and precipitation may be in the future. On the other hand, if pressure increases at a location, high pressure may be building in, bringing improving weather. Pressure data from the Naval Observatory in Washington, regularly available every three hours, prove particularly useful in applying these general rules.

These principles linking pressure and pressure changes to variations in the weather generally work best in the cold season when differences in pressure between highs and lows are largest. In summer, highs and lows tend to be weaker and pressure differences smaller, so the rules must be applied more carefully. Nonetheless, pressure data—in the form of time series and as maps from the NOAA reanalysis system—are invaluable in our analysis of the weather of the Gettysburg Campaign.

Atmospheric Moisture

"It's not just the heat, it's the humidity," a common refrain in summer in the eastern United States, rests on a firm scientific footing. Humid heat feels more oppressive to the human body, largely because about three-quarters of body cooling occurs via evaporation of perspiration—the energy to evaporate the sweat comes from the body, lowering body temperature. As the amount of water vapor (the gaseous form of water) in the air increases, the less perspiration will evaporate, limiting its usefulness as a cooling mechanism.

Some nineteenth-century weather observers regularly measured atmospheric moisture. Their data have been, to our knowledge, unused to this point in assessing the effect of weather on the Gettysburg Campaign. A major contribution of this book is the inclusion of the available moisture-related observations for that purpose, so a brief review of the key measures of atmospheric moisture is warranted.

Arguably the most well-known measure is relative humidity, but its utility is greatly misunderstood. Formally, relative humidity is the ratio of how much water vapor is in the air to how much water vapor would be required for a cloud to form, multiplied by 100 percent. High values of relative humidity (above 70 percent or so) correlate well with clouds, particularly when those high values occur in a thick layer of the atmosphere. As a simple example, check the relative humidity the next time you see fog outside—chances are, it will be close to 100 percent.

But many believe that the higher the relative humidity, the more humid the air feels. This assertion generally proves false because the relative humidity also depends on temperature. As temperature rises, relative humidity typically falls, and vice versa (see Figure 6). As a result, the relative humidity can be 50 percent or lower on a sultry summer

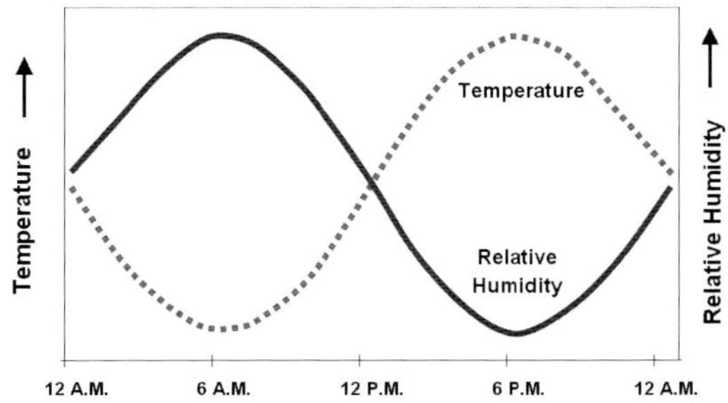

Fig. 6 Variation of relative humidity on a typical day. *Author-generated image.*

afternoon, while on a cold winter morning, the relative humidity can easily be 90 percent or higher. And that chilly winter morning surely does not feel "more humid" than the oppressive summer day! As a result, relative humidity is not consistently useful to gauge human comfort.

In contrast, a measure called the dewpoint depends almost exclusively on the amount of water vapor in the air, and thus is frequently used as a measure of human comfort (see Table 1). To visualize dewpoint, consider grass on your lawn late one evening after the sun has set and temperatures are dropping. Eventually, if enough cooling occurs, water vapor in the air will condense and dew will form on the grass—the dewpoint is the temperature at which the dew forms. It turns out that once the dewpoint reaches 65 degrees or so, most people would agree that the air feels "humid." Furthermore, at times and in places where the amount of water vapor in the air is similar, dewpoints tend to be similar.

TABLE 1. RELATIONSHIP OF DEWPOINT TO HUMAN COMFORT

Dewpoint	General Level of Comfort
60 degrees	The air starts to feel a bit humid
65 degrees	The air feels moderately humid
70 degrees	The air feels sultry and tropical
75 degrees	The air feels oppressive and stifling

In practice, observers often measure another moisture-related variable known as the wet-bulb temperature. The concept of wet-bulb temperature relies on the idea that evaporation is a cooling process. Energy is required to turn water into water vapor, so when water on a surface evaporates, the surface cools (as with the cooling of our bodies). Similarly, air will cool if water is evaporated into it because some of the energy needed to vaporize the water comes from the air itself. Formally, the wet-bulb temperature is the lowest temperature to which air can be cooled in this way.

An instrument called a psychrometer measures wet-bulb temperature. Weather observers in the 1860s used a psychrometer consisting of two thermometers mounted side by side on a platform (see Figure 7). The bulb of one thermometer, the dry-bulb, simply measures the air temperature. The bulb of the second thermometer is wrapped in a cloth "sock" soaked in pure water—this is the wet-bulb thermometer. As water evaporates from the cloth sock, the temperature of the wet-bulb thermometer (the wet-bulb temperature) will decrease—how much it drops depends on how much water vapor is already in the air. And that's the key. Given the wet-bulb and dry-bulb temperatures, other measures of atmospheric moisture such as the dewpoint can be computed.

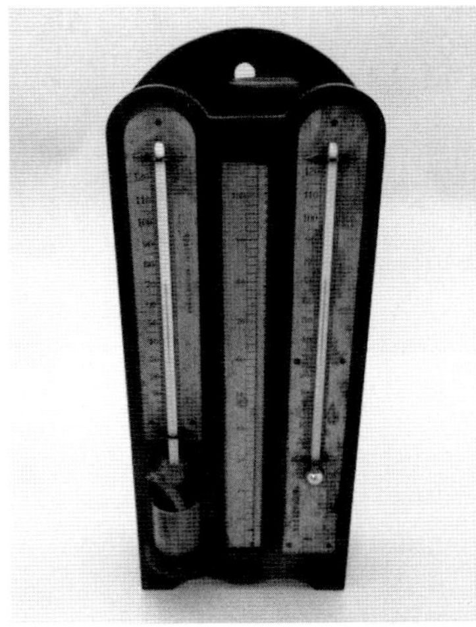

Fig. 7 A nineteenth-century psychrometer. *Courtesy of Division of Medicine and Science, National Museum of American History, Smithsonian Institution.*

So practically speaking, how will we use wet-bulb temperature? Inherent in its definition is a dependence on the temperature itself. Two locations with different temperatures but the same amount of water vapor in the air will have different wet-bulb temperatures. In contrast, dewpoint depends fundamentally on the amount of water vapor in the air. Thus, we will calculate dewpoints from the dry-bulb and wet-bulb temperature measurements and use those dewpoints to drive our conclusions.

Several potential sources of error make wet-bulb temperature measurements vulnerable to misinterpretation. Both the dry-bulb and wet-bulb thermometers must display the same temperature initially, before the wet sock is applied, ensuring that the process starts from the same base temperature. In addition, enough time must elapse for evaporation to provide the appropriate cooling effect on the wet bulb. Observers in the 1860s were told to allow the wet bulb "to stand a few moments until it indicates the temperature of evaporation," an instruction open to interpretation. Modern studies of uncertainties in measuring the wet-bulb temperature suggest error bars of ±1 degree Fahrenheit (F) are appropriate.[11] These errors, in turn, would propagate (at about the same magnitude) to estimates of quantities such as dewpoint and heat index that are derived from the wet-bulb temperature. Though we will never know for certain, it is reasonable to assume that the error bars at that time were at least that large, if not perhaps ±2 degrees F.

HEAT AND HUMIDITY: HEAT INDEX AND WET-BULB GLOBE TEMPERATURE

Once atmospheric humidity is measured—whether as dewpoint, wet-bulb temperature or relative humidity—the combined effect of temperature and humidity can be estimated. The most common measure is the heat index, widely advertised as an estimate of "how hot it really feels" when the amount of moisture in the air is considered. The concept is based on research done in the late 1970s by physicist R.G. Steadman, who called his measure a sultriness index or apparent temperature.[12]

For public consumption, the National Weather Service commonly presents heat index values in a table such as the one shown in Figure 8, with

NWS HEAT INDEX — Temperature (°F)

Relative Humidity (%)	80	82	84	86	88	90	92	94	96	98	100	102	104	106	108	110
40	80	81	83	85	88	91	94	97	101	105	109	114	119	124	130	136
45	80	82	84	87	89	93	96	100	104	109	114	119	124	130	137	
50	81	83	85	88	91	95	99	103	108	113	118	124	131	137		
55	81	84	86	89	93	97	101	106	112	117	124	130	137			
60	82	84	88	91	95	100	105	110	116	123	129	137				
65	82	85	89	93	98	103	108	114	121	128	136					
70	83	86	90	95	100	105	112	119	126	134						
75	84	88	92	97	103	109	116	124	132							
80	84	89	94	100	106	113	121	129								
85	85	90	96	102	110	117	126	135								
90	86	91	98	105	113	122	131									
95	86	93	100	108	117	127										
100	87	95	103	112	121	132										

Likelihood of Heat Disorders with Prolonged Exposure or Strenuous Activity

Classification	Heat Index	Effect on the body
Caution	80°F–90°F	Fatigue possible with prolonged exposure and/or physical activity
Extreme Caution	90°F–103°F	Heat stroke, heat cramps or heat exhaustion possible with prolonged exposure and/or physical activity
Danger	103°F–124°F	Heat cramps or heat exhaustion likely, and heat stroke possible with prolonged exposure and/or physical activity
Extreme Danger	125°F or higher	Heat stroke highly likely

Fig. 8 A standard National Weather Service heat index table with associated effects on the body. *NOAA*.

temperature on one side and relative humidity on the other.[13] Traditionally, the heat index is not calculated for air temperatures below 80 degrees because such values are usually not high enough to pose a significant risk to health, regardless of humidity. Many assumptions underlie the heat index model, including the dimensions of the person (assumed 5' 7" tall, 147 pounds), the clothing worn (long trousers and short-sleeved shirt assumed), the body's internal temperature (assumed to be 98.6 degrees F) and the speed of the wind (about 6 miles per hour). Accordingly, the heat index inherently has an error of about a degree and a half.[14]

A table showing the effects associated with various heat index thresholds typically accompanies the heat index chart, as in Figure 8. When the body is unable to cool itself effectively, or when the loss of water and salt is excessive, body temperature increases, and heat-related illness may follow. The mildest form is heat cramps, which are painful muscle cramps and spasms, especially in the legs, accompanied by heavy sweating. With heat exhaustion comes additional symptoms such as weakness, dizziness, nausea and pale, moist skin. The most severe form of heat illness is heatstroke, often bringing confusion, a rapid heart rate, fainting and loss of consciousness. Heatstroke is a life-threatening medical emergency requiring immediate attention.[15]

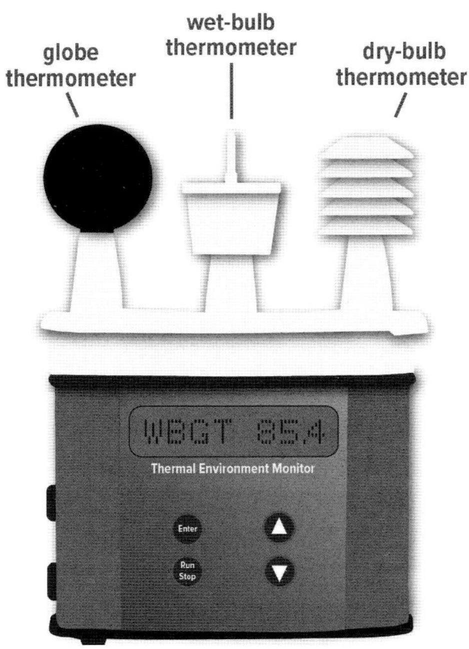

Fig. 9 Equipment to measure the wet-bulb globe temperature. *NOAA*.

WBGT / RISK	IMPACTS	ACTIONS
80-85 F / Low	Body stressed after 45 minutes	Take at least 15 minutes of breaks each hour if working or exercising in direct sunlight, Stay hydrated.
85-88 F / Moderate	Body stressed after 30 minutes. HEAT CRAMPS likely (painful contraction of muscles, weakness)	Take at least 30 minutes of breaks each hour if working or exercising in direct sunlight. Drink ½ to 1 quart of water per hour.
88-90 F / High	Body stressed after 20 minutes. HEAT EXHAUSTION likely (dizziness, nausea, vomiting, headache, fainting, disorientation, weakness)	Take at least 40 minutes of breaks each hour if working or exercising in direct sunlight. Reduce work, exercise intensity. Drink up to 1 quart of water per hour.
> 90 F / Extreme	Body stressed after 15 minutes. HEAT STROKE likely (extremely high body temp, confusion, convulsions, unconsciousness, death)	Take at least 45 minutes of breaks each hour if working or exercising in direct sunlight. Suspend all strenuous outdoor activities. Drink at least 1 quart of water per hour.
Adapted from U.S Army and OSHA guidelines and recommendations		

Fig. 10 A wet-bulb globe temperature table, with impacts and actions. *NOAA*.

One final note about the heat index. Because official temperature measurements are taken in the shade, heat index values also apply to shady locations—in full sunshine, the heat index can be up to fifteen degrees higher.[16]

The recognition that sunshine significantly influences how humans perceive heat and humidity leads to an alternative (and less well-known) measure of discomfort, the wet-bulb globe temperature (WBGT). The WBGT incorporates sunshine and wind and has been used for more than fifty years by the military, but only in the last decade or so has it seen increased use elsewhere.

As its name implies, the wet-bulb globe temperature is computed using the wet-bulb temperature, but what about the "globe" part? A globe thermometer is a hollow copper sphere, painted black, with a thermometer in the center. Its temperature, called the globe temperature, is intended to measure the warming effect of radiation (mostly sunshine) on temperature. Figure 9 shows a device used to compute the WBGT. The "regular" temperature, wet-bulb temperature and globe temperature are combined mathematically to produce the wet-bulb globe temperature. Figure 10 shows a standard WBGT table, courtesy of the National Weather Service, that links certain WBGT thresholds to effects and recommended actions. A variety of such charts exist based on location and level and type of activity.[17]

When the wet-bulb globe temperature reaches approximately 85 degrees F, human health is significantly threatened. This threshold sounds not nearly as ominous as the triple-digit heat index values that grab attention in summer, likely a big reason why the WBGT hasn't "caught on" with the public. However, organizations that oversee or manage large groups of people who might spend time in the sun, such as the military and athletic teams, as well as the Occupational Safety and Health Administration (OSHA), rely heavily on the WBGT guidelines to manage outdoor risk.

Globe thermometers are not widely available, so alternative methods have been developed to estimate the WBGT from other standard weather variables.[18] OSHA has an online calculator that computes the WBGT, given the temperature, wet-bulb temperature, wind speed and the amount of sunlight reaching the ground.[19] If the latter is not available (and for our purposes in the Gettysburg Campaign, it is not), then the calculator provides a range of WBGT values, where the highest value corresponds to direct sunlight and the minimum value is a shade estimate. Most official observers in the 1860s included an estimate of the fraction of the sky covered by clouds, plus a cloud type. The quality of these observations varies, however, and factors such as cloud thickness and the number of cloud layers affect the amount of sunlight reaching the ground. These factors are difficult or, in many cases, impossible to determine in retrospect. Nonetheless, we often have enough information to make reasonable estimates of the WBGT, and we will include these when appropriate, with necessary caveats.

Historical Reanalysis System

Weather maps—be they of temperature, pressure, dewpoint or a myriad of other variables—provide a roadmap for an operational meteorologist. By synthesizing information about the atmosphere at a given time, such maps unveil spatial patterns that help explain the "hows" and "whys" of the weather.

The idea to re-create weather maps of the past using archives of observations and modern analysis techniques is not new, but only in the last decade or so have such historical "reanalysis" efforts extended back in time into the 1800s. The most recent version of the effort is known as (take a deep breath) the NOAA-CIRES-DOE Twentieth Century Reanalysis version 3, or 20CRv3 for short.[20] The 20CRv3 reanalysis system aims to produce the best estimate of the three-dimensional state of the global atmosphere, every three hours, back to (as of this writing) 1836.

Even casual followers of weather science know that meteorologists use computer models to assist in forecasting. Essentially, supercomputers assimilate weather observations and then solve the complicated equations that govern the future behavior of the atmosphere and oceans, producing forecasts. In similar fashion, the NOAA reanalysis system also uses computer modeling, but instead of looking forward, it looks backward. Using a global database of past surface pressure observations, plus best guesses of ocean water temperature and sea ice concentrations, the system produces a virtual picture of the three-dimensional atmosphere in the form of maps of sea-level pressure, temperature, relative humidity and dozens of other variables. To acknowledge uncertainties in the observations on which the reanalysis depends, the system produces an ensemble of eighty different simulations, each using slightly different starting values. The reanalysis charts shown in this book are averages of the dozens of simulations, with the intention of capturing the best estimate of past conditions.

The reanalysis system is not gospel; rather, it is guidance. Given the sparseness of the pressure observations that are initially ingested into the system, the reconstruction system should be used as a reasonable first guess of the state of the past atmosphere. Realistically, the system is best at reproducing large-scale features such as highs and lows of pressure and waves in the jet stream and should not be expected to reproduce small-scale features such as, for example, thunderstorm complexes. The reconstruction maps do not replace the available weather observations but ideally complement and corroborate those observations and offer hints as to the meteorological reasoning behind the observed weather. Think of the reanalysis system as another instrument, one that has never been used, to reconstruct the weather of the Gettysburg Campaign.

2

PRIMARY SOURCES AND FIRSTHAND ACCOUNTS

Seeing Is Believing

You can observe a lot by watching.
—Yogi Berra

Experienced meteorologists know that the first step in preparing a local weather forecast is to look out the window. Given that observations are the key to understanding weather past, current and future, rest assured that, over time, some of the best "watchers" (as Yogi Berra put it) have been weather watchers. Even qualitative observations, for example, "it's windy outside," provide information, but instrumentation allows for the quantitative measurement necessary for comparing observations. Some of the earliest instrumented weather observations in colonial America originated in the Philadelphia area in the early to mid-1700s, but networks of observers making simultaneous observations with dependable instruments did not emerge until about a century later.

Fig. 11 James Pollard Espy, portrait by Joseph Sully. *Courtesy of National Portrait Gallery.*

Drawing useful weather maps, particularly those that unveil large-scale patterns,

Fig. 12 Joseph Henry at the Smithsonian during the 1850s. *Courtesy of Smithsonian Institution Archives, Image SIA-84-2074-000002.*

requires weather observations from far-flung points. James Espy of the Franklin Institute in Philadelphia (see Figure 11) directed one of the first attempts to create a weather observing network in the United States in the 1830s. Espy eventually moved to Washington, where he joined forces with Joseph Henry, the first secretary of the Smithsonian Institution, to create the Smithsonian Meteorological Project in 1848. The primary research objective for the new institution was establishing "systems of extending meteorological observations for solving the problem of American storms."[21] Such networks provided the data needed to see the big "weather picture."

Initially, about 150 volunteer observers from across the nation participated in the effort, all supplied with instructions and standardized forms on which to record their data. Some were given full sets of instruments, including a thermometer, barometer, psychrometer and rain gauge. Others used only a thermometer, while a third class of observers merely recorded information such as the start and end times of precipitation and changes in the look of the sky. The forms were submitted monthly by mail, so weather maps could be created only well after the fact. However, some observers transmitted their measurements of clouds, precipitation and wind once per day via telegraph to Washington, and Henry used their data to draw and display crude weather maps at the Smithsonian (see Figure 12). In essence, for the first time, "one view of the meteorological condition of the atmosphere over the whole country" in near-real time had been produced.[22]

Once the Civil War intervened, however, short-term aspirations to produce daily weather maps and long-term plans for a national weather service paused. Weather observers from the Southern states, for the most part, discontinued their efforts. For example, two volunteers in the Fredericksburg area observed before the war, but neither reported during the war. Other observers in the theater of the Gettysburg Campaign such as John Marvin in Winchester, Virginia, and Jacob Bell in Leitersburg, Maryland (near Hagerstown), either did not report or were unable to forward their observations. But some border state and most Northern Smithsonian observers continued to take observations. Fortunately, so did those at various military forts and locations, including the scientists at the Naval Observatory in Washington.

The Data

The National Oceanic and Atmospheric Administration database known as FORTS houses the historical weather observations used in this work. The database name acknowledges that U.S. Army forts began recording daily weather observations around 1820, but FORTS contains data from many other volunteer observers, including the Smithsonian network and other stations that conducted weather observations in the nineteenth century. The National Archives holds these records on microfilm, but many have been scanned and indexed and are available online through the National Centers for Environmental Information[23] and the Midwest Regional Climate Center,[24] a key partner in the digitization of the records.

The Weather Watchers and Their Observations

The primary weather observing locations used in our analysis are numbered and identified in Figures 13 and 14 along with the weather variables observed at each location. Nearly all observers participated in the Smithsonian

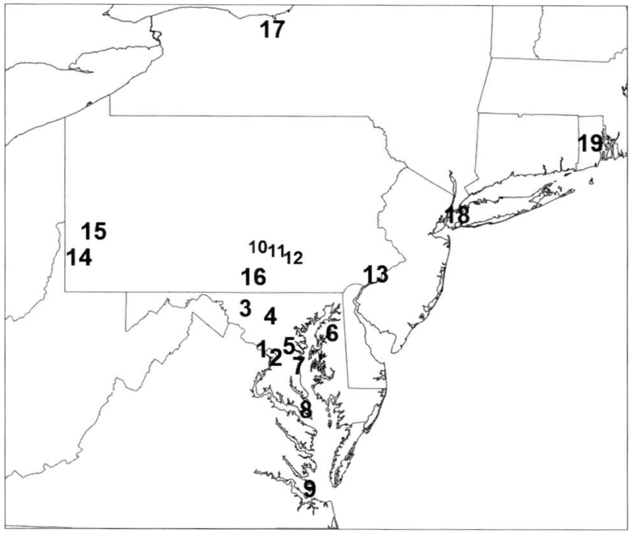

***Right*: Fig. 13**
Geographic locations of the weather observing sites used in the analysis. *Author-generated image.*

***Below*: Fig. 14**
Locations corresponding to the numbers in Figure 13, along with the weather variables measured at each location. *P* is pressure, *T* is temperature, *Tw* wet-bulb temperature, *W* wind, *C* clouds and *R* rainfall. *Author-generated image.*

		P	T	Tw	W	C	R
1	Naval Observatory*	X	X	X	X	X	X
2	Georgetown		X		X	X	X
3	Frederick, MD**	X	X	X		X	X
4	Sykesville, MD		X	X	X	X	X
5	Bladenburg, MD	X	X	X	X	X	X
6	Chestertown, MD	X	X		X	X	X
7	Annapolis, MD	X	X	X	X	X	X
8	St. Marys, MD	X	X	X	X	X	X
9	Fort Monroe, VA	X	X		X	X	X
10	Harrisburg, PA (Heisely)	X	X	X	X	X	X
11	Harrisburg, PA (Hickok)	X	X	X	X	X	X
12	Mount Joy, PA	X	X		X	X	X
13	Philadelphia, PA	X	X	X	X	X	X
14	Canonsburg, PA	X	X		X	X	X
15	Pittsburgh, PA	X	X	X	X	X	X
16	Gettysburg, PA	X	X		X	X	X
17	Rochester, NY	X	X	X	X	X	X
18	New York City, NY	X	X	X	X	X	X
19	Providence, RI	X	X	X	X	X	X

*Observations every 3 hours
**June observations only

Meteorological Project at one time or another. Given that weather often moves from west to east, the dearth of official weather observers in West Virginia and nearly all of Virginia hinders to some extent the timely tracking of weather systems. Two observers in Cincinnati, Ohio, and several in Kentucky and

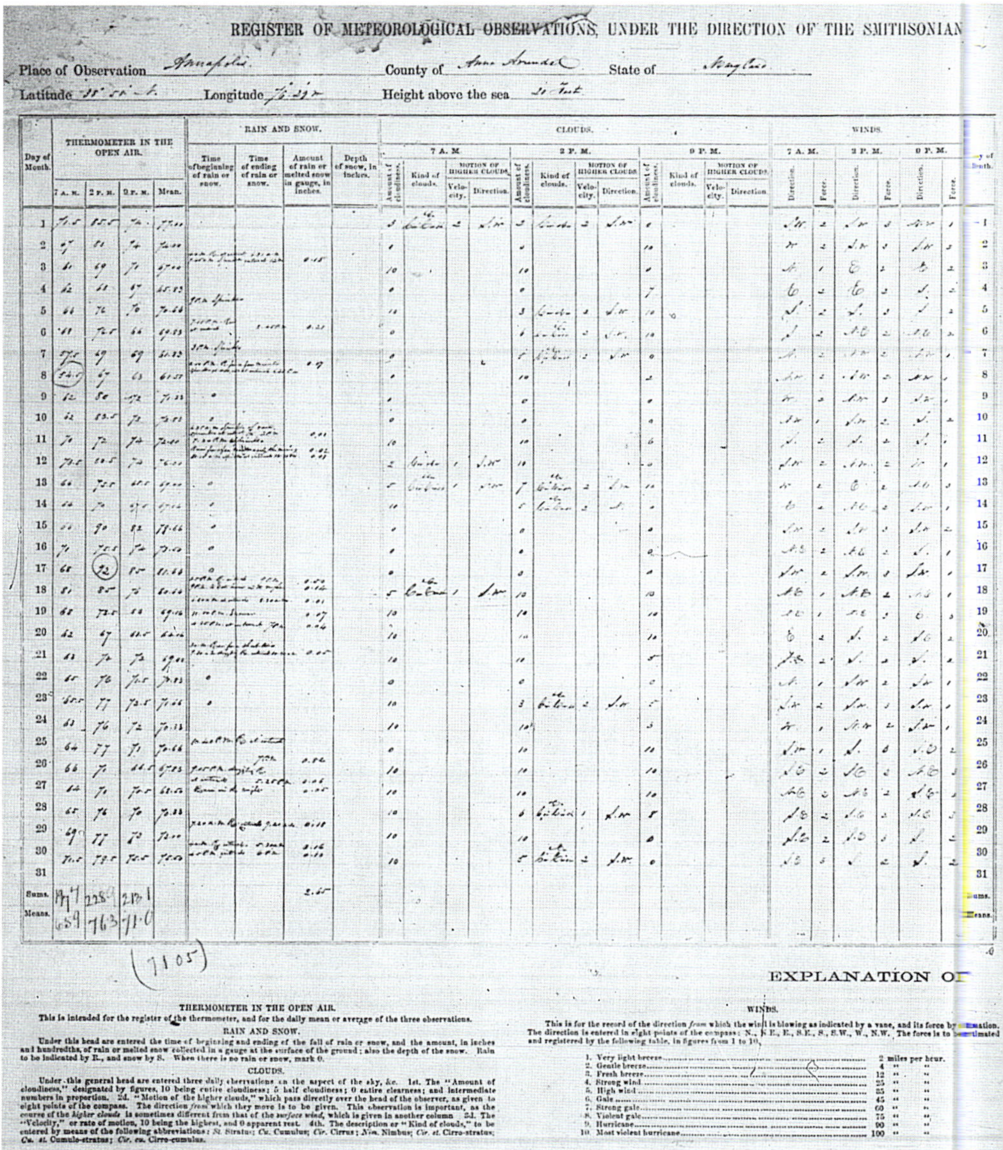
REGISTER OF METEOROLOGICAL OBSERVATIONS, UNDER THE DIRECTION OF THE SMITHSONIAN

Place of Observation Annapolis County of Anne Arundel State of Maryland

Latitude Longitude Height above the sea

EXPLANATION OF

THERMOMETER IN THE OPEN AIR.

This is intended for the register of the thermometer, and for the daily mean or average of the three observations.

RAIN AND SNOW.

Under this head are entered the time of beginning and ending of the fall of rain or snow, and the amount, in inches and hundredths, of rain or melted snow collected in a gauge at the surface of the ground; also the depth of the snow. Rain to be indicated by R., and snow by S. When there is no rain or snow, mark 0.

CLOUDS.

Under this general head are entered three daily observations on the aspect of the sky, &c. 1st. The "Amount of cloudiness," designated by figures, 10 being entire cloudiness; 5 half cloudiness; 0 entire clearness; and intermediate numbers in proportion. 2d. "Motion of the higher clouds," which pass directly over the head of the observer, as given to eight points of the compass. The direction *from* which they move is to be given. This observation is important, as the course of the *higher clouds* is sometimes different from that of the *surface wind*, which is given in another column. 3d. The "Velocity," or rate of motion, 10 being the highest, and 0 apparent rest. 4th. The description or "Kind of clouds," to be entered by means of the following abbreviations: *St.* Stratus; *Cu.* Cumulus; *Cir.* Cirrus; *Nim.* Nimbus; *Cir. st.* Cirro-stratus; *Cu. st.* Cumulo-stratus; *Cir. cu.* Cirro-cumulus.

WINDS.

This is for the record of the direction *from* which the wind is blowing as indicated by a vane, and its force by estimation. The direction is entered in eight points of the compass: N., N.E., E., S.E., S., S.W., W., N.W. The force is to be estimated and registered by the following table, in figures from 1 to 10.

1. Very light breeze .... 2 miles per hour.
2. Gentle breeze .... 4 " "
3. Fresh breeze .... 12 " "
4. Strong wind .... 25 " "
5. High wind .... 35 " "
6. Gale .... 45 " "
7. Strong gale .... 60 " "
8. Violent gale .... 75 " "
9. Hurricane .... 90 " "
10. Most violent hurricane .... 100 " "

Tennessee (not shown in Figure 13) helped fill that void. In addition, other Smithsonian observers to the northwest in Marquette, Michigan, and to the south in Charleston, South Carolina (also not shown in Figure 13), often provided clues on weather systems approaching from those directions.

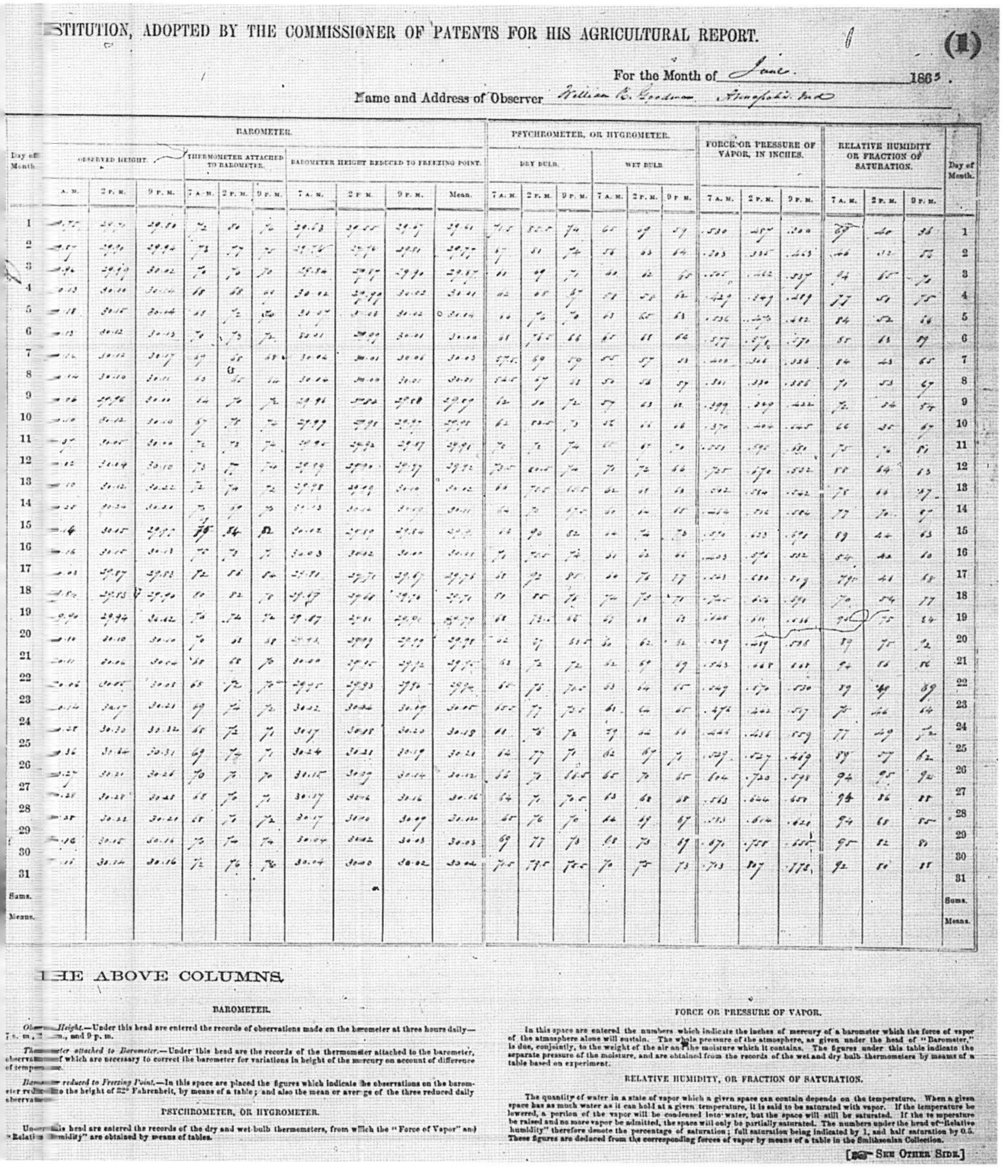

Fig. 15 Smithsonian observation sheet from Annapolis, Maryland, for June 1863. *NOAA FORTS.*

Smithsonian observers represented a variety of backgrounds and levels of experience. John Heisely, who practiced medicine in Harrisburg, had been part of James Espy's original weather observer network. So had Michael Jacobs, a professor at Pennsylvania College in Gettysburg. William Baer, a chemist in Sykesville, Maryland, began observing weather there in 1846 and a few years later was joined by his wife, Harriet, in the endeavor.

Smithsonian observers recorded data three times a day, at 7:00 a.m., 2:00 p.m. and 9:00 p.m. local time. Wet-bulb temperature was measured at most observing sites, allowing estimation of the dewpoint at those locations. All observing sites provided temperature and daily rainfall data, while nearly all observed wind, cloud cover and pressure. Only some of the pressure observations were corrected for temperature, and none were corrected for elevation, so sea-level pressure charts cannot easily be constructed from the data. Here, the NOAA reanalysis system helps to fill in the gaps.

A Smithsonian observation sheet for June 1863 from Annapolis is shown in Figure 15 on the preceding pages. The name of the observer and the latitude, longitude and height above sea level of the observing site were entered on top of the form. Temperature (in degrees F) was listed on the left, and columns were provided for the daily amount of precipitation (in hundredths of an inch) and its start and end times. Cloud cover was entered on a scale from 0 to 10, with 0 being a completely clear sky and 10 totally cloudy. Observers could also record the type of clouds and the speed and direction from which clouds directly overhead were moving. Additional columns housed the surface wind as well as an estimate of the wind "force" on a scale from 1 to 10. On that scale, Force 1 represented a "very light breeze," equivalent to 2 miles per hour (mph); Force 3, a "fresh breeze" (of order 12 mph); while Force 5 was a "high wind" equivalent to approximately 35 mph.

The right half of the Smithsonian observation sheet included columns for air pressure (in inches of mercury) and the pressure corrected for temperature. Barometers at the time consisted of a long glass tube filled with mercury, inverted in a reservoir of the heavy substance. Figure 16 is a schematic of

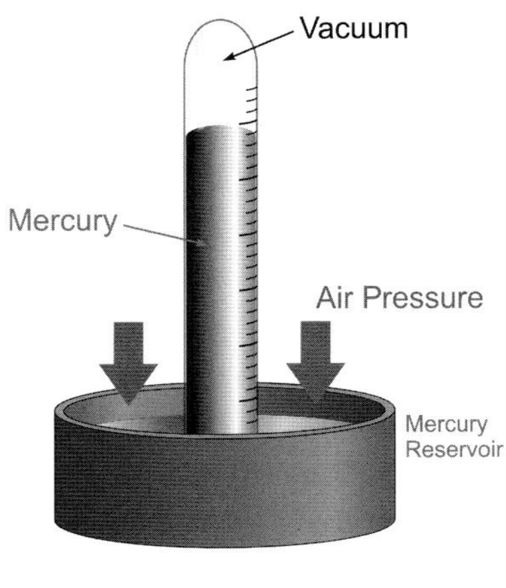

Fig. 16 Schematic of a mercury barometer. *Author-generated image.*

a so-called mercury barometer. At sea level, the weight of the air supports a thread of mercury almost thirty inches high in the tube—thus the unit. The remaining columns of the observation form included space for the wet-bulb temperature and other quantities derived from it, such as relative humidity. Many observers simply left these additional columns blank. Finally, some observers occasionally provided remarks about the weather and other topics on a separate sheet, often noting unusual features such as lightning, an aurora or the first frost of the fall.

Because Smithsonian observers recorded the weather only three times a day, we do not know the extremes in temperature, the daily high and daily low. The maximum daily temperature often occurs later in the afternoon, especially in summer. Given the high sun angle, the daily high can be several degrees above the 2:00 p.m. reading. At the other extreme, the daily minimum temperature is typically reached around sunrise, which during the Gettysburg Campaign occurred about two hours before the 7:00 a.m. observation. Thus, the daily minimum was likely several degrees lower than the 7:00 a.m. reading. Because of variations in daily weather conditions (such as cloudiness), even these general rules linking the 2:00 p.m. and 7:00 a.m. readings to the high and low temperatures will not necessarily work on any given day.

One observation site, however, did report daily maximum and minimum temperatures and provided the weather every three hours: the Naval Observatory in Washington, a treasure trove of previously underutilized meteorological information as applied to the Gettysburg Campaign.[25]

THE NAVAL OBSERVATORY

One of the oldest scientific agencies in the United States, the Naval Observatory was founded in December 1830 as the Depot of Charts and Instruments to care for the equipment and maps that the U.S. Navy needed to navigate the seas. Weather observing began there in 1838 and continued for almost one hundred years. From 1844 to 1893, the observatory was located at 24th and E Streets NW, known as Foggy Bottom.[26]

While Smithsonian observers recorded weather data three times per day, observers at the Naval Observatory reported the weather eight times each day, at midnight, 3:00 a.m., 6:00 a.m., 9:00 a.m., noon, 3:00 p.m., 6:00 p.m. and 9:00 p.m. Observations included temperature; pressure, corrected for

***Above*: Fig. 17** Naval Observatory, circa 1863. *Courtesy of Naval History & Heritage Command: Photo Section, Photo #NH 1671.*

***Opposite*: Fig. 18** Naval Observatory observation form for July 4, 1863. *NOAA FORTS.*

temperature; wet-bulb temperature; cloud cover and type of cloud; wind speed and direction; and daily rainfall. As with Smithsonian observers, the Naval Observatory also occasionally included remarks about interesting or unusual phenomena. Figure 18 is an example of an Observatory form from July 4, 1863.[27] John Eastman, a pivotal figure in the meteorological history of the agency, signed the form that day.

The Naval Observatory's three-hour observation period provides a window of largely untapped data for analyzing the weather of the Gettysburg Campaign. Of particular interest are the pressure readings, given that changes in pressure track the day-to-day movement of fronts and areas of high and low pressure that largely control weather in the mid-latitudes. On page 54, Figure 19 plots the pressure observations at the Naval Observatory for the entire campaign, from June 3 to July 14, 1863. Though pressure variations in summer typically are not as pronounced as in other seasons, significant weather changes will still be captured in the ups and downs of the barometer, particularly with eight observations per day at regular intervals. For example, the significant drop in pressure on June 17–18 signaled the approach of a front that ended a vicious heat wave.

Some remarks are necessary regarding the temperature observations at the Observatory. As previously mentioned, official temperature measurements are taken in the shade. The thermometers at the Observatory were housed in a six-foot-diameter outdoor shelter that was constructed in 1862. The wooden shelter was painted white and situated over a grassy surface. Dry-bulb (labeled "Shade" on the form) and wet-bulb thermometers were suspended five feet above the ground inside the shelter, a standard height for the measurement of temperature.[28] Similar shelters are used even today at some NOAA observing sites, making the Naval Observatory arguably state of the art for measuring temperature at the time of the Gettysburg Campaign.

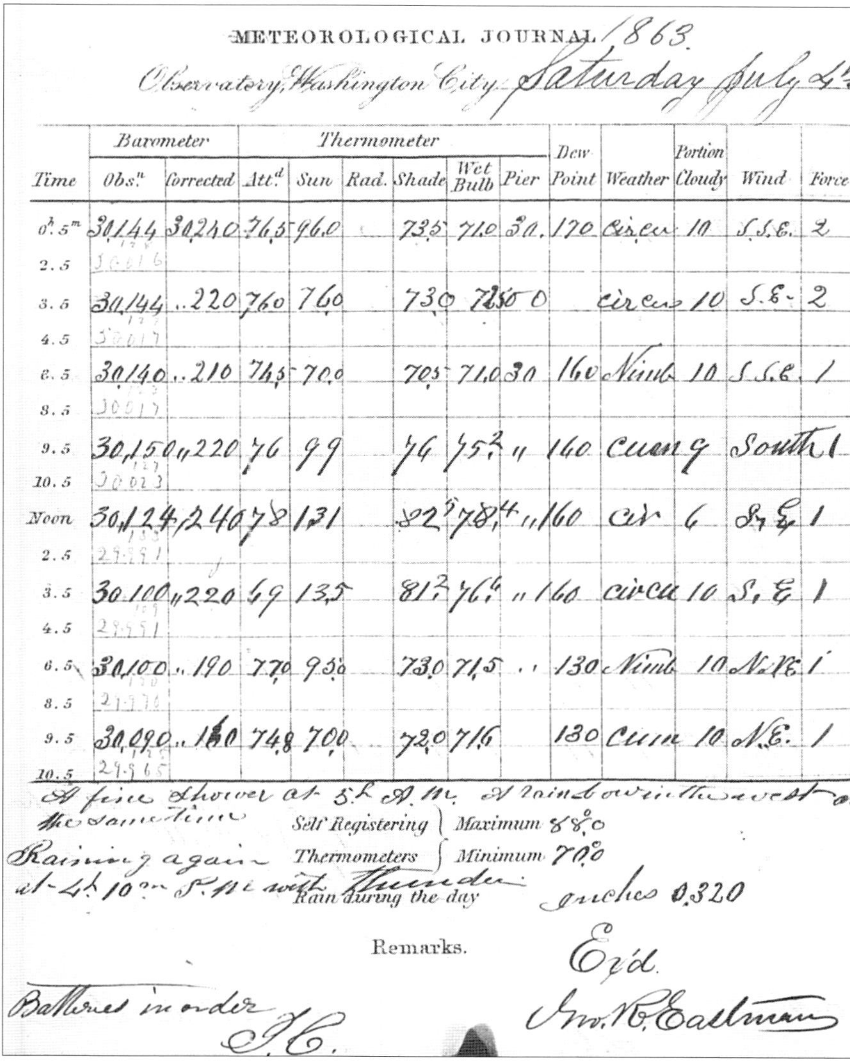

METEOROLOGICAL JOURNAL 1863.

Observatory, Washington City Saturday July 4th

	Barometer		Thermometer						Dew		Portion		
Time	Obs.n	Corrected	Att.d	Sun	Rad.	Shade	Wet Bulb	Pier	Point	Weather	Cloudy	Wind	Force
0h. 5m	30144	30240	76.5	96.0		73.5	71.0	30.	170	Cir. cu	10	S.S.E.	2
2.5	30016												
3.5	30144	..220	76.0	76.0		73.0	72.5	0		cir cu	10	S.E.	2
4.5	30017												
6.5	30140	..210	74.5	70.0		70.5	71.0	30	160	Nimb	10	S.S.E.	1
8.5	30017												
9.5	30150	..220	76	99		74	75.2	"	160	cum	9	South	1
10.5	30023												
Noon	30124	240	78	131		82.5	78.4	"	160	cir	6	S.E.	1
2.5	29991												
3.5	30100	..220	69	135		81.2	76.6	"	160	cir cu	10	S.E.	1
4.5	29951												
6.5	30100	..190	77.0	95.0		73.0	71.5	..	130	Nimb	10	N.E.	1
8.5	29976												
9.5	30090	..180	74.8	70.0		72.0	71.6		130	Cum	10	N.E.	1
10.5	29965												

A fine shower at 5h A.M. A rainbow in the west at the same time

Raining again at 4h 10m P.M. with thunder

Self Registering Thermometers: Maximum 88.0; Minimum 70.0

Rain during the day inches 0.320

Remarks.

Batteries in order J.C.

Exd. Jno. R. Eastman

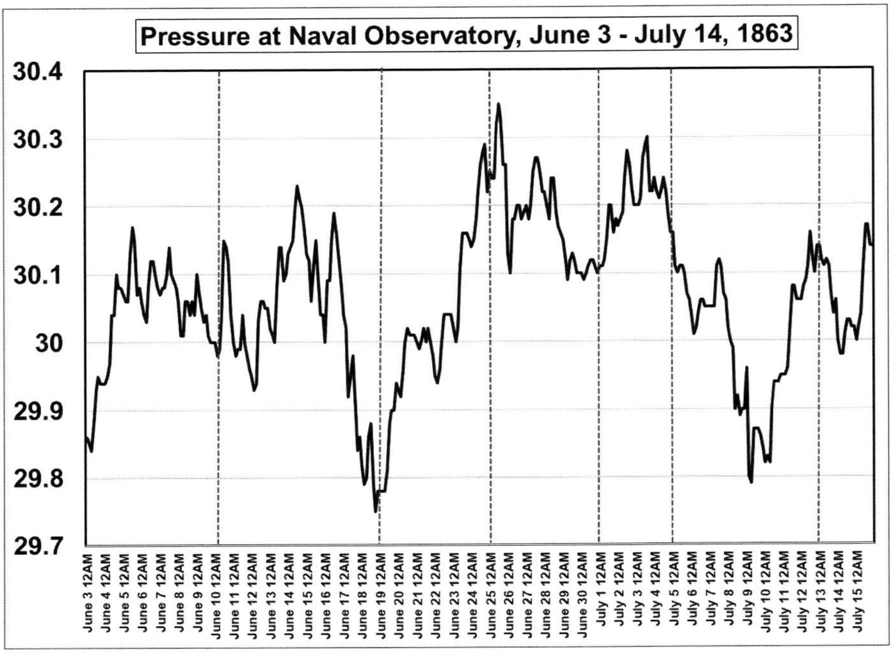

Fig. 19 Pressure at the Naval Observatory from June 3 to July 14, 1863, in inches of mercury. Vertical lines delineate the periods covered in chapters 3–9. *Data from NOAA FORTS.*

The Naval Observatory also used two special "self-registering" thermometers, one for the daily maximum temperature and one for the daily minimum. These thermometers were also placed in the shelter and reset at midnight. Thus, in contrast to observing sites on the Smithsonian network, the Naval Observatory provided daily high and low temperatures, the *only* location near the Gettysburg theater with such information.

Finally, the Naval Observatory provided an additional temperature measurement from a special thermometer placed a few inches above the grass in a non-shaded location on the Observatory grounds: essentially, an estimate of what the temperature felt like in the sun close to the ground. Called a "solar temperature" or "sun temperature," its value was entered in the "Sun" column on the observation form. To some extent, this special temperature describes the heat load experienced by someone sitting or lying in the sun.[29] Because cloud conditions and surface covering can vary greatly over short distances, extrapolating this sun temperature to other locations in the theater requires care. But this measurement represents another unique approach to our reconstruction of weather conditions during the campaign.

OTHER SOURCES

Aside from the aforementioned primary source weather observations, useful information also came from nonofficial civilian accounts penned by various diarists. These invaluable chroniclers reported from a variety of locations throughout the geographic region covered by the campaign. Newspapers also contained valuable data, most notably the *Alexandria Gazette* and the *Baltimore Sun*.

In the end though, the "boots on the ground" approach proved to be a truly outstanding source of information on the weather during the campaign. Undeniably, the soldiers' words spoke volumes. And why not? What would you write about if you lived outdoors? Those who served during the Gettysburg Campaign wrote about many topics—home and family, their surroundings, their dissatisfaction with army leadership, the lack of decent food, the despised enemy and various other concerns. But more than anything, they wrote about the one thing there was no escaping: *the weather*.

Fortunately, many of these accounts survive. We drew from a source base built on approximately 1,500 such recollections from over 250 sources, covering all branches and organizational levels of each army. At times the soldiers' accounts remained somewhat vague as to their exact location, but often the account told us where the soldiers were. Of course, with no standard time in existence in 1863, times cited by chroniclers occasionally could be problematic.

Despite some of the inherent shortcomings of the soldiers' accounts, overwhelmingly the weather-related details are nothing short of extraordinary. In fact, these daily accounts and recollections provided crucial pieces of the meteorological assimilation puzzle that allowed understanding and description of the prevailing weather conditions during the forty-two-day campaign. Over this time, both armies experienced just about everything Mother Nature could throw at them, from extreme heat to torrential rains. In the final analysis, no account of the weather during the Gettysburg Campaign could exist without paying testament to the enlightening firsthand testimonials of those who lived it. Some wrote in amazingly descriptive and eloquent prose. Others offered succinct assessments of the weather but did so every day, or nearly so. Regardless, these nonofficial weather observers left us with priceless evidence of not only their suffering from the elements but also their ability to persevere through it all. And that alone makes their stories worth telling.

PEOPLE, STORIES AND MATTERS TO REMEMBER: JOHN ROBIE EASTMAN, U.S. NAVAL OBSERVATORY, WASHINGTON

Sometimes it's better to be lucky than good. Discovering that John Robie Eastman recorded weather observations at the U.S. Naval Observatory in Washington from June 3 to July 9, 1863, proved a phenomenal stroke of luck. Why? Because integrity of data matters. And while many of the Smithsonian Meteorological Project's weather observers were uniquely qualified for their duties and steadfast in their efforts (Gettysburg's Professor Jacobs is a prime example), the U.S. Naval Observatory eclipsed all others when they assigned Eastman the duties of recording weather observations there.

Over the course of his lifetime, John Eastman wore numerous hats, including scientist, author and U.S. Navy admiral. At the time of his death, obituaries in newspapers across the nation paid tribute to the man and his many accomplishments. Interestingly, Eastman's duties as a weather observer were largely overshadowed by his achievements as an astronomer. Yet for those of us concerned with the weather's impact on the Gettysburg Campaign, the importance of the data he gathered during June and July 1863 cannot be overstated. These records, largely overlooked and unused by historians until now, represent a quantum leap that permits a much more thorough

Fig. 20 John Robie Eastman. *Courtesy of the U.S. Naval Institute Archives.*

analysis of the weather conditions at the time and a better understanding of the effect of these conditions on the soldiers of the armies who served during the campaign.

Born in Andover, New Hampshire, on July 29, 1836, John Robie Eastman spent his youth attending area schools and working on the family farm. A distant cousin to Daniel Webster, the young Eastman demonstrated a bent for all things academic in his formative years. He served as a teacher for several years prior to enrolling at Dartmouth College in 1860.[30] Having entered Dartmouth as a third-year student, Eastman completed his Master of Arts degree in 1862[31] and then accepted an appointment to the U.S. Naval Observatory in Washington, where extant documents confirm that he acted as an official weather observer from 1862 to 1865.[32] On February 17, 1865, his earnest efforts at the Observatory resulted in his appointment as professor of mathematics with the U.S. Navy. Given the relative rank of lieutenant commander, Eastman was assigned to various astronomical duties. During his tenure with the Observatory, he also received his doctorate from Dartmouth.[33] His work and research at the Observatory included directing and coordinating the publication of *The Second Washington Star Catalogue*, a remarkable tome that includes some 80,000 observations made at the Observatory between 1866 and 1891 (one source indicates that Eastman's observations dominated the work). He traveled far and wide to observe and study numerous eclipses both while at the Observatory and afterward, including total solar eclipses at Syracuse, Sicily (December 1870); West Las Animas, Colorado (July 1878); and Barnesville, Georgia (May 1900).[34]

Though Eastman retired in 1898, he remained active in astronomical and scientific circles, working tirelessly to revise, recompute and correct results of observations of the sun, moon, planets and comets. This work culminated in the 1903 publication of *Transit Circle Observations of the Sun, Moon, Planets, and Comets*. He also served as the president of the Philosophical Society of Washington and the first president of the Washington Academy of Sciences.[35]

Even after residing in Washington for some thirty-six years, Eastman never lost his love of farming. In his later years he spent most of his time enjoying the farm on which he was born while also serving in the New Hampshire Legislature in 1905 and on the Board of Directors of Dartmouth from 1906 to 1909.[36] Eastman passed away on September 26, 1913, at age seventy-seven. He was buried, along with his wife of some forty-six years, at Andover's Proctor Cemetery.[37]

3

THE BEGINNING

The Calm Before the Storm, June 3–9, 1863

The day was quite warm; a shower in the p.m. A portion of the First Corps—General [Longstreet's] *started up the river today.*[38]
—Jedediah Hotchkiss, June 3, 1863

In what turned out to be a great understatement regarding both the campaign and the weather, the famous Confederate topographical engineer Jedediah Hotchkiss recorded this comment in his diary on June 3, 1863. Little did he know what was to come.

Setting the Stage

Situation Report—A Brief Summary of Troop Movements and Dispositions

Historians sometimes disagree regarding the Battle of Gettysburg's significance in the course of the Civil War. Certainly, the Union victory at Gettysburg represented a landmark event. As the largest and bloodiest battle ever fought in North America, it stands above all others. But did the Battle of Gettysburg represent *the* turning point in the war? Perhaps authors Vossler and McCausland best capture its consequence in their *Battle Tested! Leadership Lessons for 21st Century Leaders*. Rather astutely, they point out

Fig. 21 Jed Hotchkiss. *Courtesy of Mary Baldwin College.*

that twelve Civil War campaigns preceded Gettysburg and twelve came afterward. They further note that Winston Churchill's observation pertaining to the Allied victory at El Alamein in Egypt during World War II might well apply to the Union victory at Gettysburg: "Now this is not the end. It is not even the beginning of the end. But it is, perhaps, the end of the beginning."[39]

If true, the end of the beginning began on June 3, 1863. As it happened, between June 3 and June 9, 1863, both the Confederate Army of Northern Virginia and the Union Army of the Potomac were located within thirty-five miles of Fredericksburg, Virginia. General Robert E. Lee's forces gradually began a generally westward movement away from Fredericksburg on June 3. His First Corps (Longstreet's) as well as his Second Corps (Ewell's) initially headed toward Culpeper. Meanwhile, Lee's Third Corps (Hill's) remained at Fredericksburg. As elements of Lee's army moved out, the Army of the Potomac under Major General Joseph Hooker, who remained uncertain of Lee's intentions, maintained its positions near Fredericksburg. Only the Union cavalry, the eyes and ears of the army, responded as they sought to gain intelligence on Confederate movements. On June 9, the Union cavalry surprised the Confederate cavalry at Brandy Station, a few miles from Culpeper. The resultant battle between some 20,000 troops became the largest cavalry battle to ever take place in North America.

The Weather—Background

Collectively, the weather threats posed to the armies from June 3 to June 9, 1863, were relatively tame compared to those in other periods of the campaign. Figure 2A (color section) provides the daily high and low temperatures, maximum daily heat index (when at or above 80 degrees F) and daily rainfall at the Naval Observatory for the entire Gettysburg campaign. For context, the average daily high and average daily low temperatures during the period June 3–9 were around 80 degrees F and 60 degrees F, respectively. The color coding conveys the departure from

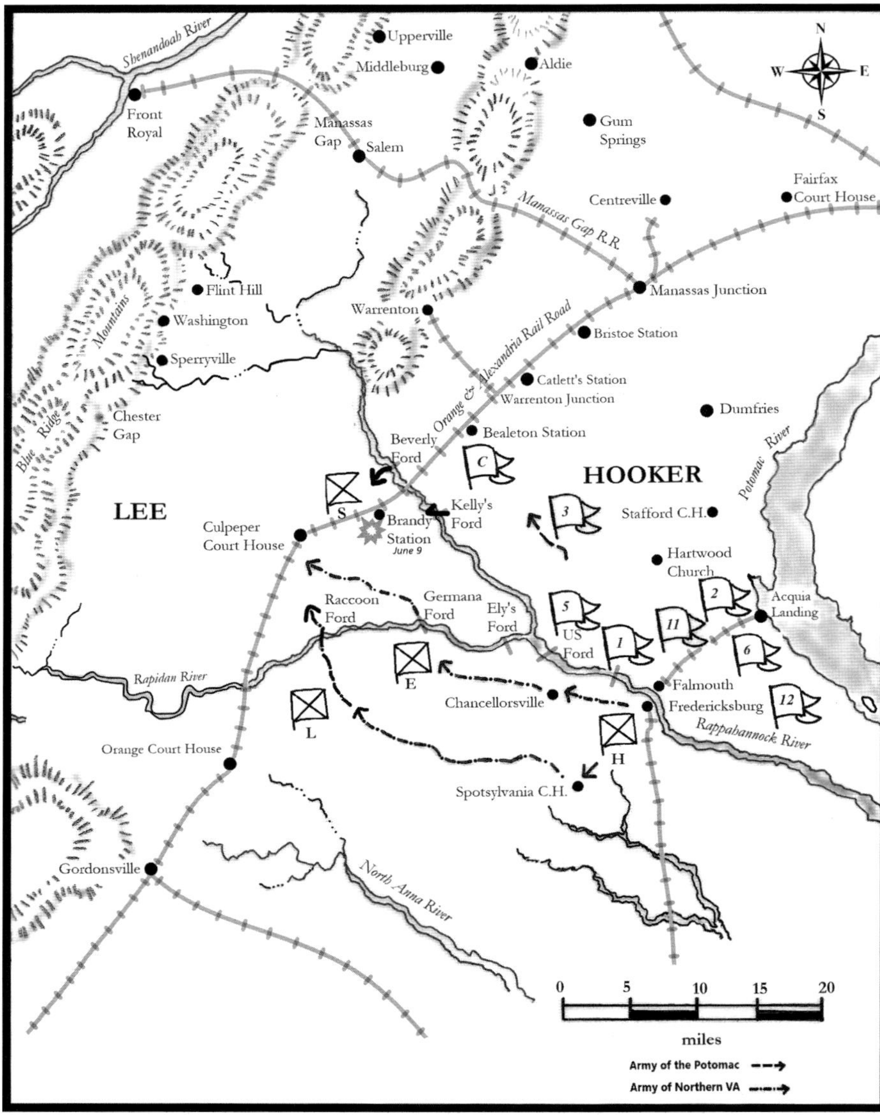

***Above*: Fig. 22** Gettysburg Campaign, June 3–9, 1863. For all maps, swallowtail flags denote Army of the Potomac infantry corps (1st, 2nd, 3rd, 5th, 6th, 11th, and 12th) and cavalry (*C*), X-marked flags denote Army of Northern Virginia infantry corps (*H* for Hill, *L* for Longstreet, *E* for Ewell) and cavalry (*S* for Stuart's Cavalry Division). *Courtesy of J. Heiser.*

***Opposite, left*: Fig. 23** General Robert E. Lee. *From Dawes,* Service with the Sixth Wisconsin Volunteers.

***Opposite, right*: Fig. 24** General Joseph Hooker. *From Dawes,* Service with the Sixth Wisconsin Volunteers.

average for the daily high and low temperatures and is intended to provide, at a glance, a sense for how each day's temperature extremes compared to their respective average.

Figure 25 focuses on June 3–9, and in addition to showing the daily high (triangle), daily low (circle) and maximum daily heat index (square), plots the temperature (solid line) and dewpoint (dashed line) every three hours at the Naval Observatory. If precipitation was observed, the daily amount appears along the bottom. For reference in assessing the impact of the weather on human comfort, the dashed horizontal line marks 65 degrees F, a dewpoint value generally associated with conditions that would feel humid to most people. Notice that dewpoints remained below this threshold at every observation time.

The Primary Source Data

Two Smithsonian weather observers in the Fredericksburg area diligently recorded data before the Civil War, but neither continued during the conflict. Thus, the nearest official weather observers at the time were in Washington, about fifty-five miles to the north-northeast, at the Naval Observatory and at Georgetown. The reports from the Observatory provide the richest dataset for the purposes of this analysis.

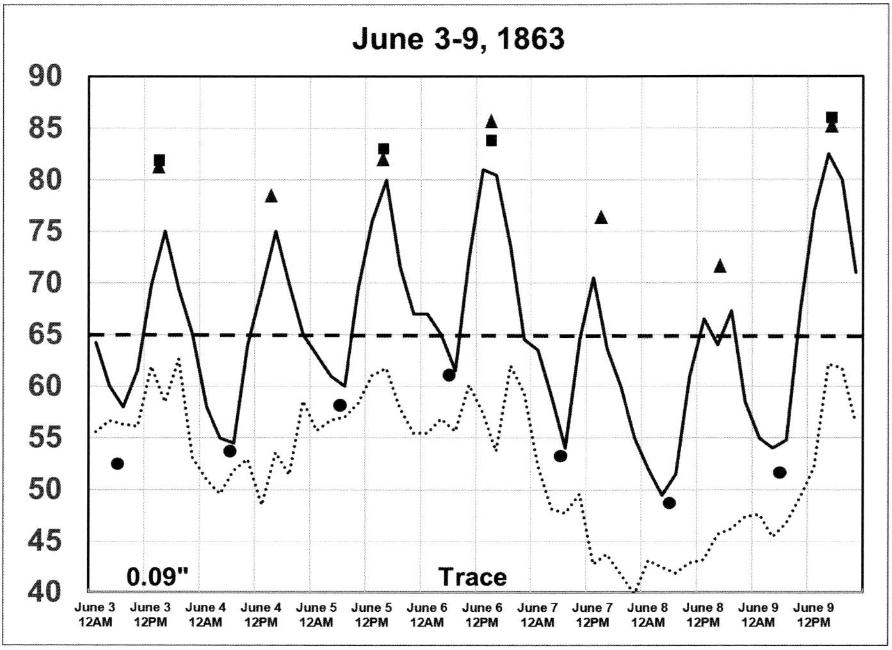

Fig. 25 Plot of temperature (solid) and dewpoint (dotted) every three hours at the Naval Observatory for June 3–9, 1863. Circles indicate daily low temperatures, triangles daily high temperatures and squares the estimated daily maximum heat index. If rain occurred, the amount is noted. (Trace means less than 0.01") *Data from NOAA FORTS.*

As previously established, the modern-day climates of Washington and Fredericksburg are, on average, very similar, with average daily high and low temperatures within a degree or two of each other. During the first week of the campaign, the armies were concentrated in the region from Fredericksburg to Culpeper. Temperature and precipitation data are available from both locations as far back as the early twentieth century, a time when the climate would not have differed substantially from the 1860s. The data show that, on average, high temperatures at the two locations in June differed by less than one degree F during that reference period and low temperatures by less than two degrees F. Average June precipitation varied by less than a quarter inch, both close to four inches for the month.[40] These small differences solidify our assertion that the Naval Observatory data provide a reasonable proxy for the general weather conditions experienced by the armies during this part of the campaign. On any given day, of course, variations in cloud cover and precipitation can create differences in local weather, and observations from soldiers often were useful in filling those gaps.

DAY-TO-DAY ANALYSIS

The first two days of June 1863 were generally warmer than average, particularly during the day. Clear to partly cloudy skies had dominated, and no rain was reported by any official observer in the mid-Atlantic. That would soon change. Skies at the Naval Observatory clouded over by 9:00 p.m. on June 2, and observers in Washington and Annapolis reported light rain the morning of June 3. A reconstruction of the average surface weather map on June 3 (see Figure 3A, color section) shows a zone of relatively low pressure along the East Coast, which likely housed a front (indicated by the thick line) that would have been the culprit for the much-needed rain. Writing about the 149th Pennsylvania Volunteer Infantry of the First Corps encamped near Fredericksburg, historian Richard E. Matthews noted, "The third day of June was remembered by the men of the 149th as the first day with rain since the return from Chancellorsville."[41] About forty miles to the south at Mangohick Creek, Army of Northern Virginia Surgeon Charles Edward Lippitt of the 57th Virginia reported a "severe hail storm," likely associated with the front.[42]

As that zone of lower pressure eased off the Atlantic coast on June 4, high pressure in the Midwest on June 3 slid east, ushering in a cooler and drier air mass. The barometer at the Naval Observatory signaled this change in weather as the pressure there generally rose through noon on June 5, while dewpoints settled into the comfortable range. In fact, high temperatures near 80 degrees F and overnight lows in the 50s prompted Mary Gray Caldwell, a resident of Fredericksburg, to write, "The weather still continues good, neither too warm or too cold."[43] But some soldiers, undoubtedly those exposed to a midday sun now less than three weeks from the solstice, referred to "very warm" days and "dry, hot, dusty marching."[44]

Teasing a possible change in the weather, air pressure at the Naval Observatory trended lower by the end of June 5, and Sergeant William Wilkin with the 1st West Virginia (Union) Cavalry near Manassas and vineyard owner Marcus Buck near Front Royal both reported a shower that evening.[45] Farther north, John Heisely in Harrisburg and Professor Jacobs in Gettysburg both recorded some rain as well. These signs of a moistening atmosphere were likely assisted by southerly and southeasterly winds reported into the wee hours of June 6 at the Naval Observatory.

Meanwhile, large rises in air pressure well to the north and west in Rochester, New York; Cincinnati, Ohio; and Marquette, Michigan, signaled that a second, more significant center of higher air pressure (and the cooler, less humid air associated with it) was poised to move east into the mid-Atlantic. Indeed, breaks in the heat, and especially humidity, often arrive in stages in the mid-Atlantic in summer. Here, the cold front that represented the leading edge of "Stage 2" began to approach. Ahead of that front, the high temperature reached 85.5 degrees F at the Naval Observatory. Corporal Calvin Heller of the 153rd Pennsylvania, just north of Fredericksburg, called the day "nice and warm," while the 15th Georgia's Private Thomas Ware, near Culpeper, said it was a "pleasant…Very warm day."[46]

Fig. 26 Private Thomas Ware. *Courtesy of UNC-Wilson.*

By far, however, soldiers most clearly recalled the weather on June 6 for what happened late in the day. Clues emerge from the official observers, including evening rain in Gettysburg and Harrisburg and a shower at 6:30 p.m. with lightning and distant thunder at the Naval Observatory. The *Baltimore Sun* reported "a tremendous hail storm" twenty miles northeast of that city "in the neighborhood of Havre-de-Grace."[47] Various soldiers affirm that rain reached both armies later that day, described variously as "a very severe storm," "a thunder shower which has cooled the air amazingly" and "a little shower of rain this evening."[48] Such differing descriptions are not uncommon, as rainfall intensities can vary greatly across short distances with the broken lines of showers and thunderstorms that typically accompany summer cold fronts. The result was that most troops saw at least some rain later on June 6, while for an unfortunate few such as Private John Camden West of the 4th Texas Infantry, "It rained a good deal during the night and kept me thoroughly soaked."[49]

The late-day rains on June 6 were followed by arguably the most comfortable three-day period of weather during the entire Gettysburg Campaign. High pressure anchored over the western Great Lakes (see Figure 3B, color section) sponsored persistent and, at times, gusty northwesterly breezes that dominated June 7 and June 8 in Washington, ushering cooler and drier air into the mid-Atlantic. Very comfortable dewpoints of 50 degrees F or lower were observed there from 3:00 a.m. on June 7 to 9:00 a.m. on June 9. The temperature at the Naval Observatory on June 8 reached only 72 degrees F, tied for the coolest day of the campaign there, while overnight lows dropped to near 50 degrees F on three consecutive nights. That prompted a few soldiers such as Private Ira S. Pettit of the 11th U.S. Infantry, just west of Fredericksburg, to comment about the night of June 7, "Quite cold last night."[50]

Most soldiers, however, complimented Mother Nature in this period. According to Chaplain Alanson Haines of the 15th New Jersey, June 7 was "fair and beautiful, and the storm clouds had all passed away,"[51] while, on June 8, Mary Gray Caldwell in Fredericksburg summarized the period this way: "The weather is really like fall weather, cool and windy. It has been in this way for two or three days."[52]

It is often said that "all good things must come to an end," and that applies particularly to a period of low humidity in summer in Virginia. A warmup coupled with an increase in dewpoint commenced on the afternoon of June 9 under largely sunny skies, and the combination of temperature and humidity produced a maximum heat index estimated at 86 degrees F in Washington. Still, the day was dry, and fresh westerly winds took a bit of the edge off the heat. Notably, on June 9 mentions of two weather-related characteristics, repeated time and time again later in the campaign, began to appear in soldiers' observations. Private John T. Mark of the 147th Pennsylvania, near Fredericksburg, remarked that during a general review, "it was awful dusty,"[53] while the 1st Virginia's First Lieutenant John Dooley, after marching some forty miles in two days, wrote, "The sun is very afflicting during the day and some of the men break down."[54]

Fig. 27 Captain John E. Dooley. *Courtesy of Georgetown University Library.*

Little did anyone know how much Mark's and Dooley's observations portended what was to come.

PEOPLE, STORIES AND MATTERS TO REMEMBER: UNIFORMS—A BIT OF CLARITY

It happens every time. Guaranteed. No matter the audience, the retort remains the same. Mention the word *heat* in conjunction with the U.S. Civil War and someone within earshot quips, "It must have been terrible, *especially considering those wool uniforms the soldiers were wearing!*" Granted, donning a wool uniform during summer, especially on long marches and in battle, seems counterintuitive. That said, it's not that simple. To be accurate, one must actually ask, did all the soldiers wear wool? If not, what did they wear? And finally, how did what they wore (wool, cotton, etc.) affect their ability to cope with heat and humidity?

During the first few years of the war, uniforms on both sides shared great variations in types, colors and materials.[55] But by mid-1863, a high degree of standardization in uniforms prevailed. Most Union soldiers wore uniforms made of wool, both the frock coat and blouse (sack coat), but evidence points to an increasing use of shorter, waist-length jackets.[56] Yankee soldiers' trousers typically consisted of heavy wool, also known as "kersey."[57] Differing from their counterparts, most Confederate soldiers wore uniforms made of a cotton-wool blend material commonly referred to as "jean cloth." And overwhelmingly, by the summer of 1863, most Rebels would have worn waist-length jackets typically referred to as "shell jackets."

Regarding which uniform soldiers might prefer in summer heat, modern living historians indicate that jean cloth proves much more comfortable than wool in extremely warm weather. They also pointed out that this cotton-wool blend usually "breathes" much better than wool. As one put it succinctly, "As for heat tolerance, I think I would rather be a Reb in the summer and a Yank in the winter."[58]

In addition to their outerwear, many soldiers wore undergarments commonly referred to as "drawers," year-round. As one museum specialist noted, "Both governments issued depot-produced undergarments to their soldiers, typically flannel for Union soldiers and cotton for Confederates."[59]

Uniform color also mattered. Typically, Yankee soldiers' uniforms consisted of a dark blue sack coat and light blue pants.[60] Meanwhile the typical Confederate wore either gray or light brown (butternut) colored uniforms, including their pants and "shell jackets" (see Figures 10A, 11A and 11B, color section).[61] Regardless, the dark blue coats worn by the majority of Union soldiers absorbed more sunlight and, in turn, transferred this heat to the soldier. As a result, the average Union soldier felt the heat more on any given sunny day than his Confederate counterpart.

Interestingly, the men who served during the Gettysburg Campaign opined very little about their uniforms, whether made of wool, cotton or a combination thereof. They wrote more about their poor footwear, or lack thereof, and their blistered feet, than anything else. And ironically, several sources point to a better-shod Rebel than Yankee in the Gettysburg Campaign.[62] In truth, by the early summer of 1863, soldiers in both armies faced more pressing concerns. If they complained about anything, grousing centered on the burden of carrying some forty to fifty pounds of clothing, blankets, half of a tent, cartridge box, bayonet, canteen, rifle and more on lengthy forced marches.

In the end, this fact seems clear: not *every soldier* in the Gettysburg Campaign wore a wool uniform. If a soldier wore wool, he typically served in the Army of the Potomac. The Confederates were fortunate in that most wore a cotton-wool blend known as jean cloth and their lighter colored shell jackets did not magnify the heat like the deep blue sack coats often worn by their counterparts. However, their jean cloth uniforms retained moisture more than pure wool, while the Union soldiers' wool uniforms wicked sweat away better than the Confederates' wool-cotton blend. Thus, as far as the pros and cons of uniforms worn by all soldiers during the Gettysburg Campaign, the Southerners may have gotten the better end of the deal, as their clothing likely allowed them to suffer somewhat less from heat-related circumstances. But neither uniform was perfect. Regardless, the extreme heat and torrential rains experienced by both armies during the Gettysburg Campaign likely proved an equalizer.[63]

4

THE APPROACH

Hotter Than Hades, and Then Some, June 10–18, 1863

There were many prostrations—men staggering from the ranks and falling as if shot. There were a number of cases of fatal sunstroke, and some dying almost as quickly as if struck by a bullet in a vital part.[64]

—Sergeant James A. Wright of the 1st Minnesota Infantry

Flesh and blood cannot sustain such heat and fatigue as we have undergone this day. It is terrible! All along the roadside since 9 o'clock this morning I have seen men dropping, gasping, dying—or already dead![65]

—Private Randolph A. Shotwell of the 8th Virginia Infantry

SETTING THE STAGE

Situation Report—A Brief Summary of Troop Movements and Dispositions

Within a day of the Battle of Brandy Station, General Lee ordered the Army of Northern Virginia to continue its march northward. Finally, on June 12, Major General Hooker began to move the Army of the Potomac away from the vicinity of Fredericksburg. By then, Lee's army effectively had stolen a march on Hooker. Eminent historian Edwin B. Coddington explained it best when he wrote, "At the beginning of the campaign most of the Federal

Troop Location Map

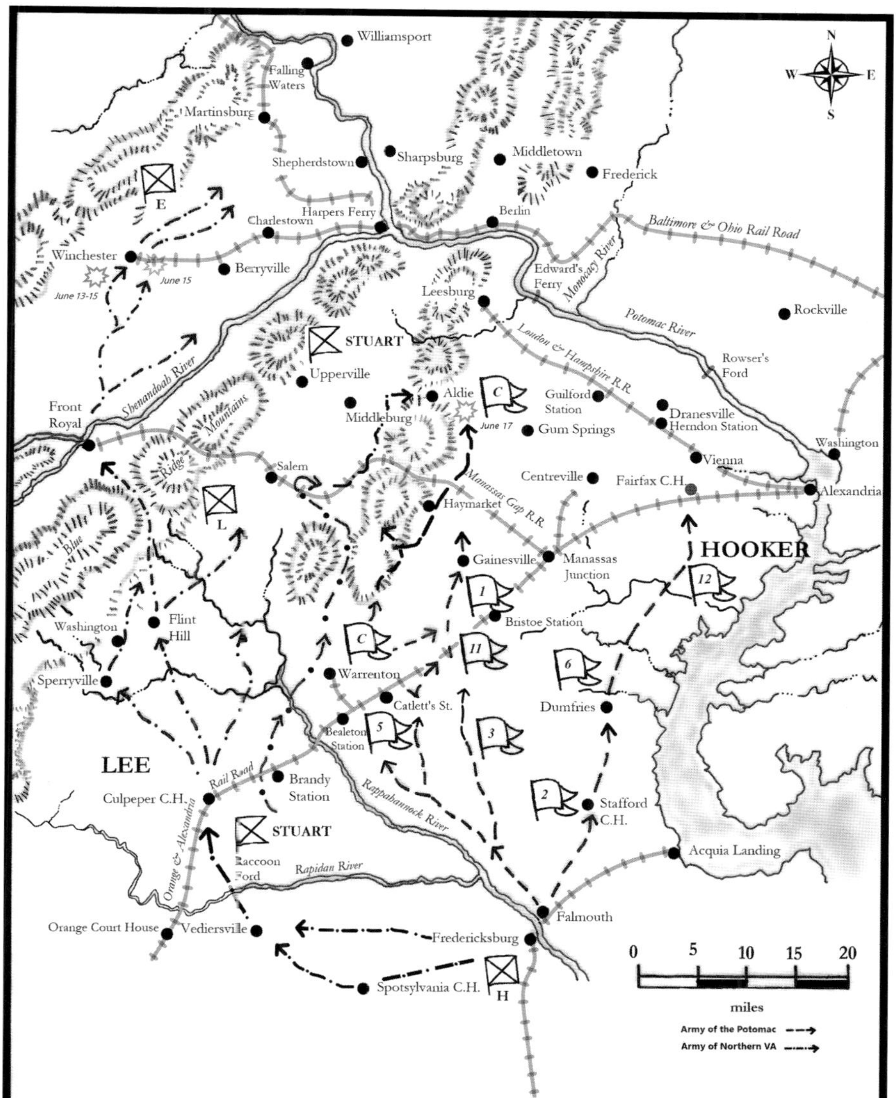

Fig. 28 Gettysburg Campaign, June 10–17, 1863. This map covers troop movements only through June 17 to best convey relevant army movements detailed in this chapter. *Courtesy of J. Heiser.*

troops had remained in more or less fixed positions while their adversary slyly moved away from them. Almost before anyone knew it, the Army of the Potomac was facing an emergency: It was in danger of being cut off from Washington."[66] To remedy this situation, Hooker needed to move his forces with alacrity. And the men of the Army of the Potomac paid the price for Hooker's earlier timidity in the form of a series of lengthy marches, some upward of twenty-five miles per day. And much of it in weather that proved to be rare in June for its extreme heat and humidity.

As both armies moved northward, a series of significant cavalry battles ensued. The first occurred on June 17 at Aldie, where the Union troopers sought to penetrate the Confederate cavalry forces guarding the mountain passes to screen the northward movement of Lee's army. Meanwhile, by this date the advancing Confederate forces under General Ewell had won significant victories at Winchester and Stephenson's Depot, effectively clearing the lower Shenandoah Valley of Union opposition. As the sun set on June 18, Lee's army ranged from north to south along a line some one hundred miles long. Meanwhile, Hooker moved his army northward along the path of the Orange and Alexandria Railroad with elements beginning to push westward to interrupt Lee.

The Weather—Background

Modern-day weather forecasting is truly a scientific revolution. Although improvements in the accuracy of forecasts have generally occurred slowly over time, those advances are real and measurable. For example, the error in a five-day National Weather Service high temperature forecast averages about four degrees F, the same as the error in a three-day forecast twenty years ago. A seven-day high temperature forecast today misses the mark, on average, by about five degrees F, the same as the error in a five-day forecast twenty years ago.[67] Stated another way, the ability to forecast temperature accurately has advanced at the rate of about one day per decade. What Lee or Hooker wouldn't have given for even a reasonably accurate five- to seven-day weather forecast on June 10, 1863! The military value of such information would have been immense and measured in the reduction of suffering and the saving of lives.

As the first month of meteorological summer, June continues the general warming trend of May in the mid-Atlantic. Cooler Canadian air masses occasionally break the heat, especially early in the month, though days when temperatures do not reach 70 degrees F are rare and generally caused by clouds and rain. Much more typical in June are stretches of warm, humid weather that create oppressive conditions: in short, a heatwave. Often, these periods of above-average heat and humidity end with powerful thunderstorms that pack torrential rains, strong winds and, at times, hail. The heatwave that settled over northern Virginia during mid-June 1863 followed this pattern, but the heat and humidity proved neither typical nor usual. Moreover, the timing could not have been worse.

The Primary Source Data

With the forces of the Army of the Potomac generally moving north from Fredericksburg and closer to Washington during the period June 10–18, the Naval Observatory data are likely even more representative of weather conditions endured by the Union army. Meanwhile, most of Lee's forces were aligned farther west in a south-to-north fashion from Culpeper to Martinsburg, where elevations were generally in the five-hundred to seven-hundred-foot range. As a result, temperatures experienced by Confederate forces likely averaged about two degrees lower than the Washington observations. From a practical standpoint—particularly given the weather conditions that would dominate this period—such a difference would have a minimal impact on the way the weather felt to soldiers.

DAY-TO-DAY ANALYSIS

In terms of sheer misery brought upon both armies by the weather, the period from June 10 to June 18, 1863, stands above all others during the Gettysburg Campaign for the combination of heat and humidity.

Maximum temperatures were above average on eight of the nine days, including four consecutive days that surpassed the daily average by more than 10 degrees F (see Figure 2A in the color insert). Increasing dewpoints compounded the misery caused by the heat, and as a result, the heat index became relevant.[68] Figure 29 resembles Figure 25 in chapter 3 (see page 62) but for June 10–18. During the period June 3–9, the dewpoint never reached the threshold of 65 degrees F generally associated with conditions that feel "humid" to most people, but the dewpoint exceeded that value at one or more official observation times *every day* from June 10–18. In fact, the

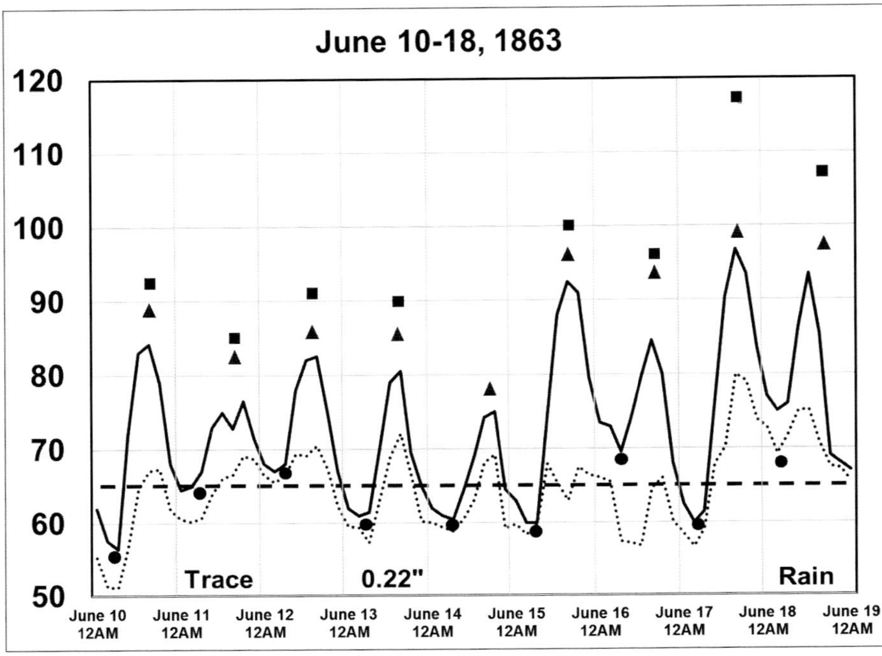

Fig. 29 Plot of temperature (solid) and dewpoint (dotted) every three hours at the Naval Observatory for June 10–18, 1863. Circles indicate daily low temperatures, triangles daily high temperatures and squares the estimated daily maximum heat index. If rain occurred, the amount is noted. *Data from NOAA FORTS.*

dewpoint stayed above that threshold for thirty consecutive hours early in the period and then most of the time during June 17 and June 18, the last two days—and peak—of the heat wave, when the dewpoint remained above 70 degrees F much of the time.

Weatherwise, June 10–18 began generally benign, just as the prior seven-day period ended. No observer in the mid-Atlantic, official or unofficial, reported rain on June 10. Instead, soldiers' remarks included observations of a deepening dryness. Arriving at camp near Warrenton Junction, Lieutenant Norman Ball of the 16th Pennsylvania Cavalry reported "a very dusty ride,"[69] while Private Henry R. Berkeley of Kirkpatrick's Battery of the Army of Northern Virginia's Second Corps indicated, "We marched from Culpeper to Little Washington, some twenty-three miles; a very hot and dusty day."[70] Indeed, the temperature peaked at 89 degrees F on June 10 at the Naval Observatory as winds shifted to southerly by afternoon, drawing in more humid air. The estimated maximum heat index reached 92 degrees F, a harbinger of things to come.

Farther west, Smithsonian observers near Louisville and Nashville measured significant pressure falls and nearly an inch of rain on June 10, while about a half inch fell in Cincinnati, portending the next weather system to come east. The NOAA reconstruction system places a storm in the western Ohio Valley in the wee hours of June 11 with attendant fronts that marked the leading edge of the next round of cooler, drier air (see Figure 4A, color section). The counterclockwise circulation around that storm, coupled with the clockwise flow around an area of high pressure off the Carolinas, provided moist southerly winds that kept dewpoints high for both armies but also made for a cloudier day, keeping temperatures in the 70s most of the time. More than a half inch of rain fell west of the Alleghenies in Pittsburgh on June 11, but as sometimes happens when fronts try to move into the mid-Atlantic in summer, precipitation weakens east of the mountains. The Naval Observatory reported only a light shower shortly before 9:00 p.m. Only a few soldier accounts mentioned rain on June 11, and then only sprinkles; instead, Lieutenant Edwin Houghton of the 17th Maine Infantry, north of Fredericksburg, spoke for many when he wrote, "The weather was very warm, and the roads extremely dusty."[71]

Air pressure bottomed out around sunrise at the Naval Observatory on June 12 (see Figure 19, page 54), signaling the passage of what was left of the storm and front. By afternoon, the observer reported northwest winds at "Force 4" (estimated at approximately twenty-five miles per hour), briefly ushering in more comfortable air for the overnight period. But before that short break, June 12 became the first of many days when weather affected the health of soldiers. As the Union forces went on the move, the heat index in Washington likely climbed above 90 degrees F for a time that afternoon. Drummer boy Henry M. Kieffer of the 150th Pennsylvania, which marched twenty miles that day, remarked, "Very warm, dust plenty, water scarce, marching very hard."[72] Chaplain Warren Cudworth of the 1st Massachusetts traversed nearly thirty miles that day "through clouds of dust in some places so dense, that vision was impossible beyond a few yards; and a large number of the men fell out by the wayside, utterly overcome by heat and fatigue."[73] Fellow member of the 1st Massachusetts, fifer Charles Bardeen, added: "It was an awful hot day. Many dropped dead on the road."[74] Little did they know that Mother Nature soon had much worse to offer.

The early morning hours of June 13 provided some relief from the previous day's discomfort. The temperature bottomed out at 60 degrees F at the Naval Observatory, with the dewpoint slipping into the 50s overnight. But as commonly happens in the mid-Atlantic in summer, humidity returned quickly, and buoyed by some sunshine, the afternoon heat index approached 90 degrees F once again, setting off a round of scattered thunderstorms across the theater. "Raining at 10 to 4 with sharp lightning and heavy thunder," wrote John Eastman at the Naval Observatory, who reported 0.22 inches of rain, while the nearby Georgetown observer recorded 0.73 inches. Of the day, Private Isaac Taylor of the 1st Minnesota wrote, "Quite pleasant—some clouds," then added, "thunder shower at sunset."[75] Private Ira Pettit of the 11th U.S. Infantry reported, "A heavy thunder shower prevailed from 6 until 8 o'clock after we started and marched until nearly midnight towards Warrenton Junction. Very hot; some died from sunstroke."[76] Confirming that rain was not confined to the Union forces, Private Thomas Ware of the 15th Georgia remarked, "Cloudy night with thunder and lightning" near Culpeper,[77] while just south of Winchester, Second Lieutenant Robert Funkhouser of the 49th Virginia noted that it "rained very hard about night and we got pretty well drenched."[78]

Fig. 30 Sergeant Patrick Taylor and Private Isaac Taylor. *Courtesy of NPS, GNMP, Museum Collection, GETT #3554.*

The rain proved to be neither widespread in coverage nor sufficient in amount to curb complaints about dust in the coming days. For the next four days, no more rain fell on the armies, confirmed by both official and unofficial sources, setting the stage for one of the most consequential weather-related effects on the Gettysburg Campaign.

Skies in Washington remained overcast into early afternoon on June 14, suppressing the afternoon maximum temperature to 79 degrees F, the lowest high temperature there in almost a week. Clouds broke earlier in some areas to the west and south in Virginia, leading to another difficult day of marching for Union forces. Henry Kieffer remembered, "From five o'clock of that morning till three the following morning…we were hurried along under a burning June sun."[79] Private Thomas Cooper of the 26th Pennsylvania was more graphic: "On the 14th our march from Bealeton to Manassas is remembered as one of the hottest, many of the division and corps falling from sunstroke, so that when night came the losses, if they had been compiled, would have held comparison with a battle."[80] Observations from the Naval Observatory of light winds that day were confirmed by Captain Jonathan Hager of the 14th U.S. Infantry who noted, "We very soon reached the country where there had been no rain....There was scarcely a breath of air stirring to sweep away the clouds of dust which enveloped the column...while the sun seemed to do its utmost to make veterans of us all."[81]

Few if any clouds likely accompanied the sunset in the western sky that evening. With light winds and relatively dry air, temperatures fell quickly after sunset, and the thermometer at the Naval Observatory bottomed out at 59 degrees F early on the morning of June 15. Clear skies and dry air also allow for rapid warming once the sun rises, particularly true so close to the solstice, and temperatures rose quickly on June 15, the first of a punishing four-day stretch of summer weather, covered in-depth in the "When Weather Mattered the Most" focus piece that follows.

The dryness that preceded the coming heat wave likely played a role in its intensity. Sunshine absorbed at the earth's surface not only warms the ground but also evaporates water on it. In very dry conditions, with reduced surface moisture, more of the sun's energy goes toward heating. So, all else being equal, a drier surface typically leads to a warmer day.

Table 2 shows the amount of rain in the four-week period May 18–June 14 preceding the heat wave at official observing sites in the vicinity of Washington. For comparison, average rainfall for those four weeks at these locations generally ranges from 3.0 to 3.5 inches, so most places received only 10 to 30 percent of average. To place this dry period in context, consider the Naval Observatory's total of 0.31 inches. When compared to the May 18–June 14 period in the modern-day records of Washington (which start in 1872), only two other years had less rain during those four weeks.[82] Not coincidentally, in those two years, June ranked as the warmest and tenth warmest on record. The bottom line: exceptionally dry weather preceded the June 1863 heat wave, and the dry ground likely exacerbated the potential for heat.

Two maps from the NOAA reanalysis system, shown in Figures 4B and 5A (see color section), capture the weather pattern that dominated June 15–18, 1863, in the mid-Atlantic. Figure 4B shows the surface pressure pattern averaged over the first two days of the period. An elongated zone of higher

TABLE 2. RAINFALL (IN INCHES) IN THE PERIOD MAY 18–JUNE 14, 1863

Frederick, MD	0.00
Naval Observatory, DC	0.31*
Annapolis, MD	0.52
Sykesville, MD	0.00
Bladensburg, MD	0.89
Chestertown, MD	1.12
Georgetown, DC	0.73

*May have been slightly higher

pressure, known as a "ridge" to meteorologists, stretched from the Midwest to the mid-Atlantic. High pressure typically sponsors sinking air which is conducive to fair skies and little rain. Figure 5A shows the average relative humidity about 10,000 feet above the ground during that two-day period. High values of relative humidity at that altitude, typically 70 percent or greater, often correlate well with clouds, while values less than 30 percent typically signal clear skies. Observations from the Naval Observatory during this period indicated cloud-free skies most of the time except when the report read "hazy," a common description of the milky skies that often accompany heat and humidity in the eastern United States.

Next, our first "When Weather Mattered the Most" focus piece introduces the new and enhanced understanding of the meteorological circumstances facing both armies alongside an in-depth interpretation of the weather's effect on the soldiers. This boots on the ground perspective not only reveals how the elements truly felt to the soldiers but also provides historians with an expanded window of interpretation as viewed through the lens of the weather.

WHEN WEATHER MATTERED THE MOST: THE MID-JUNE HEATWAVE—PUTTING EVERYTHING IN PERSPECTIVE

For years, historians have known it was very warm in northern Virginia in the period June 15–18, 1863. Two weeks into the Gettysburg Campaign, sundry soldiers' accounts attest to this fact. And according to Robert K.

Krick's 2007 book *Civil War Weather in Virginia*, temperatures in the region may have reached upward of 96 degrees F.[83] However, historians did not know how hot the weather actually felt to the soldiers. Previous studies have not considered heat index. This dearth of data represented a crucial gap of knowledge because numerous soldiers suffered serious consequences from the combination of heat and humidity during this period. Without heat index data, historians have questioned the validity of the soldiers' accounts. Beyond this, the question lingered: Did the intensity of the heat during this period represent an unusual circumstance for the region in June? Fortunately, previously unused primary source records from the Naval Observatory, and subsequent meteorological analysis, answered these important questions. As a result, we now understand how hot the weather likely felt to the soldiers during this time frame. And we also understand the highly unusual nature of the deadly mid-June heatwave.

Eventful weather can influence military campaigns. Indeed, history offers numerous such circumstances. And the mid- to latter part of the second full week of the Gettysburg Campaign represents a prime example. After an initial period of relative inactivity during the early phases of the campaign, the Army of the Potomac's commanding officer, Major General Joseph Hooker, finally realized the Confederate army had begun, surreptitiously, to slip away to the northwest. Upon this realization, Hooker considered the option of advancing on Richmond, but Lincoln indicated to him that Lee's army, not the capital of the Confederacy, must remain his target. Lacking any additional, more specific, direction from Lincoln and his chain of command in Washington, Hooker initiated a series of movements. His goal was to shadow Lee's Army of Northern Virginia as much as possible while keeping his army between Lee's army and Washington. Historian Edwin B. Coddington, in his highly regarded *The Gettysburg Campaign: A Study in Command*, summed up the situation at the time:

> *These movements which resulted in the realignment of the two armies occurred during a heat wave, so typical of the month of June. The weather affected everyone, in some cases disastrously so.... To catch up with the enemy one corps after another wheeled into long columns and hour after hour tramped northward over rough roads, though stifled by the broiling sun and blinded by the clouds of dust. For the men in blue these forced marches marked the real beginning of a campaign memorable for such hardships, when it was not an unusual occurrence to cover thirty-five miles in twenty-four hours.*[84]

For the Army of the Potomac, these movements began in earnest on June 12, a few days prior to the onset of the heatwave. The fast-paced and lengthy marches of June 12–13 could not have held the Union soldiers in good stead for the near future. The Confederate soldiers, who had already marched for several days, also stood much more susceptible to the forthcoming weather-related circumstances because of their recent exertions. And though Coddington captured the situation accurately in stating that June heatwaves were somewhat typical in the region, the intensity of the mid-June 1863 heatwave proved to be entirely atypical.

The extreme conditions experienced by Union and Confederate soldiers beginning in earnest on June 15 caused widespread suffering, heatstroke and even death. Yet the degree to which a soldier may have suffered depended largely on chance. Here a soldier's fate hung not on a random bullet but on several other factors. While some troops had the good fortune of experiencing less arduous marches, a large number suffered through lengthy forced treks, some upward of twenty-five miles in length. And for some, these tramps took place on consecutive days during the heatwave. Worse yet, some of these dreadful marches occurred on June 17, the hottest and most dangerous day of all.[85] Meanwhile, opportunities to obtain water and meaningful respites proved scarce. Few escaped the misery and suffering, whether Union or Confederate.[86]

As a baseline, Figure 31 shows modern-day average maximum and minimum temperatures for June 17, essentially the middle of the heat wave. These values are likely a degree or so higher than those in the nineteenth century due to climate change and another degree or two higher in the larger cities because of urbanization, especially at night. These averages, particularly the highs, illustrate a relatively small spread in typical conditions across the area of interest, especially in the eastern part where, for all

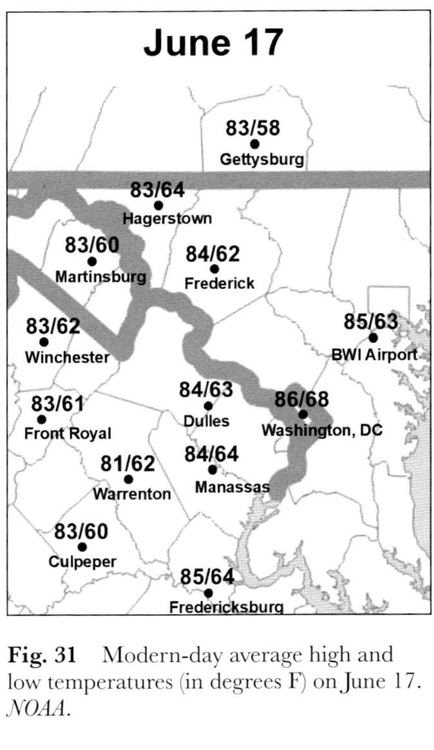

Fig. 31 Modern-day average high and low temperatures (in degrees F) on June 17. *NOAA.*

TABLE 3. TEMPERATURES (IN DEGREES F) AT THE NAVAL OBSERVATORY, JUNE 15–18, 1863

	June 15	June 16	June 17	June 18
12:00 a.m.	63	73.5	62.5	77
3:00 a.m.	60	73	60	75
6:00 a.m.	60	69.5	61.5	76
9:00 a.m.	74.5	74	76	86.2
12:00 p.m.	88	79.5	90.3	93.5
3:00 p.m.	92.5	84.5	96.8	85.4
6:00 p.m.	91	80	93.5	69
9:00 p.m.	79.5	68	83.5	68
Max/Min	96/59	93.5/68	99/60	97.3/68

intents and purposes, the Washington averages are equivalent to those in Fredericksburg.

The primary source data indicate that the mid-June heatwave of 1863 ranks near the top end of severity for recorded June heatwaves in the region. Table 3 provides the relevant temperature observations for June 15–18, 1863, at the Naval Observatory, where daily high and low temperatures were also observed. Those extremes are indicated by the triangles (highs) and circles (lows) in Figure 29 on page 72 and are also shown in Table 3. Daily high temperatures reached the 93–99–degree F range four consecutive days, with readings above 90 degrees F for more than six hours on June 17, the peak of the heatwave. The Georgetown observations parallel the heat at the Naval Observatory, with temperatures at 2:00 p.m. of 92, 94, 94 and 96 degrees F, respectively, during the four-day stretch.

The highest estimated heat index at an observation time at the Naval Observatory on June 15 was 95 degrees F, based on a temperature of 91 degrees F and a dewpoint of 67 degrees F at 6:00 p.m. The temperature for the day peaked at 96 degrees F, which likely occurred between 3:00 p.m. and 6:00 p.m. Pairing that maximum temperature with a reasonable estimate of 66 degrees F for the dewpoint at that time yields a maximum heat index for the day in the 99–100–degree F range. Notably, the temperature stayed mainly in the 70s that night, dropping below 70 degrees F only briefly.

On June 16, the highest estimated heat index at any observation time was 86 degrees F, based on a temperature of 84.5 degrees F and a dewpoint of 65 degrees F at 3:00 p.m. Coupling the daily high temperature of 93.5 degrees F with observed late-afternoon dewpoints consistently in the 65–66–degree F range yields a maximum heat index for the day of 96 degrees F. Though that value still falls in the middle of the "Extreme Caution" category of the heat index, June 16 was the least dangerous of the four days.

In contrast, the third day of the heatwave, June 17, proved to be the apex of this atypical period. Remarkably, the estimated heat index that fateful day reached 117 degrees F at 3:00 p.m., based on an observed temperature of 96.8 degrees F and a rare dewpoint of 80 degrees F. The heat index almost surely spiked slightly higher an hour or two later, given that the dewpoint was still 79 degrees F at the 6:00 p.m. observation and the high temperature for the day reached 99 degrees F. According to Figure 8 in chapter 1 (page 39), heat indices in the 117–119–degree F range are at the high end of the "Danger" category, with heat cramps or heat exhaustion likely and heatstroke possible. And remember, the heat index is a shade measurement—exposure to sunlight could add up to 15 degrees F to the shade value. The estimated wet-bulb globe temperature, which includes the impact of sunlight, was in the 89–91–degree F range. Modern guidelines (see Figure 10 in chapter 1, page 41) categorize these conditions as "high to extreme risk," indicating the body becomes stressed after fifteen to twenty minutes and recommending at least a quart of water per hour and at least forty minutes of rest each hour if working in direct sunshine. Sadly, the beleaguered soldiers of both armies had little if any opportunity for either proper hydration or regular and lengthy periods of rest.

Importantly, the temperature at 9:00 p.m. on June 17 only dropped to 83.5 degrees F. Coupled with an observed dewpoint of 74 degrees F, the resultant heat index was still 90 degrees F at that late hour. Such conditions likely spoiled any chance for soldiers to gain meaningful rest and relief from the heat.

To put these extreme heat index values into historical context, we looked at more than sixty recent years (1962–2023) of hourly June observations from downtown Washington and nearby Dulles International Airport. Over that period, only five days downtown and two days at Dulles featured at least one hour with a heat index of 110 degrees F or higher. The highest observed hourly June heat index in either place is 115 degrees F, two degrees below the estimated value at 3:00 p.m. on June 17, 1863. Given that the modern-day readings likely reflect at least slightly the impact of climate change and urbanization, the 117-degree F value on June 17, 1863, is remarkable for this area in June. In fact, even including July and August, only one day at Dulles and six days in downtown Washington in the period 1962–2023 exceeded a heat index of 117 degrees F.[87]

The heatwave lasted one more day. On June 18, the maximum heat index at an observation time was 105 degrees F at noon, based on a temperature of 93.5 degrees F and a dewpoint of 75 degrees F. The wet-bulb globe temperature, computed using the observed 4/10 cloud cover at that time, was still in the "high risk" range of 88–90 degrees F. The temperature peaked at 97.3 degrees F, likely between noon and 2:00 p.m. given that the sky had nearly clouded over by 3:00 p.m. A reasonable estimate of the heat index at the time of the maximum temperature is 108 degrees F, based on an estimated dewpoint of 73 degrees F. The temperature had dropped to 85.4 degrees F at 3:00 p.m., resulting in a heat index of 90 degrees F at that time. Thunderstorms began at 3:10 p.m. at the Naval Observatory with "considerable hail during the storm about the size of peas," and by 6:00 p.m. the temperature had decreased to 69 degrees F.

The length of the June 15–18 heatwave suggests another approach to putting this hot spell in historical context. Recall that the high temperatures at the Naval Observatory on those four days were 96, 93.5, 99 and 97.3 degrees F, respectively. Daily high temperature data from Washington, available starting in 1872, provide a largely apples to apples comparative dataset given that late nineteenth-century and early twentieth-century measurements come from a time uncontaminated by climate change and urbanization. In the fifty years from 1872 to 1921, only three periods of four consecutive days in June included maximum temperatures of 93 degrees F or higher, and no periods longer than that. A similar comparison with modern-day Dulles, using the sixty-three-year period 1962–2024, shows only three stretches of four days in June with maximum temperatures of 93 degrees F or higher.[88] The bottom line: Based solely on high temperatures, a four-day hot stretch in June like that of June 15–18, 1863, is extremely uncommon.

Moreover, taken together, these findings certainly shed new light on the soldiers' accounts of suffering from the heatwave. The brutal blast of heat and humidity that hit both armies during mid-June 1863 is best described by the men who experienced it.

Union soldier Sergeant Henry C. Morhous of the 123rd New York Infantry described the twenty-five-mile march made by the Twelfth Corps on June 15.[89] His words certainly proved emblematic of the suffering experienced by other infantrymen in the Army of the Potomac on this terrible day: "It was one of the hottest days ever experienced by the regiment while on a march....Many received a sunstroke that day, and some died....No good water was to be had along the line of march; but some drank too much of what they could get, and they were the first to succumb to the heat."[90] The suffering on June 15 did not affect only the boys in blue. Confederate Private John Camden West's account demonstrates how he and his fellow members of the 4th Texas Infantry struggled from the intense heat: "This was one of the hottest days and one of the hottest marches I have yet experienced. Over 500 men fell out by the road side from fatigue and exhaustion, and several died where they fell."[91]

One soldier put the situation in perspective regarding those who lost their lives due to the lengthy forced marches in the brutally hot weather. In reflecting on the march of June 15, Sergeant James A. Wright of the 1st Minnesota Infantry wrote, "It was one of the most heart-breaking marches of our experience, and many men wilted in the scorching heat and dust like mown grass. There were many prostrations—men staggering from the ranks and falling as if shot. There were a number of cases of fatal sunstroke, and some dying almost as quickly as if struck by a bullet in a vital part."[92]

Fig. 32 Suffering from the heat. *Courtesy of D. Gallon.*

Most of the Union army remained idle on June 16. Ironically, that day was the least oppressive of the heatwave. Only soldiers in the Second and Sixth Corps suffered through forced marches that day. Unfortunately, these marches came on the heels of similarly long marches on June 15. That said, the brief respite from the extreme temperatures of June 15 did not go unnoticed, as James Wright recalled:

Fig. 33 One falls out from sunstroke, the other lends a hand. *Courtesy of D. Gallon.*

"The afternoon march was trying—though the heat was not quite so bad as the day before, as there was a breeze—but it was very severe and many prostrations."[93]

Little did any of these chroniclers suspect what Mother Nature had in store for them on June 17. As First Lieutenant A.P. Smith of the 76th New York Infantry recalled, "The day was extremely hot." He also pointed to the ultimate cost of marching in the unbearable heat: "Many fell down in the ranks from sun-stroke and exhaustion."[94] A fellow soldier from the Army of the Potomac, Private Robert G. Carter of the 22nd Massachusetts Infantry, left a detailed account of soldiers desperate for any semblance of water to quench their insatiable thirst: "Men, horses, mules, all rushed pell-mell into the warm, disgusting pools and puddles, and drank the filthy fluid to quench their thirst….Several men were sun-struck in the column during the day…. Colonel Gleason of the 25th New York of our brigade died of exhaustion and sun-stroke, and it was said that seventeen men died in the division on this day's march."[95]

Those soldiers who trudged along with the Confederate army faced equally difficult conditions. While Private Randolph A. Shotwell of the 8th Virginia wrote with a certain expressive flair, his account's sheer descriptive qualities demand our attention. In fact, considering what we now know regarding the life-threatening conditions on June 17, Shotwell's account seems perfectly valid: "Dead or alive? I am sure I hardly know which! Flesh and blood cannot sustain such heat and fatigue as we have undergone this day. It is terrible! All along the roadside since 9 o'clock this morning I have seen men dropping, gasping, dying—or already dead!" Shotwell did his best to describe the shocking scenes and tally the cost: "Is it strange that one sees hundreds of men gasping for breath, and lolling out their tongues like madmen? Is it any wonder that *coup de soleil* is of hourly occurrence? Some of the men say that fully two dozen men were killed today by sun stroke. I saw that number 'down' but whether they recovered subsequently I cannot say."[96]

Finally, after another brutal period of extreme heat during the first half of June 18, the heavens let loose. Only the Army of the Potomac's Twelfth Corps completed a lengthy march on June 18. And though most escaped the oppression of the early heat that day, Yankee and Rebel alike felt the force of the ferocious late-day thunderstorms. Division Commander Brigadier General Alpheus S. Williams of the Twelfth Corps described the day this way: "The early morning was the hottest we had felt. One perspired freely standing still at sunrise." Regarding the weather later in the day, Williams added, "The storm of rain, hail, thunder, and lightning had become terrific, but the men felt new life from the cool wetting."[97] Infantry soldier First Lieutenant John E. Dooley of the 1st Virginia Infantry also summed up the strong thunderstorm that quelled the heatwave: "We have a very heavy rain—then a storm of hail—great big lumps come down thick and fast and feel anything but agreeable when they thump us on the head; after the hail more rain and as we have no shelter we just take in all that pours down."[98]

Fig. 34 "We Drank from the Same Canteen." *From Billings,* Hardtack and Coffee.

Fig. 35 Struggling to survive. *Courtesy of D. Gallon.*

In looking back at the strenuous and taxing marches that took place during the brutal heatwave, Lieutenant Colonel Selden Connor of the 7th Maine Infantry summed things up this way: "It has been the hardest march in my experience. It was hot; the roads were dusty and filled with trains and the men fell out by the road-side [*sic*] in scores overcome by the heat and exertion. Numbers died by sunstroke."[99] And Private Charley Goddard of the 1st Minnesota Infantry tried to measure the cost of marching during such heat and humidity: "Since I last wrote we have been doing some 'tall' marching. There has been no less than 70 men [who] fell dead out of this Corps...caused by the hard marching and excessive heat, there has been a great many disabled, also—about 1200 disabled and dead."[100]

This quantitative analysis of the June 1863 heatwave certainly provides context to these statistics as they pertain to the misery experienced by the soldiers of the Army of the Potomac. Moreover, this analysis also supports the severity of the suffering as recorded in *The Medical and Surgical History of the War of the Rebellion*. This landmark document makes it clear that the "Army of the Potomac outpaced all other armies with regard to reported cases of sun stroke." Specifically referring to June 1863, the document states that the Army of the Potomac furnished 58 percent of the sunstroke cases among all Union armies while it represented only 18.2 percent of the strength of commands

Fig. 36 Lieutenant Colonel Selden Connor. *Courtesy of Maine State Archives.*

that rendered reports. For comparison, troops operating in June 1863 in the Department of the Cumberland and Tennessee furnished only 17.5 percent of the sunstroke cases while these armies constituted 43 percent of the commands reporting. Now we know why.[101]

In the final analysis, here is what the data show: The heatwave of mid-June 1863 proved to be far worse than previously thought by historians. And June 17, the third day of the heatwave, stands out as one of the most oppressive days on record in the area. Nonetheless, one is left to consider the irony that many of the troops serving in both armies experienced lengthy forced marches just prior to, and most especially during, this merciless period. Moreover, the same ill-fated odds applied to the cavalry forces from both armies who saw action in the Battle at Aldie on June 17, the hottest day of all. Perhaps with such large numbers of contending forces in close proximity to one another, the chances for long forced marches and spirited cavalry clashes increased during the third week of the Gettysburg Campaign. However, the odds of all this happening during one of the worst June heatwaves on record certainly represented quite a "long shot." Unfortunately for the men of the contending forces, this long shot came in, in spades.

But irrespective of the odds, the consequences were certain. The human body can endure only so much heat without proper rest and hydration. Many men, as well as horses and mules, did not get nearly enough of either during the historic heatwave. The resultant effects varied, whether it be on the campaign or the men themselves. On one hand, it meant either delayed or shortened marches for the armies. On the other, it caused large numbers of soldiers to fall out with heatstroke. And as mentioned previously, for a significant number of these men, the result was death.[102]

Beyond this, an enhanced understanding of the weather conditions experienced by the armies during the period June 15–18, 1863, leaves historians to wonder about its ultimate effect on the overall campaign. Certainly, in pondering these new findings regarding the intensity of the heatwave, we must reconsider the possibility that the overall effect on future episodes of the campaign proved greater than previously understood.

PEOPLE, STORIES AND MATTERS TO REMEMBER: CONGRESSIONAL MEDAL OF HONOR RECIPIENT SAVED SUNSTRUCK SOLDIER

Seventy-two. That's the total number of Medals of Honor awarded to soldiers for heroic actions during the Gettysburg Campaign: sixty-four cited events during the Battle of Gettysburg, six during pre-battle actions and two after the battle. Many medals recognized soldiers who captured enemy flags in the heat of battle. Some came because of a soldier's heroism in rescuing a fellow soldier who had fallen due to enemy fire. But only one medal—just one—stemmed from the rescue of a soldier who suffered sunstroke.[103] The Medal of Honor recipient's name—Nathan Mullock Hallock.

The onset of the four-day heatwave on June 15 called for plenty of hydration and frequent breaks. And though the Third Corps did enjoy a brief respite during the predawn hours of June 15, that break came on the heels of a difficult ten-mile march on June 14. Unfortunately for the stalwart soldiers of Major General Daniel E. Sickles's Third Corps, even longer treks would lie in their future. Another fifteen miles in the

Fig. 37 *The Old Braves*, by Charles Reed. Though depicting a scene a few days after the heatwave as veterans of the Army of the Potomac marched past the outer defenses of Washington, this image also reflects the condition of the members of the Army of the Potomac during this period. *Charles W. Reed Collection, Manuscripts Division, LOC.*

increasing heat added to their misery, and the pace of the march slowed accordingly. On June 15, the haggard men marched some fifteen hours, from about 6:00 a.m. until around 9:00 p.m. The strain on the foot soldiers proved devastating. Men fell out in scores from the heat. The 17th Maine's Captain Charles Mattocks recalled, "We had a most horrible march. 8,000 men fell out from this Corps from sheer exhaustion.…This is the most of a scorcher we have had yet."[104] Another soldier from the corps claimed at least fifty men suffered sunstroke.[105]

Fig. 38 Private Nathan M. Hallock. *Courtesy of Middletown, New York Historical Society.*

The plight of Lieutenant Lewis Wisner represents just one such example. Wisner served with the 124th New York Infantry, the so-called Orange Blossoms from Orange County, New York. He collapsed and fell unconscious in the vicinity of Bristoe Station on the Orange and Alexandria Railroad. Fortunately for Wisner, Company K's commanding officer ordered one soldier from the regiment to stay behind to help him. Here, Private Nathan Mullock Hallock drew the short straw.

Fig. 39 Lieutenant Lewis Wisner. *Courtesy of Rick Carlile.*

Soon after, while Hallock steadfastly aided Wisner, the company of Vermont soldiers left behind to guard Bristoe Station, the only nearby group offering possible protection to Wisner and Hallock, departed, leaving the two New Yorkers without cover. Meanwhile, previous calls for an ambulance continued to go unheeded. Worse yet, roaming bands of Confederates fast approached. With this, Wisner urged Hallock to leave him so that he (Hallock) might escape. But Hallock's retort spoke volumes with regard to his

Fig. 40 Medal of Honor of the appearance and type awarded to Nathan M. Hallock. *Courtesy of NPS, GNMP, Museum Collection, GETT #44192.*

character, "Lieutenant, if necessary I will go with you to prison or death, but I will never desert you." As the adage goes, some of the greatest heroes do the right thing when no one is watching. Hallock represents one such hero. Meanwhile, spying Wisner and Hallock, the nearby Confederates opened fire. Reacting quickly, Hallock somehow found a way to half-carry and half-drag Wisner to a nearby refuge.[106]

Finally, some ten hours after Wisner fell ill, the long-awaited Union army ambulance approached. But the persistent Confederates still lay in wait. Wary of the situation, the ambulance driver refused to get too close. Hallock knew that to save Wisner he needed to reach the ambulance. Undeterred, Hallock once again summoned up the strength and energy to move Wisner's limp frame to safety. In the mad dash for the ambulance, bullets flew fast and furious. Yet somehow both Hallock and Wisner escaped unscathed. In the end, Hallock had saved Wisner from certain capture or possible death. And in the process, he had indeed lived up to his oath—*I will never desert you.*[107]

To honor Hallock's heroic act, an appreciative nation awarded him the Congressional Medal of Honor. He received news of the high honor on July 31, 1897. The citation read as follows:

> *At Bristoe Station, VA., June 15, 1863, this soldier, then a private, Co. K, 124th New York Volunteers, at imminent peril, saved from death or capture, a disabled officer of his company by carrying him to a place of safety under a hot musketry fire.*[108]

5
THE APPROACH

Fair Weather Folly, June 19–24, 1863

I rather wish that we march continually; this idleness is unendurable.[109]
—Captain Frederick C. Winkler, 26th Wisconsin Infantry

Setting the Stage

Situation Report—A Brief Summary of Troop Movements and Dispositions

After a full-court press of forced marching in extreme heat over the previous several days, the Army of the Potomac gained a much-needed rest between June 19 and June 24. Ironically, this stretch of days proved relatively benign weatherwise, albeit somewhat wet. Most of the marching during this period involved limited repositioning, nothing like the lengthy marches that had taken place during the heatwave. The only actions of significance centered on the ongoing series of cavalry clashes, namely those at Middleburg, Virginia, on June 19 and Upperville on June 21. These were fierce actions replete with mounted and dismounted charges as well as artillery fire. At Upperville, Colonel Strong Vincent's brigade of infantry, drawn from the Army of the Potomac's Fifth Corps, marched to the support of the Union cavalry and provided timely assistance. In the end, the Confederate cavalry pulled back toward the mountain gaps, but their slow and tenacious retrograde movements prevented the prying eyes of the Union cavalry from

Troop Location Map

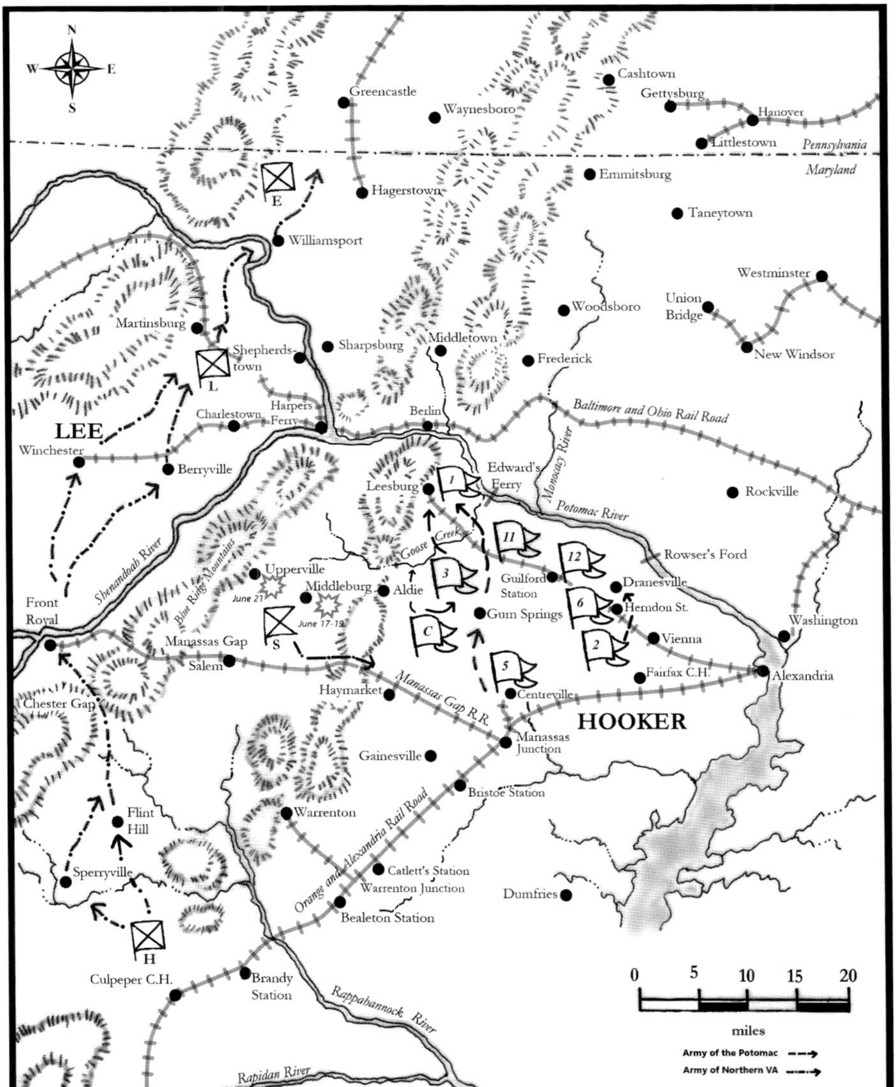

Fig. 41 Gettysburg Campaign, June 18–24, 1863. This map includes June 18 troop movements to best convey relevant army movements detailed in this chapter. *Courtesy of J. Heiser.*

Fig. 42 Lieutenant General Richard S. Ewell. *LOC.*

gaining information on Lee's main body of forces as they continued their northward movements.[110]

As the main body of the Army of the Potomac rested and prepared to cross the Potomac River into Maryland, in the vicinity of Goose Creek and Edward's Ferry, Robert E. Lee's infantry once again gained an advantage over their idle adversaries. With Longstreet's Corps assigned the responsibility of guarding the right flank of the army, Ewell's Corps marched down the Shenandoah Valley and then crossed a slightly rain-swollen Potomac into Maryland. In a matter of days, lead elements of Ewell's Second Corps reached as far north as Chambersburg, Pennsylvania. A.P. Hill's Third Corps crossed the Potomac and by June 24, Longstreet's First Corps was prepared to do the same. Meanwhile, Confederate cavalry commander James Ewell Brown "Jeb" Stuart contemplated his future actions. By June 24, he had decided to implement a plan to cross the Potomac River with his most trusted brigades. Stuart intended to ride completely around the Army of the Potomac to gather intelligence and disrupt its rear by cutting communications and access to its supply base in Washington.[111]

The Weather—Background

Summer officially arrived on the evening of June 21, 1863, but as Mother Nature had demonstrated the previous week, extreme heat and humidity do not heed the boundaries of the astronomical seasons. In part, this explains why meteorologists dub the three-month period from June to August in the Northern Hemisphere as "meteorological summer."

On the summer solstice, the sun reaches its maximum altitude above the horizon of any day of the year, and daylight in the mid-Atlantic is almost fifteen hours long. With such a high sun angle and long days, cooler air masses that nose into the mid-Atlantic are usually modified quickly. In fact, the cold fronts that serve as the leading edges of the refreshing air often stall and eventually just "wash out" in the region. The result is that lots of clouds and occasional rain typically accompany the frontal leftovers. That is likely what happened early in the June 19–24 period of the Gettysburg Campaign. The cold front that ended the heatwave—or what was left of that front—got stuck in the mid-Atlantic for a few days.

The Primary Source Data

Figure 43 summarizes the period of June 19–24, 1863, based on data from the Naval Observatory. The format follows that of similar diagrams in chapters 3 and 4. The contrast between this part of the campaign and the previous period of June 10–18 in terms of temperature and humidity could not be more dramatic. The period June 19–24 featured only one day with a

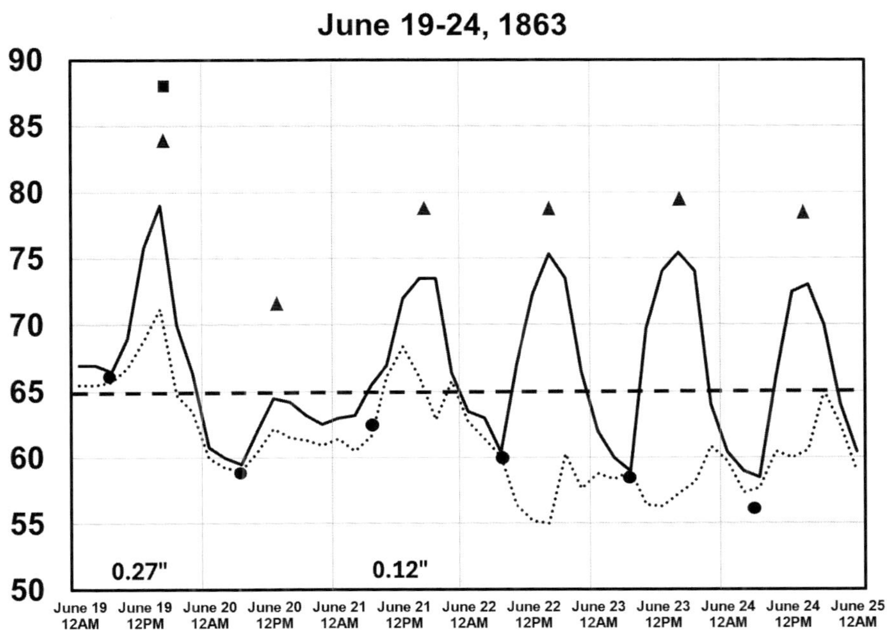

Fig. 43 Plot of temperature (solid) and dewpoint (dotted) every three hours at the Naval Observatory for June 19–24, 1863. Circles indicate daily low temperatures, triangles daily high temperatures and squares the estimated daily maximum heat index. If rain occurred, the amount is noted. *Data from NOAA FORTS.*

maximum temperature above 80 degrees F; only one day with a maximum heat index approaching 90 degrees F; and just a few days when the dewpoint reached 65 degrees F—in short, much more favorable conditions for marching.

Day-to-Day Analysis

The barometric pressure at the Naval Observatory began to rise on the morning of June 19 as an area of high pressure passed to the north through New England. Although rising pressure often portends decreasing clouds and a reduced chance of rain, the clockwise circulation around high pressure in that location means that winds in the mid-Atlantic eventually blow from the east. And in fact, the wind at the Naval Observatory—after having briefly blown from the northwest and then north—took on an easterly bent by noon on June 19 that persisted for two days. Figure 5B (see color section) shows the average surface pressure pattern for the two-and-a-half-day period starting the evening of June 18, annotated with winds inferred from the pressure pattern and the approximate position of any fronts and pressure systems. The stalled front that ended the heatwave extended west–east through southern Virginia to the Atlantic Ocean, while a north–south–oriented front cut through the Ohio and Tennessee River valleys. In concert with the mired front, the wind from the east off the ocean, also reported at other nearby Smithsonian observing locations, portended persistent clouds and scattered rains in the campaign theater for the next three days.

Table 4 shows daily rainfall amounts at Frederick, the Naval Observatory, Sykesville and Gettysburg for the period June 19–24, quantifying the soggy nature of the first three days of the period. When it was not raining, clouds dominated. From 6:00 p.m. on June 18 until 3:00 p.m. on June 21, the Naval Observatory reported overcast skies at every observation time except for the afternoon of June 19, when skies remained 80 to 90 percent cloudy. Similarly, Henry Hanshew, the observer at Frederick, recorded cloudy skies from 7:00 a.m. on June 18 to 7:00 a.m. on June 21, except for one observation of 8/10 cloud-cover and another of 9/10.

In association with the new air mass and the cloud-filled skies, the afternoon high temperature on June 19 at the Naval Observatory reached only 84 degrees F, a thirteen-degree drop from the previous day. Although dewpoints remained in the muggy upper 60s, many soldiers noted the

Table 4. Daily Rainfall (in Inches) for the Period June 19–24, 1863

	Frederick	Sykesville	Gettysburg	Naval Observatory
June 19	0.38	0.50	0.70	0.27
June 20	1.44	-	0.13	-
June 21	-	-	0.15	0.12
June 22	-	-	-	-
June 23	-	-	-	-
June 24	-	-	-	-

change in temperature. As Captain Asa Bartlett of the 12th New Hampshire Infantry remarked, "During the day the mercury fell thirty or forty degrees," undoubtedly an exaggeration in terms of actual temperature drop but certainly capturing the tenor of the large overall change from sun and heat to clouds and mud.[112]

One of the more interesting quantitative observations that day centered not on air, but water. Private Samuel Pickens of the 5th Alabama Battalion noted, "This morning our Brigade waded the Potomac at Williamsport." He added, "The river was about 200 yds or probably wider. The water was just above the knees—swift & beautifully clear."[113] This yardstick for both width and depth of the Potomac provides a baseline for comparative purposes in the second week of July during the retreat from Gettysburg when Lee's forces attempted to recross the Potomac at Williamsport.

By far, soldiers' accounts on June 19 centered on what came late in the day: torrential rains. Captain E.C. Strouss of the 57th Pennsylvania noted that the men started for Gum Springs (not far from present-day Dulles International Airport) late in the afternoon, but "We had not gone far when a severe storm of rain, thunder and lightning set in."[114] Lieutenant William Crennell of the 140th New York, near Aldie, remarked, "About 6 o'clock it commenced to pour down in torrents and continued most of the night."[115] Confederate forces farther west, where easterly winds got a slight boost from the terrain, may have had it worse. Private Thomas Ware of the 15th Georgia Infantry, who was with Hood's Division at Snickersville, about halfway between Winchester and Leesburg, noted that "it commenced raining at 9 p.m. & rained as fast as I ever saw it for 1 hour & then slowly all night. All got very wet."[116] To the southwest, near Front Royal, Surgeon Spencer Welch of the 13th South Carolina remarked that after getting to camp about 10:00 p.m., "it began to rain furiously. We were in an open grass field and so we had to stand up and take it. It was a very heavy rain and the night was the worst I ever experienced."[117] Several diarists commented on the darkness of the night, testimony to the thick clouds and the waxing crescent moon.

That night, temperatures dropped to 59 degrees F at the Naval Observatory and recovered only to 72 degrees F on June 20, tied with June 8 for the lowest maximum temperature of the campaign, as clouds dominated the daylight hours. An east-southeasterly wind peaked at Force 3 (approximately twelve mph) in late afternoon, with the maritime flow locking in clouds and priming the atmosphere for additional rain. Most soldier accounts agree that some rain fell during the day of June 20, with Lieutenant Crennell of the 140th New York near Aldie observing, "Disagreeable weather a drizzling rain most of the day with occasional heavy showers."[118] Surgeon Charles Lippitt of the 57th Virginia, just east of Winchester, noted that "sometimes the rain fell in showers & the whole day was misty and cold."[119]

Now a few days into a rainier pattern that followed the dryness of the first two weeks of the Gettysburg Campaign, soldier comments about heat and dusty marching gave way to remarks about water, especially as elements of the Army of Northern Virginia neared the vicinity of the rising Shenandoah and Potomac Rivers. Adding details about the previous night's rain and relating those thunderstorms to the travails of June 20, Private Randolph Shotwell of the 8th Virginia Infantry described the impact on the Shenandoah east of Berryville: "The hail storm of yesterday chilled the water to winter temperature….The passage was like wading through the same amount of ice-water."[120] First Lieutenant John Dooley of the 1st Virginia observed that the river was "swollen by the late rains, is now very swift and over 3½ feet in depth; it takes us above our waists."[121]

As with the previous two days, June 21 dawned cloudy at the Naval Observatory and across the theater. Accounts differ regarding the raininess of the day and the amount of sunshine in the afternoon, but most reporters found temperatures agreeable. Indeed, readings stayed in the 70s all day in Washington, with the Naval Observatory reporting "light showers at intervals during the forenoon." The pressure subtly but steadily began to fall in the afternoon, eventually bottoming out in the wee hours of June 22, probably indicating the passage of yet another front—in fact, likely the north–south–oriented front that appears in Figure 5B (see color section) in the Ohio and Tennessee River valleys. Any showers and thunderstorms that accompanied that front must have been scattered, given only a few reports of late-day rain. One came from a rather distinguished observer, Charles Marshall, sometimes aide-de-camp, military secretary and assistant adjutant general on the staff of General Lee. He noted that on June 21, General Lee "proceeded to a place a short distance beyond Milwood in Clark County, where we encamped that night. There was a very severe storm, I remember."[122] Fifty miles east at the Naval Observatory, John Eastman reported that it was "raining at 11 p.m. with thunder and lightning" that lasted at least to midnight.

These thunderstorms signaled the beginning of a significant change in the weather across the theater. One dramatic clue comes courtesy of

***Left*:** **Fig. 44** Colonel David W. Aiken. *Courtesy of the South Caroliniana Library, University of South Carolina, Columbia, SC.*

***Right*:** **Fig. 45** Captain Sam Keene. *Courtesy of Maine State Archives.*

Colonel David W. Aiken, commanding officer of the 7th South Carolina Infantry. Writing about the wee hours of June 22 in the Blue Ridge east of Winchester, he emphasized a very chilly morning: "That night on the mountain was one of the severest I ever spent, I wrapt up in my overcoat & cape…when I awoke almost freezing. I got up and walked up & down the mountain to get warm…but it was only a chattering of teeth until morning."[123] Meanwhile, clear skies greeted the June 22 sunrise at the Naval Observatory for the first time in five days, with a morning low temperature of 60 degrees F, a dewpoint in the upper 50s and brisk west to northwest winds. For the third straight day, in what would eventually become a stretch of nine days, the maximum temperature at the Naval Observatory stayed in the 70s, undoubtedly made even more refreshing by breezes estimated in the ten-to-twenty-mph range much of the day. To the west, both Captain Sam Keene with the 20th Maine, near Aldie, and Confederate engineer Jedediah Hotchkiss, near Boonsboro, described the day as "pleasant"[124]

The NOAA reanalysis surface weather map for the morning of June 23 shows that the front that brought the change in the weather two days earlier had moved well south and east of the Gettysburg Campaign theater (see Figure 6A, color section). Air pressure began to rise significantly at the Naval Observatory as the area of higher pressure over the Midwest nudged closer during the day. The clockwise circulation around that high continued to funnel relatively dry air into Maryland, Virginia and Pennsylvania from the northwest. Elements of the Army of Northern Virginia already in south-central Pennsylvania experienced a "clear" day according to William Heyser, the former Smithsonian observer in Chambersburg.[125] Dewpoints remained in the comfortable 50s nearly the entire day at the Naval Observatory. Captain Theodore Dodge of the 119th New York, who was with the Eleventh Corps near Dranesville (just ten miles or so west of Washington), proclaimed, "The weather is fine, clear, breezy." He then turned amateur weather forecaster, continuing, "I think we shall have it fine for some time."[126] This would prove to be an overly optimistic prediction, for sure.

Another relatively cool night followed, and on June 24, for the third consecutive morning, the temperature dropped to 60 degrees F or lower at the Naval Observatory. Pressure continued to rise until the late afternoon, and as is characteristic near the center of high pressure, winds weakened in contrast to previous days. Other changes were afoot as well. The dewpoint at the Naval Observatory reached 65 degrees F, albeit briefly, for the first time in three days, while clouds more prominently covered the skies. In addition, scattered reports of late-day rain from soldier observers west of Washington in the Union Second Corps, in the Union cavalry and on General Lee's staff, signaled that the atmosphere had already regenerated its moisture. That pattern shift set the stage for a cloudy, and often wet, six-day period for the armies leading up to the Battle of Gettysburg.[127]

When Weather Mattered the Most: Weather and Warfare—Timing Is Everything

It is a familiar phrase but one worth repeating about weather and warfare: *Timing is everything*. Unfortunately, the Weather Gods can be fickle, and often man pays the price. Here is yet one more example.

Given a choice, General Hooker certainly would not have wanted his army to conduct lengthy forced marches between June 12 and June 18, 1863. Why? Because, as we have seen, the bulk of the marching done during that time frame occurred during the hottest weather of the entire Gettysburg Campaign. Regardless, the urgency of the situation facing the Army of the Potomac by mid-June 1863 did not allow for any wiggle room. Having delayed moving his army as long as possible, General Hooker had to act quickly to interpose his army between Washington and the advancing Army of Northern Virginia. And Hooker needed to make up ground fast, Weather Gods be damned.

In a cruel twist of fate, during the ensuing six-day stretch, between June 19 and June 24, temperatures and humidity levels grew much more suitable for hard marching. Indeed, strong thunderstorms on the evening of June 18 ushered in much more temperate weather, and June 19–24 proved to be a relatively cloudy and cool period. Ironically, during this six-day period, most of the Union army corps either remained idle or marched less than a total of ten miles each. Only the Second and Twelfth Corps marched as much as twenty miles each.[128] The rub was that this extended respite took place during some of the best marching weather of the entire Gettysburg Campaign. Here again, unfolding operational circumstances, not weather, dictated when and if Hooker's forces marched.

Irrespective of such concerns, the facts remain clear. While the First, Second, Fifth, Sixth and Eleventh Corps rested, temperatures in the region in the period June 19–24 ranged from nighttime lows generally in the 56–62 degrees F range to daytime highs of 72–80 degrees F, based on observations at the Naval Observatory. During this period, overcast skies largely prevailed, particularly June 19–21, thereby offering an abundance of shade for soldiers on the march. Moreover, comfort levels, as measured by the dewpoint and heat index, were quite tolerable.

Fig. 46 Private Wilbur Fisk. *Courtesy of University Press of Kansas.*

Certainly, after a week of exceptionally difficult forced marches, Union forces welcomed a brief respite during temperate weather. Without a doubt, having a few days to recover after such an arduous period proved critical to the soldiers' well-being and readiness for further campaigning. But seven days of rest may have been more than the soldiers needed or wanted. Captain Frederick C. Winkler of the 26th Wisconsin opined on this subject: "I rather wish that we march continually; this idleness is unendurable."[129] And the 2nd Vermont's Private Wilbur Fisk, when considering his division's lengthy idleness at Bristoe Station, indicated, "We had staid [*sic*] there five days. All was quiet along the lines during the time, affording us ample opportunity for leisure and rest, more than we really needed. Herein is the great objection to camp life; when we rest we have more rest than we require, and when we are called upon to act, we have more action than any necessity of our physical being demands, decidedly more than our inclinations ask for."[130]

Might General Hooker have planned differently had he enjoyed the benefit of modern weather forecasting? Previously, knowing his army faced a punishing heatwave, might he have begun to move his army sooner? Later, after the forced marches ended, might he have moved out after a day or so rather than resting his troops for an entire week? Furthermore, could such decisions have allowed him to avoid the dreadfully long marches his men made on the eve of the battle?

Of course, these are all hypothetical scenarios. That said, we do know why he dallied, how long he delayed and the misery that resulted from his decisions. We also know that many of Hooker's men suffered the lingering effects of these marches, such as horrifically bloodied and blistered feet, for the remainder of the campaign. On the other hand, we know that following the weeklong respite, Hooker's army experienced another round of forced marches, in increasingly difficult weather.[131] And after all of this, they engaged the Confederate army at Gettysburg.

But most importantly, while most men who fell out during the mid-June heatwave eventually rejoined their respective regiments, many lost their lives due to heatstroke. How many lives might have been saved had Hooker marched earlier in June, avoiding the mid-June heatwave, or taken advantage of the somewhat cooler spell the week after? From one perspective, Hooker can no more be blamed for the ill-timed marches he ordered than his predecessor, Major General Ambrose E. Burnside, can be blamed for not anticipating the weather that resulted in his army's ill-fated "Mud March." However, from another perspective, as commanding officer of the Army of the Potomac, he ultimately became responsible for the ramifications of his operational decisions.

Meanwhile, as Hooker's army rested, Lee's army moved out. On the heels of Confederate victories at Winchester and Stephenson's Depot in mid-June, most of the boys in gray and butternut continued to advance northward during the subsequent meteorological respite. Distances covered by the three corps of Lee's army from June 18 to June 24 totaled between approximately thirty miles to upward of ninety miles each.[132] Although these marches covered considerable ground, many soldiers reflected on how the prevailing moderate weather mitigated the treks' overall effect on their well-being. What's more, freed of the constant thoughts of suffering felt while marching in intense heat, some such as Sergeant J.E. Whitehorne of the 12th Virginia Infantry even felt compelled to admire the scenery: "This county is equally as pretty in Scenery [*sic*] as Clarke....The soil is fertile—Streams clear and pure, wood magnificent and beautiful. We are luxuricating [*sic*] on good apple butter & milk, just having a good time generally. The troops are in first class condition, and very confident—morale splendid."[133]

In the end, all of this points to a prime example of how a lack of understanding of the weather during the campaign directly affected the men left to suffer because of this ignorance. And as we shall see, this lack of understanding continued to haunt both armies during the remainder of the Gettysburg Campaign.

PEOPLE, STORIES AND MATTERS TO REMEMBER: A FATHER'S LAMENT

In peace sons bury their fathers. In war, fathers bury their sons.[134]
—Herodotus, Greek historian

The day bright and warm, but to me, and my family, one of gloom and darkness. At about 1 o'clock P.M. I received a note from my brother William, informing me that my dear, precious boy, Walter, had been wounded in the Cavalry fight at Upperville, on yesterday. I immediately got on my horse and started in that direction, by way of Berry's ferry. Very soon the fatal truth was communicated to me, first by wounded soldiers returning, and a few miles further on, in letters from Cousins [sic] *Horace and Isaac N. Cloud. My first-born son, my pride, had fallen by a shot fired from the enemy, while making a charge for the protection of Chew's Battery.*[135]
—Marcus Buck, Monday, June 22, 1863

Marcus Buck's diary entry hits like a ton of bricks. His son Lieutenant Walter Buck of the 7th Virginia Cavalry was dead. And Marcus Buck's life would never be the same.

Fig. 47 View of Front Royal from Belmont Vineyards, circa 1890. *Courtesy of Warren Heritage Society, Warren County, VA.*

Belmont Vineyards, once located near Front Royal, Virginia, was well known in the mid-1800s. Owned and operated by Marcus Buck, the family winery and farm sat majestically on the hilltops of the Blue Ridge Mountains. The view from the family homestead was stunning. But when war came to the Shenandoah Valley, everything changed, slowly but surely.

Fig. 48 Lieutenant Walter Buck. *Courtesy of Rick Armstrong.*

Marcus Buck kept meticulous notes on the weather almost every day. He grew not only grapes for his winery but other crops as well. And as for all farmers, in both the North and South, the weather mattered. Indeed, nothing was more important than the weather—nothing, that is, except family. Thanks to Marcus Buck, we have numerous invaluable accounts of the weather in the valley region during the Gettysburg Campaign. But his story, and the price he paid for war, forever stands out above all the rest.

Today, the remnants of the vines that once provided the feedstock for Marcus Buck's winery continue to grow in the wilds of the Shenandoah National Forest.[136] Meanwhile, the last vestiges of the family homestead continue to rot. Most of those passing on the nearby Skyline Drive Highway likely remain unaware of the once-thriving farm and the tragedy that befell the family who once lived there.

The passing of Walter Buck continues to serve as a stark reminder of the sad truth of all wars: young men die. Tragically, many young men. Marcus Buck's son Walter represents just one of the estimated 750,000 or more who died as a result of the U.S. Civil War.

6

THE APPROACH

Rain Was the Order of the Day, June 25–30, 1863

I don't think I ever before saw at this time of year such a long continued, misty, drizzling storm as we have been marching though since we crossed the Potomac.[137]
—*Lieutenant Colonel Rufus R. Dawes, 6th Wisconsin Infantry*

Setting the Stage

Situation Report—A Brief Summary of Troop Movements and Dispositions

On the heels of Confederate victories at Winchester and Stephenson's Depot in mid-June, most of the boys in gray and butternut had remained in motion during the subsequent meteorological respite of June 18–24. Distances covered by the three corps of Robert E. Lee's Army of Northern Virginia during the time frame measured between approximately thirty miles to upward of ninety miles each.[138] And as the fourth week of the campaign opened, Lee's army continued to spread its wings far and wide. Ewell's Corps, minus Early's division, proceeded northward through Pennsylvania's Cumberland Valley with the goal of capturing Harrisburg, the state capital. Meanwhile, Early's division moved east across South Mountain in search of supplies and information on their adversary. Moving first through Gettysburg, where they brushed aside hastily assembled local militia,

Early's men continued toward York and then Wrightsville to support Ewell's movement on Harrisburg. At the same time, Hill's Corps moved into position near Chambersburg and Cashtown while Longstreet's Corps brought up the rear, with Pickett's Division crossing the Potomac on June 25 and the rest of the corps following the next day. As Longstreet proceeded northward toward a position where he might support either Ewell or Hill, Major General James E. Brown "Jeb" Stuart's cavalry, the "eyes and ears" of Lee's army, crossed the Potomac into Maryland. Before long, they found themselves cut off from communications with Lee (see color section, Figures 12A and 12B).

Fig. 49 Major General James Ewell Brown "Jeb" Stuart. *From Longstreet,* From Manassas to Appomattox.

The Gettysburg Campaign started with Lee stealing a march on Hooker. As a result, Hooker had to play catch-up, with the soldiers suffering the physical consequences. Cruelly, less than two weeks later, a similar pattern played out. On June 25, Hooker began to move the Army of the Potomac into Maryland, and once again the foot soldiers paid the price for the need to keep up. Over the ensuing five days, the seven corps of the Union army faced a series of forced marches, with some corps making daily marches of twenty, twenty-five and even thirty-plus miles. The weather at the time often became rainy and the muddy roads resultantly difficult. And though the heat proved not nearly as intense as it had been earlier in the campaign, the discomfort level grew generally worse day by day. Meanwhile, on June 28, startling news arrived in the Union army camp. Soon the soldiers of the Army of the Potomac learned Major General George Gordon Meade had been appointed as their new commanding officer.

General Meade's ascension to the role of commanding officer of the Army of the Potomac occurred as Ewell's Corps prepared to advance on Harrisburg. But fate took a hand when Lee learned, much to his surprise and chagrin, that Hooker's army had finally begun to move. Here Lee suffered the consequences of the lack of timely intelligence, due primarily to the

Troop Location Map

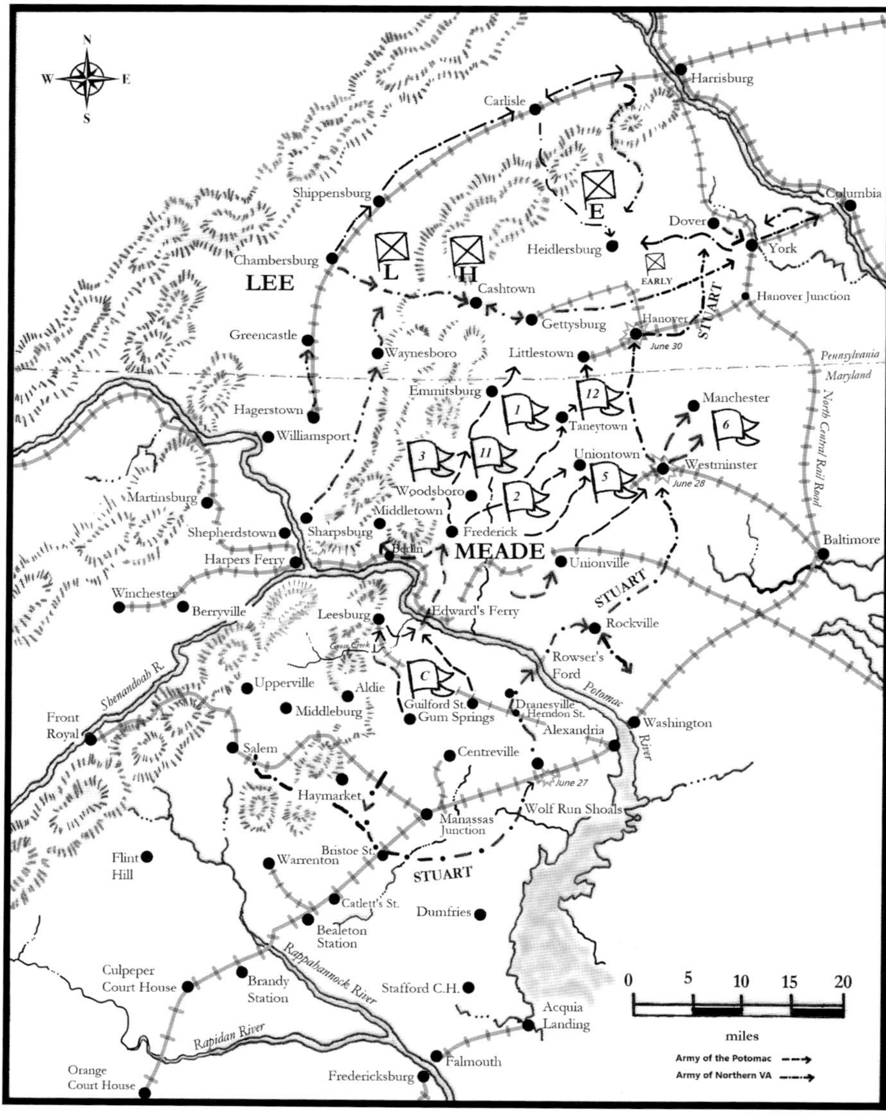

Fig. 50 Gettysburg Campaign, June 25–30, 1863. *Courtesy of J. Heiser.*

absence of reporting from General Stuart and his cavalry. Only the report of a Confederate spy alerted Lee that a portion of the Union army had reached a position only thirty miles or so from his army. To avoid the risk of having his widespread forces attacked piecemeal by the enemy, Lee called off Ewell's advance and instead ordered a concentration of his army near Cashtown. Thus, as Lee's army moved to come together, Meade cautiously moved his cavalry and seven infantry corps north across a thirty-mile-wide front to locate Lee's army. With the Confederate army concentrating and the Union forces fanning out, the stage was set for a colossal collision. And as this situation unfolded, the regional road network at the crossroads town of Gettysburg soon turned the community into a virtual bullseye between both armies.

The Weather—Background

Bermuda is a British overseas territory in the North Atlantic Ocean at about thirty-two degrees latitude, some 650 miles east of the nearest point on the East Coast. The stuff of urban legend (think Bermuda Triangle) for nearly seventy-five years, Bermuda is also part of meteorological jargon because of its location. During the summer, a center of high pressure sometimes sets up in its general vicinity and persists there for days. The broad clockwise flow around this so-called Bermuda High sends warm and moist southerly and easterly breezes off the Atlantic Ocean and Gulf of Mexico into the Eastern United States. Many who reside in the mid-Atlantic hear weather forecasters invoke this aptly named pressure system to explain warm and humid conditions during the summer.

Multiple lines of evidence suggest that a Bermuda High–type pattern began to develop during the period of June 25–30, 1863, particularly affecting the humidity, and this pattern would carry over into the battle. Because weather in the mid-latitudes generally is controlled by traveling areas of high and low pressure, maps of pressure averaged over many days often smooth out pressure systems, yielding a composite chart of little meteorological value. But the period from June 25 to June 30, 1863, was different. Figure 6B (see color section) shows the average pressure pattern over these six days, annotated with winds to emphasize how such a pattern favored maritime air enveloping the mid-Atlantic. Notably, the average center of high pressure sits north and west of where a typical Bermuda High parks, and the position shown in Figure 6B favors more of an easterly flow off the Atlantic Ocean than in the classic case. Such a scenario leads to increases in humidity but not necessarily heat. That's precisely what happened during this period. Although the exact location, intensity and shape of the high varied during the period, this six-day average provides a window into the dominant weather pattern. The proof lies with the actual weather observations.

The wind data at the Naval Observatory showed that, of the forty-nine wind measurements from midnight on June 25 to midnight on July 1, more than 70 percent of the time the wind blew from either the east, east-southeast, southeast, south-southeast or south. Although wind speeds generally remained light, a modern weather forecaster—knowing the time of year, the average pressure pattern and this set of relatively consistent wind observations—would conclude that this period likely would feature high (or increasing) humidity that potentially primed the atmosphere for clouds and occasional rain. This proved an apt description of weather conditions for June 25–30.

Figure 51 tracks the weather during this six-day period as measured at the Naval Observatory. The graphs show temperature (solid) and dewpoint (dotted), along with daily maximum (triangles) and minimum (circles) temperatures and maximum daily heat index (squares, if 80 degrees F or higher) and daily rainfall. During this period, high temperatures remained in

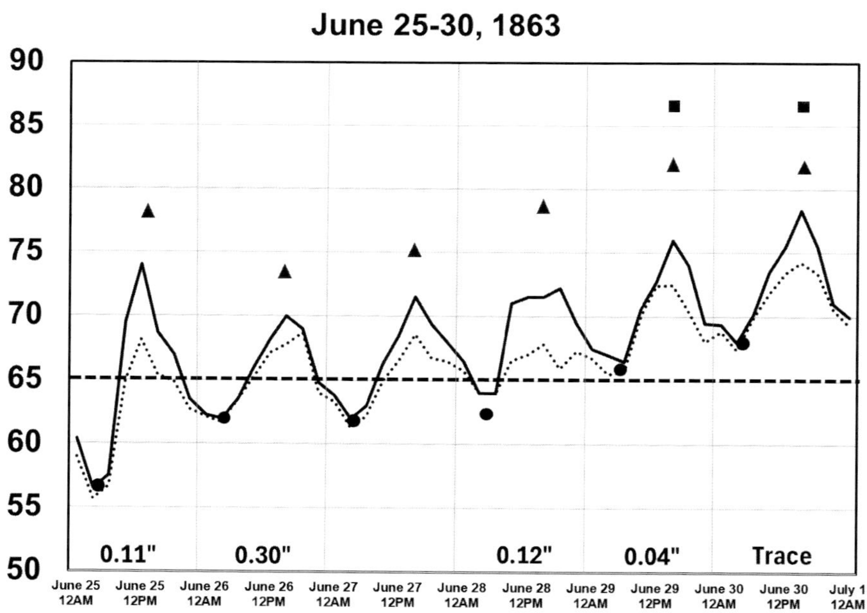

Fig. 51 Plot of temperature (solid) and dewpoint (dotted) every three hours at the Naval Observatory for June 25–30, 1863. Circles indicate daily low temperatures, triangles daily high temperatures and squares the estimated daily maximum heat index. If rain occurred, the amount is noted. *Data from NOAA FORTS.*

the relatively narrow range of 73–82 degrees F, suppressed by considerable cloudiness; the highs on June 26–27, in particular, were well below average (see Figure 2A, color section). With relatively low maximum temperatures, the maximum daily heat index exceeded 80 degrees F on only two days, June 29 and June 30. However, the dewpoint exceeded 65 degrees F at least part of the time each day, and after 6:00 a.m. on June 27 the dewpoint remained at or above that threshold through June 30 at all but two observation times (and at those two times, the dewpoint was 64 degrees F). For the first time in the campaign, the dewpoint remained consistently high for such a long period. In fact, truly tropical air dominated much of the time on June 29 and June 30 as the dewpoint exceeded 70 degrees F on back-to-back days for the first time since June 18–19.

Though persistently high dewpoints at the surface made life uncomfortable for the soldiers, muggy air near the ground does not necessarily translate into consistent cloud cover, but that occurred here. From midnight on June 26 to noon on June 30, overcast skies (10/10 cloud-covered) were reported at the Naval Observatory at thirty of the thirty-seven observation times—thirty-three of the thirty-seven when including 9/10 cloud coverage. In Frederick, where observations were taken only three times a day, skies were 10/10 cloud-covered at twelve of the thirteen observation times, while in Gettysburg eleven of thirteen, with twelve of thirteen if also counting 9/10 cloud coverage. This was a consistently very cloudy period across the theater.

These wind, dewpoint and cloud observations, although conducive to rain, do not guarantee it. Yet rain fell on five of the six days at the Naval Observatory. Table 5 expands the geographic landscape and shows daily rainfall at several observing locations close to the theater of operations. These observations indicate that rainfall was heaviest and most widespread on June 26; June 28 was the driest day of the period; and additional rain fell on June 29 and 30. The pressure variations at the Naval Observatory that week, shown in Figure 52, suggest a reason for this timing: two subtle disturbances superimposed on the general pattern of higher pressure. The first is captured in the rapid pressure drop that began on the morning of June 25, with pressure bottoming out in the wee hours of June 26. Air pressure recovered somewhat after that, began falling again on June 28 and then remained relatively low on June 29–30. Compared to pressure changes in other seasons, these pressure lulls are relatively modest, but in summer when atmospheric moisture levels are high, even minor pressure falls often correlate with an enhanced risk of precipitation.

Consider one final point about the rain during the period June 25–30. Most of northern Virginia, central Maryland and south-central Pennsylvania averages an inch or so of rain per week in late June. By that standard, rainfall was generally average to slightly above average during those six days. Given the number of miles soldiers marched during this period, however, the question remains: How quickly did the ground dry and allow for solid footing? In general, the sunnier and windier the weather, the faster the surface dries. Plus, the drier the air, the faster water on the ground evaporates. In this case, the lack of significant sunshine and strong winds, coupled with high humidity, slowed evaporation from the ground. The dirt roads took a long time to dry out.

In summary, while heat ebbed during the period June 25–30, high humidity, persistent clouds and frequent rains dominated the Gettysburg

TABLE 5. DAILY RAINFALL (IN INCHES) FOR THE PERIOD JUNE 25–30, 1863

	June 25	**June 26**	**June 27**	**June 28**	**June 29**	**June 30**
Frederick	||	||	0.45	-	0.75	-
Sykesville	-	0.75	-	-	-	0.25
Gettysburg	||	1.28	-	-	||	0.15
Naval Observatory	0.11	0.30	-	-	0.04	Trace
Annapolis	||	0.82	0.11	-	0.18	0.26
Harrisburg (Heisely)	-	1.29	-	-	-	**

Double vertical lines indicate that rain fell on that day but was not officially recorded until a subsequent day. The Harrisburg observer indicated a starting time for rain on June 30 but did not enter an amount.

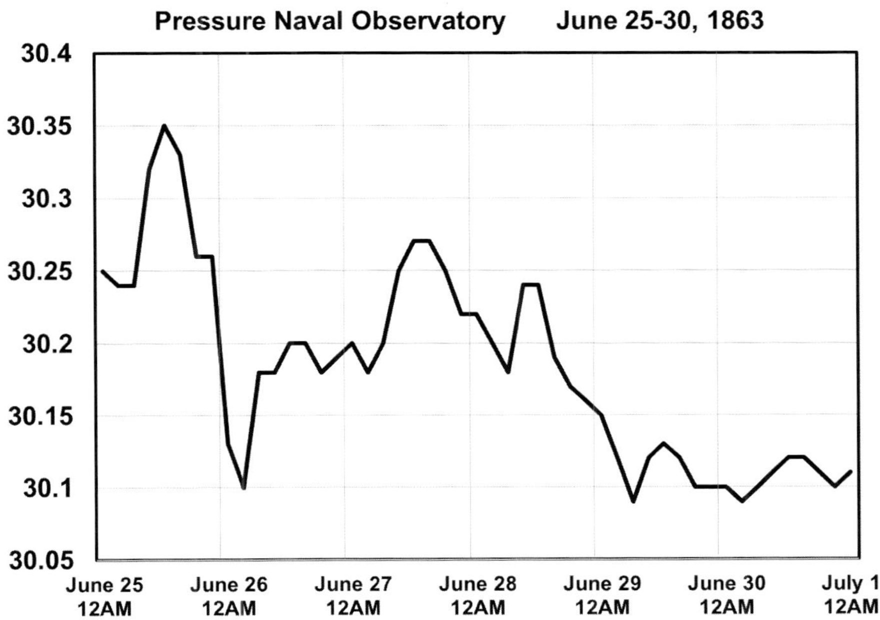

Fig. 52 Plot of pressure (in inches of mercury) at the Naval Observatory, June 25–30, 1863. *Data from NOAA FORTS.*

area. What follows is a day-by-day account of this period of forced marches, interweaving the weather with the travails of the soldiers.

The Primary Source Data

Because Union forces remained not far to the west and northwest of Washington during much of this period, the Naval Observatory remains a reliable source of weather observations. With the rapid repositioning of the Army of the Potomac during this period, observations from Frederick, Sykesville, Gettysburg and Harrisburg become increasingly useful as well. In addition, the Pennsylvania observation sites are conveniently close to the positions of the Army of Northern Virginia.

(Note: In this chapter we present our "Day-to-Day Analysis" of the weather as part of our "When the Weather Mattered the Most" feature.)

When Weather Mattered the Most: Road Warriors

To paraphrase a one-time popular song, "They had a long way to go and a short time to get there." As it happened, the seven corps of the Army of the Potomac covered a combined 618 miles during the last six days of June 1863.[139] The shortest distance any individual corps marched during this time frame was 79 miles, while the longest distance was 95 miles. How in the world did they do it?

Fortunately, the soldiers whose feet and backs bore the brunt of these historic wartime tramps left numerous firsthand accounts of their experiences. Historians' interpretations of these accounts elaborate on all that these "Road Warriors" accomplished during this trying six-day window. Now, a better understanding of how the weather shaped these events only increases our appreciation of the resultant effects of the elements on the hardy veterans of the Army of the Potomac.

Thursday, June 25

As the sun rose in Washington on the morning of Thursday, June 25, the weather seemed quite nice. The heatwave had broken the previous Thursday, and afternoon temperatures most days since then had remained in the 70s. Concerns about the weather soon gave way to fears about the war. Robert E. Lee's Army of Northern Virginia was on the march northward, and some citizens were fraught with worry. Though it served as the nation's capital, Washington seemed more Southern in look and feel than most Northern cities. Moreover, its geographic location, with Virginia on one side and border state Maryland on the other, offered an ever-present threat to the seat of the nation's government. Everyone from political leaders to the city's full-time residents counted on the Army of the Potomac to quash this unfolding second Confederate invasion of the North.[140] Most importantly, they expected General Joseph Hooker to secure their homesteads and their lives, at all costs.

Early morning temperatures at the Naval Observatory on June 25 measured in the upper 50s. Winds were light, and mostly clear skies prevailed. Meanwhile, in Frederick, Smithsonian observer Henry Hanshew recorded 61.5 degrees F at 7:00 a.m., also under clear skies. Thus, with the Union army encampments roughly equidistant between Washington and Frederick, the weather seemed to offer Hooker's army an invitation to rejoin the march. But looks were deceiving.

At the time, the bulk of Hooker's forces rested between the Potomac River to the east and the Virginia towns of Aldie to the west, Fairfax Court House to the south and Leesburg to the north. After several days of rest, Hooker deployed two pontoon bridges across the Potomac at Edward's Ferry.[141] The Eleventh Corps left Confederate soil first. Later in the day, the Third Corps followed, and then came the storied First Corps under the watchful eyes of its commanding officer Major General John Fulton Reynolds (see color section, Figure 12C).[142]

Fig. 53 Major General John F. Reynolds. *LOC.*

As the troops moved out and June 25 wore on, temperatures in the area reached well into the 70s. Gentle southerly winds prevailed, but skies became increasingly cloudy, with observers in Washington and Frederick reporting overcast skies by midafternoon. Clouds transitioned from the high, thin cirrostratus variety to a thicker cumulus type, and air pressure began to fall, a combination that often portends a turn to inclement weather.[143] Regardless, there was plenty of marching to be done.

Here, Chaplain Warren Cudworth of the 1st Massachusetts Infantry bore witness to the arduous nature of the march, which was hampered greatly by the onset of ferocious rains, cold winds and slippery footing:

> *A march followed, by the way of Edwards' Ferry, to the mouth of the Monocacy River, which, for length, severity, and discomfort, exceeded any thing* [sic] *the army ever had been through before....It was nearly five o'clock in the afternoon when the Maryland side of the Potomac was reached; and a heavy rain had set in, accompanied by a raw, cold wind.... The rain, which fell in torrents, raised the canal so that in some places its waters poured over the embankment into the Potomac River; and the flood led many soldiers to mistake the path, and plunge head first into the canal....*

> *Three hundred and sixty men belonging to the First* [Massachusetts] *left Gum Spring in the morning; but only forty laid down in the rain, seventeen hours after, on the banks of the Monocacy. The rest had given out.*[144]

The First Corps crossed last that day. And here, First Lieutenant A.P. Smith of the 76th New York Infantry testified to his disdain for the rain and mud:

> *The rain had already set in, making the roads slippery and heavy, they marched twenty miles, passing through Poolesville, and going into camp near Barnesville, Maryland. The Regiment was stationed in a cornfield where the water stood from three to six inches between the rows of corn. Of all the songs and rhymes written to show the beauties of the different season and the multifarious phases of human existence, we do not remember of any in which the author fell into ecstacies* [sic] *over sleeping in a mud-puddle.*[145]

By the time poor Smith bedded down, the weather observer at the Naval Observatory recorded 64 degrees F, cloudy skies and steady rain through midnight. In nearby Frederick, the Smithsonian observer reported 65 degrees F at 9:00 p.m. with overcast skies as well, while Jacob Sahm, a citizen observer in Frederick at the local Quynn's Hardware store, noted rain at sunset. Meanwhile, some thirty miles north of Frederick, Smithsonian observer Michael Jacobs recorded 63 degrees F at 9:00 p.m. with overcast skies, rain and light winds out of the south. Jacobs was in Gettysburg.[146]

The marching on June 25 proved difficult for many. The Eleventh and Third Corps both covered about twenty-five miles, and the First Corps trudged some fifteen. Incidentally, the same rain that harassed these troops also haunted the Union cavalry, some of whom crossed the Potomac that day, as well as the remaining four infantry corps still in Virginia. Of the latter group, only the Second Corps experienced lengthy marching on June 25. Regardless, as the day closed, most of Hooker's remaining forces prepared to cross the Potomac the next day.

Meanwhile, Lee's Confederates did not escape the elements either, whether on the march (Longstreet and Hill) or resting (Ewell). This day also marked the start of Confederate commander Major General James Ewell Brown Stuart's ill-fated cavalry foray. Dr. Charles Lippitt, a surgeon with the 57th Virginia, described the weather facing all the Rebels rather succinctly when he wrote that it "rained all night & was still inclement."[147]

Fig. 54 Nowhere to bed down. *Courtesy of D. Gallon.*

Most importantly from a Union perspective, June 25 marked an inauspicious renewal of movement for the ground-pounding infantry in Hooker's Army of the Potomac, as they pursued an ever-elusive foe. Soldiers of each Union corps that entered Maryland that day must have wondered why they always seemed to be on the march during either dangerous heat or drenching rains. Many likely wondered whether this trend would continue. The answer was not long in coming.

Friday, June 26

Weather data for June 26 from the Naval Observatory as well as Smithsonian observers in Frederick, Sykesville and Gettysburg reveal a general, but very slight, decrease in daily temperatures compared to the previous day. Meanwhile, the cloudy skies that had arrived on June 25 continued. Of note, although winds were light, they had generally shifted to a cooler northeasterly direction. Most importantly, there was even more rain.[148] The soldiers offered ample evidence of the accuracy of the weather observers' records.

As the Second Corps of the Union army crossed the Potomac at Edward's Ferry, Sergeant James A. Wright of the 1st Minnesota Infantry took mental notes on scenes he never forgot, leaving us one of the most descriptive passages written during this portion of the campaign:

> *Men who had left the Rappahannock twelve days before with new shoes on their feet were now practically bare-footed; and there were quite a number with feet so badly bruised or blistered that they walked like foundered horses.*

Wright recalled the bridge crossing in vivid detail:

Fig. 55 Sergeant James Wright. *Courtesy of Christopher Herrick and the Minnesota Historical Society Press.*

> *As it grew dark the pontoon men lighted torches.... The sun went down behind banks of clouds; and it was scarcely dark before a thunderstorm broke over us; and we were drenched with what felt like ice-cold water.... Driven by furious wind, whirling masses of clouds surged across the sky; the rain came down at a horizontal slant of about 45 degrees; successive flashes of lightning alternatively illuminated the scene or left it in total darkness; and peals of thunder shook the hills. In the intervals of light the marching column could be seen with heads bowed to the wind, moving slowly over the heaving pontoons across the storm-swept river. It was a scene to challenge a poet or painter, but I have never read a poem or seen a picture of it. But that midnight passage of the Potomac by the Second Army Corps while the storm was on was a sight worth seeing and remembering. If some "special artist" had been on the spot to have sketched it, it would have made as inspiring a picture as Washington Crossing the Delaware—a Civil War companion piece—but I imagine they were all asleep at that hour in some village hotel or farmhouse and never heard of it.*[149]

Indeed, June 26 had been a raw and nasty day. The temperature at the Naval Observatory peaked at 73.5 degrees F, while 2:00 p.m. readings at Sykesville and Frederick reached 67 and 68 degrees F, respectively. Daily rainfall totals included 0.30 inches at the Naval Observatory, 0.75 inches at Sykesville and 1.28 inches in Gettysburg. Nearly all soldiers' accounts mention the rain and its aftereffects, including "slippery and heavy" roads that "retarded progress" and at times were "almost impassable." Regarding the rain itself, men wrote of "sleeping in the mud" that night and waking that morning "completely saturated." They described the ever-present rain as ranging from "drizzly" to "pouring."

Despite the uncooperative elements, the army marched on. And by days end, only the massive Sixth Corps, some 15,000 men strong, remained on the Virginia side of the Potomac. Hooker's army had endured another day of double-digit miles of marching. Meanwhile, much of the Confederate army was on the move this day as well, and those soldiers suffered similarly from weather-related issues. First Lieutenant John Dooley of the 1st Virginia Infantry described the circumstances facing the Confederates: "The morning dawns but no sun breaks forth to cheer our second invasion and as our column advances along the road mud, deep and slippery, impedes our march at every step." Commenting further, he added, "As we advance into Pennsylvania the road becomes almost impassable, so slippery is the mud whilst a cold steady rain falls constantly upon our ranks, increasing every moment our burdens and the difficulties of our march."[150]

Saturday, June 27

The official weather observations for June 27 indicate another relatively cool day, with temperatures ranging from the low 60s in the early morning to midday highs in the low 70s. Complete cloud cover ruled the day, with the Smithsonian observer in Frederick recording nearly a half inch of early morning rain. Light northeasterly winds prevailed in the morning but took on a southerly component later in the day as the Bermuda High once again flexed its muscles. John Koogle, a civilian diarist in Myersville, Maryland, between Frederick and Hagerstown, described the day quite succinctly: "weather rainy."[151]

Fig. 56 Rain on the march. *Courtesy of D. Gallon.*

Meanwhile, General Hooker continued to spread his army of seven infantry corps across a wide east and west arc to cover the approaches to Washington and Baltimore. Here, the Weather Gods finally smiled on the soldiers of the Army of the Potomac. First Corps artillery commander Colonel Charles S. Wainwright attested to this welcome relief: "We had a nice march today, one really to be enjoyed. The weather had cleared off fine, but not hot; the road was capital, wide and smooth; and the country exquisite."[152] Of course, Wainwright's account came from the perspective of an officer fortunate enough to opine from horseback. Differing somewhat, a number of foot soldiers offered comments along the lines of that provided by Private R.W. Mckee of the 139th Pennsylvania Infantry: "Cloudy all day—and rained some at intervals....More pleasant marching to-day than yesterday, but still a little muddy."[153] Others, like Quartermaster Lieutenant William H. Crennell of the 140th New York Infantry, not only commented on the lingering effects of the incessant rains but also noted the splendor of the surrounding scenery: "Started from camp about ½ past five found the roads very bad both from being rocky and muddy crossed the Monocacy (river) and brought up about three miles from Frederick. The country traveled through today is the most bea[u]tiful seen since I have been in the service."[154]

Fig. 57 Lieutenant Colonel Rufus Dawes. *Courtesy of The Dawes Arboretum.*

Regardless of the variable weather conditions, the marching continued in earnest. Though the Eleventh Corps finally enjoyed a day of well-earned rest, most corps covered double-digit distances. Only the First Corps marched fewer than ten miles, while the others covered fifteen to twenty. For most soldiers, however, the past seventy-two hours had been difficult at best. Lieutenant Colonel Rufus Dawes of the 6th Wisconsin Infantry summarized his experiences of the past few days in his diary entry for June 27:

> *What do you think of trudging along all day in a soaking rain; getting as wet as a drowned rat, taking supper on hard tack and salt pork, and then wrapping up in a wet woolen blanket and lying down for a sleep, but waked up during the night three or four times to receive and attend to orders and finally turning out at three o'clock in the morning to get the regiment ready to march? Well—that is soldiering.*[155]

Fortunately for most of Lee's forces, by day's end, they had completed the bulk of the hard marches that led them to Gettysburg.[156] But for the Union soldiers, the series of forced marches that brought them to the battlefield had yet to reach a crescendo. Meanwhile, Hooker's ongoing disagreements with his superiors in Washington reached a boiling point. As a result, Hooker finally offered to resign and President Lincoln quickly relieved him, appointing Major General George G. Meade to the post.[157]

Sunday, June 28

Sunday, June 28, proved to be no average day. At 3:00 a.m., General Meade received the momentous news that he had been appointed the new commanding officer of the Army of the Potomac.[158] Meade was not so certain this promotion represented good news. He expressed these sentiments in a letter to his wife: "Well, I've been tried and condemned without a hearing, and I suppose I will have to go to execution."[159] To be sure, he faced an unenviable task. By the time Meade assumed command, Lee's forces ranged widely and largely unchallenged across south-central Pennsylvania. And in no small matter of concern, Lee's army boasted, in essence, an undefeated record at the time.[160] Regardless, Meade faced a two-part mission: first, to keep Lee from threatening the nation's capital and other major Northern cities and, second, to maneuver onto favorable ground from which he (Meade) could bring the Army of Northern Virginia to battle and defeat it. To accomplish these goals would demand quick action by the Army of the Potomac. Perhaps it was better that the soldiers did not know the weather conditions they would face.

Weatherwise, June 28 started just like the previous few days. Morning temperatures in the area occupied by Meade's army measured in the mid- to upper 60s. Skies remained mostly cloudy with light to gentle easterly breezes. No official observers in the area reported rain that day, the only such day in the June 25–30 period. Regardless, soldiers who wrote about the weather on June 28 offered somewhat conflicting accounts. It appears the skies were quite changeable, with scattered pockets of light rain and overcast skies mixed with times of sunshine and corresponding rises in temperature. At 2:00 p.m., the Smithsonian observer in Sykesville recorded a temperature of 74 degrees F, while one of Harrisburg's official observers recorded 77 degrees F. The high temperature for the day at the Naval Observatory in Washington was

78.5 degrees F. Though these temperatures are below average for late June, the "discomfort level" as measured by dewpoints in the upper 60s combined with the forced marches in occasional sunshine left some soldiers feeling the heat, literally.[161]

Lieutenant Colonel Rufus Dawes of the 6th Wisconsin noted, "We left South Mountain in a great haste on the 28th and marched to Frederick city though a drizzling rain as usual.…I don't think I ever before saw at this time of year such a long continued, misty, drizzling storm as we have been marching though since we crossed the Potomac."[162] As the 1st Minnesota's James Wright reflected, "Early Sunday morning, June 28th, we were in line and again bore banners northward. The day was fair, and the heat increased as the sun rose higher, until it was oppressively hot. The road was hilly, and we marched rapidly with only brief halts."[163] As R.W. McKee of the 139th Pennsylvania summarized his day, it was "cloudy all day, but quite warm, especially in P.M." He added, "Roads in good marching order, neither dusty nor muddy."[164]

As it happened, June 28 also proved to be a critical day for the Army of Northern Virginia's commanding officer. Late that day, Lee learned, quite surprisingly, that at least one portion of the Union army was closer than he anticipated. Lee had operated blindly since June 25, when General Stuart had departed with his cavalry on his infamous mission, intending to ride around the Army of the Potomac. From that moment forward, Lee remained generally unaware of the whereabouts of his adversary. On the evening of June 28, the northernmost elements of Lee's army rested on the doorstep of Harrisburg, the westernmost portion of his army occupied the Chambersburg area in the Cumberland Valley, and the easternmost elements rested about fifty miles east near York. When Lee learned from a spy named Henry T. Harrison, who was working for General Longstreet during the campaign, that a large portion of Meade's army had moved as close as thirty-some miles from his headquarters, he was

Fig. 58 Major General George G. Meade. *From E. Forbes,* Thirty Years After.

Fig. 59 Harrison. *From Longstreet,* From Manassas to Appomattox.

shocked! Understandably alarmed, he immediately sent orders to his far-flung corps commanders to concentrate. Lee knew he needed to draw his forces together to prepare for battle. And he needed to do so quickly.

In the meantime, as the sun set on the Army of the Potomac on June 28, most of its soldiers notched yet another hard march in their campaign belts. Only the First Corps, which had moved about eight miles, and the Fifth Corps, which had rested that day, escaped lengthy marches on this fateful Sabbath. Each of the remaining corps, however, marched double-digit distances, with the Eleventh Corps advancing an estimated twenty-two miles. Despite these continued demands, the soldiers shouldered the burden well. The weather, more or less, had been their friend that day. For Meade's men, this had been a blessing. Yet as the calendar turned at midnight, the onset of rain portended a coming day of misery.

Monday, June 29

On June 29, as the two combatants drew closer together, the stakes increased. Lee began to concentrate his forces while Meade continued to move north and northeast in a thirty-mile-wide arc. As both armies jockeyed for position, a small crossroads town in south-central Pennsylvania's Adams County emerged as a potential flash point. Gettysburg was uniquely situated with no fewer than ten roads converging there like spokes on a wagon wheel, each drawing both armies toward its hub. Although the weary foot soldiers of the Army of the Potomac likely remained unaware of the proximity of their adversaries, the demands on the Union soldiers to be "on their game" increased exponentially as they drew nearer to their foe. And until a battle was joined, their "game" was marching.

The day broke with cloudy skies and patchy fog as documented by the Smithsonian observers in Sykesville, Gettysburg and Harrisburg.

Wind direction varied among locations that morning, but by 2:00 p.m. all observers reported winds from either the south or southeast. Temperatures ranged from the mid-60s in the early morning to the low 80s by afternoon when breaks in the clouds appeared. Moreover, for the first time since June 19, the combination of temperature and humidity resulted in a heat index that likely exceeded 85 degrees F in Washington. Rain returned, too, in some instances with a vengeance. The official observer in Frederick reported 0.75 inches. Skies began to clear late in the day, but between sunrise and sunset on June 29, the soldiers of the Army of the Potomac had to shoulder the burden of both the weather and the great distances they marched.[165]

The First, Third and Eleventh Corps each faced arduous treks of over twenty miles on June 29. According to the regimental historian of the First Corps' 14th Brooklyn, who may as well have spoken for soldiers in all three corps, the day proved insufferable: "It rained heavily nearly all day, and the roads were in a frightful condition." As for the effects of these rains, he added, "The men were so fatigued that whenever the wagon train was temporarily blocked many of them sank down in their tracks, in the mud and rain, and snatched a little sleep."[166] Before the day ended, the Twelfth Corps had trekked some twenty miles and the Sixth Corps nearly thirty miles. And accounts from both groups echoed those of their comrades from the aforementioned corps. That said, none marched farther in misery that day than the stalwart men of Major General Winfield S. Hancock's Second Corps.

Late-arriving orders forced these men to make up time, and as a result they marched like dogs on the hunt. Many, though steadfast and hardened veterans of multiple campaigns, counted their experience this day as "the most remarkable day's march during its service."[167] One veteran even stated that on this day his corps "completed the longest march made by infantry during the war...a distance of thirty-four miles."[168] Other soldiers later challenged this claim, but the point was moot. Any march in

Fig. 60 Major General Winfield S. Hancock. *From Johnson and Buel, eds.,* Battles and Leaders of the Civil War, *vol. 3.*

excess of thirty miles in the course of an estimated fourteen hours, in less-than-ideal weather conditions, stands as a testament to human endurance.

James A. Wright's 1st Minnesota was part and parcel to the suffering as the Second Corps trudged some thirty-two to thirty-four miles, all the while under the added duress from carrying their burdensome paraphernalia:

> *It must be remembered that each soldier carried a rifle which—with bayonet, etc.—weighted about 11 pounds. Also, 100 rounds of ammunition, knapsack, haversack, canteen, coffee pot, and whatever cooking utensils he had; his blanket, tent cloth, rubber, all extra clothing, and whatever else he might have—writing paper, envelopes, keepsakes, or a book. These* impediments, *which must have weighed full 40 pounds, were useful and necessary, but often a real impediment to rapid transit, and could not be thrown away and replaced at will....It was a misty, murky morning with a sultry air and cloud-covered skies....The day proved a hot one.*

Wright continued to recall his suffering years later when he wrote:

> *Chafed shoulders and blistered feet were the rule, for we had wetted the latter frequently and had been sweating freely. The most of us had been marching with our blouses and shirts open, and when the sun ceased to shine we took off our hats, but still the heat was oppressive, and the sweat oozed from our bodies, and the* ache *increased in our weary shoulders and over-strained muscles as the march continued.*[169]

At the end of the day, rare was a soldier who was not completely exhausted. Many had fallen out with sunstroke. Those who survived the experience must have wondered what it all meant, these seemingly endless forced marches in miserable weather. And most likely they wondered when, if ever, it might end.

Tuesday, June 30 (The Eve of Battle)

The Union cavalry likely suspected battle was imminent, particularly Brigadier General John Buford's and Brigadier General Judson Kilpatrick's divisions. Two brigades of Buford's men screened Meade's left flank, and as Meade's "eyes and ears" they served their commanding officer very well. Buford's reports alerted Meade to the presence of a significant number of enemy forces both west and north of Gettysburg. With this information, Meade set his jaw and determined to do battle with the much-vaunted army of Robert E. Lee. His initial contingency was to hunker down in a defensive position south of Gettysburg, the so-called Pipe Creek Line. But fate decreed otherwise.

Temperatures the morning of June 30 ranged from the upper 60s to the low 70s. At 2:00 p.m., Frederick observer Henry Hanshew recorded 76.5 degrees F while Professor Jacobs in Gettysburg recorded 79 degrees F, suggesting that the afternoon maximum there likely topped 80 degrees F. Multiple days of a general easterly flow from the Atlantic Ocean had raised dewpoints in the area into the 70–75–degree F range, bringing a truly tropical feel to the air. Another 0.25 inches of rain fell in Sykesville, with 0.15 inches in Gettysburg. Both observers described the day as "showery." The heat index from Frederick to Gettysburg, the area where the Union forces maneuvered that day, likely reached into the upper 80s during the hottest part of the day.[170]

Several of Meade's hard-pressed corps made relatively short marches on June 30, while the exhausted Second and Eleventh Corps breathed a sigh of relief as they remained in camp after covering thirty-two to thirty-four miles and twenty-five miles, respectively, the previous day. The First and Third Corps, already strategically positioned, marched less than ten miles each. Nevertheless, for the Fifth, Sixth and Twelfth Corps, hard marching became the order of the day. Sergeant A.P. Morrison of the Fifth Corps' 9th Pennsylvania Reserves set the tone when he wrote, "Reveille at 4 o'clock; it rained on us very hard last night and this morning…found the road exceedingly heavy and slippery." Morrison and his comrades

Fig. 61 Brigadier General John Buford. *LOC.*

trudged northeastward through Liberty, Johnsville and Union Bridge, finally halting near Union Mills after twenty-five arduous miles.[171] They now sat only a few miles from the Pennsylvania line and fifteen miles southeast of Gettysburg.

As the regimental historian of the Sixth Corps' 37th Massachusetts recorded, "There was a heavy rain-fall during the forenoon, wetting everybody completely and making the roads quite difficult." Yet, as this group trekked through New Market, Westminster and finally reached Manchester it appears "the afternoon was pleasant and comparatively comfortable for marching."[172] Another member of the Sixth Corps, First Lieutenant and Adjutant George W. Bicknell of the 5th Maine Infantry, also commented on the nice weather but added, "These long and continued marches began to leave their effects upon the men. Feet were blistered. Frames were sore and weary."[173] In the Third Corps, the 17th Maine's Captain Charles Mattocks echoed Bicknell's remarks when he wrote, "We are suffering for shoes in the Regt. Some men are actually barefoot. A supply has been expected for the past week."[174]

All in all, the men of the Sixth Corps did remarkably well, especially considering that their twenty-mile march of June 30 brought the total number of miles marched to ninety-one miles for the hardy soldiers of the Sixth Corps over five days. Howe's division could add even more to this total as they marched an additional eighteen miles the evening and night prior to the commencement of this six-day period. Yet their trials were not over. The Sixth Corps' endurance capability would be tested even further on the night of July 1 through the late afternoon of July 2 when it undertook another thirty-plus-mile forced march. Moreover, that march also involved an overnight tramp that took them straight to the battlefield.

Fig. 62 Captain Charles Mattocks. *Courtesy of Maine State Archives.*

However, on June 30, Major General Henry W. Slocum's Twelfth Corps stretched their legs the most, as they trudged thirty miles.[175] Interestingly, as the leading edge of the army's right flank, their route brought them close to armed conflict that day. This occurred when Union cavalry under General

Kilpatrick encountered General Stuart's wayward horsemen in a spirited clash of arms at Hanover, about fourteen miles east of Gettysburg. While comments on the weather often dominated recollections of long marches, a potential brush with the enemy such as this one turned the soldiers' concerns to those of entering battle. In the end, the men of the Twelfth Corps saw no action this day. Regardless, the possibility of battle proved just the elixir needed for sore feet, fatigued bodies and overall exhaustion. In fact, adrenaline often forms the lifeblood of battlefield courage. Sergeant Samuel Toombs of the 13th New Jersey provided proof of this notion:

Fig. 63 "A Footsore Straggler." *From Billings,* Hardtack and Coffee.

> *As we neared the Pennsylvania line the spirits of the men grew exultant. There was a novelty in the situation of affairs which affected the troops wonderfully, and increased their anxiety to meet the enemy on loyal territory…when within two miles of Littlestown, Penn.,* [Littlestown is just north of the state line] *word was received that the enemy were marching upon that place. Our column at once halted, and the order to load rifles was passed down the line. Skirmishers were deployed, and we moved forward at a rapid pace until we came in sight of the town, where we halted.*[176]

Through the forced marches on the eve of battle during the period June 25–30, 1863, the soldiers of the Army of the Potomac had more than proven their fortitude and resolve. Challenged by frequent periods of rain that turned the roads into quagmires, the men soldiered on. Left to sleep in drenched fields in rain-soaked clothing, the stalwart souls somehow kept up their spirits. Forced to trudge great distances, day upon day, the "Road Warriors" of the Army of the Potomac painted their names in the annals of history. In the end, only one question remained: Could they show the same grit, determination and mettle in the forthcoming battle at Gettysburg?

PEOPLE, STORIES AND MATTERS TO REMEMBER: THE OBSERVERS, HARRIET BAER AND PROFESSOR WILLIAM BAER, SYKESVILLE, MARYLAND

History is rife with stories of women whose pioneering efforts in sundry realms resulted in meaningful strides in the advancement of this nation's scientific history. And while most of these stories have been well documented, a few remain untold. Harriet Baer's contributions to the field of meteorology represent one such instance.

Interestingly, the story of Harriet's mark on the field is tied closely to her husband's work. Professor William Baer gained great fame, both for his service to the nation during the War of 1812 and in his profession as an "agriculturist" and chemist. But one of his most significant contributions to science centered on his reliance on Harriet to fulfill his obligations as an official weather observer for the Smithsonian.

Harriet Mantz Baer, born on June 8, 1789, and her husband, William, born on February 2, 1788, were both raised in Frederick, Maryland. At age twenty-five, William volunteered and served with several different regiments during the War of 1812.[177] He then embarked on a fruitful life in the world of science, including a stint as director of the Maryland Chemical Works. According to one report, William enjoyed few educational advantages, but his earnest academic pursuits enabled him to become "one of the best practical chemists in the country." In agricultural chemistry it was said "he was, perhaps, the most intelligent man in the United States." The same report indicated that "in meteorology he was especially distinguished."[178] He lectured far and wide throughout Maryland and surrounding states about agriculture, and it appears he shared his passion for meteorology with his wife.

After living in Frederick for many years, the Baers moved to Sykesville, about fifteen miles west-northwest of Baltimore, to a home they dubbed Schellman Hills (or Hall), in deference to their familial roots.[179] Here occurred one of the earliest known instances of a woman's active involvement in support of observational meteorology. The *Maryland Weather Book* indicates that William and Harriet recorded and reported various weather data in Sykesville from January 1846 through December 1865. The Smithsonian's *Meteorological Stations and Observers of the Smithsonian Institution in North America and Adjacent Islands, from the Year 1849 up to the Year 1869* indicates that William served as observer from 1849 to 1852, Harriet and William shared duties in 1853–54 and Harriet observed

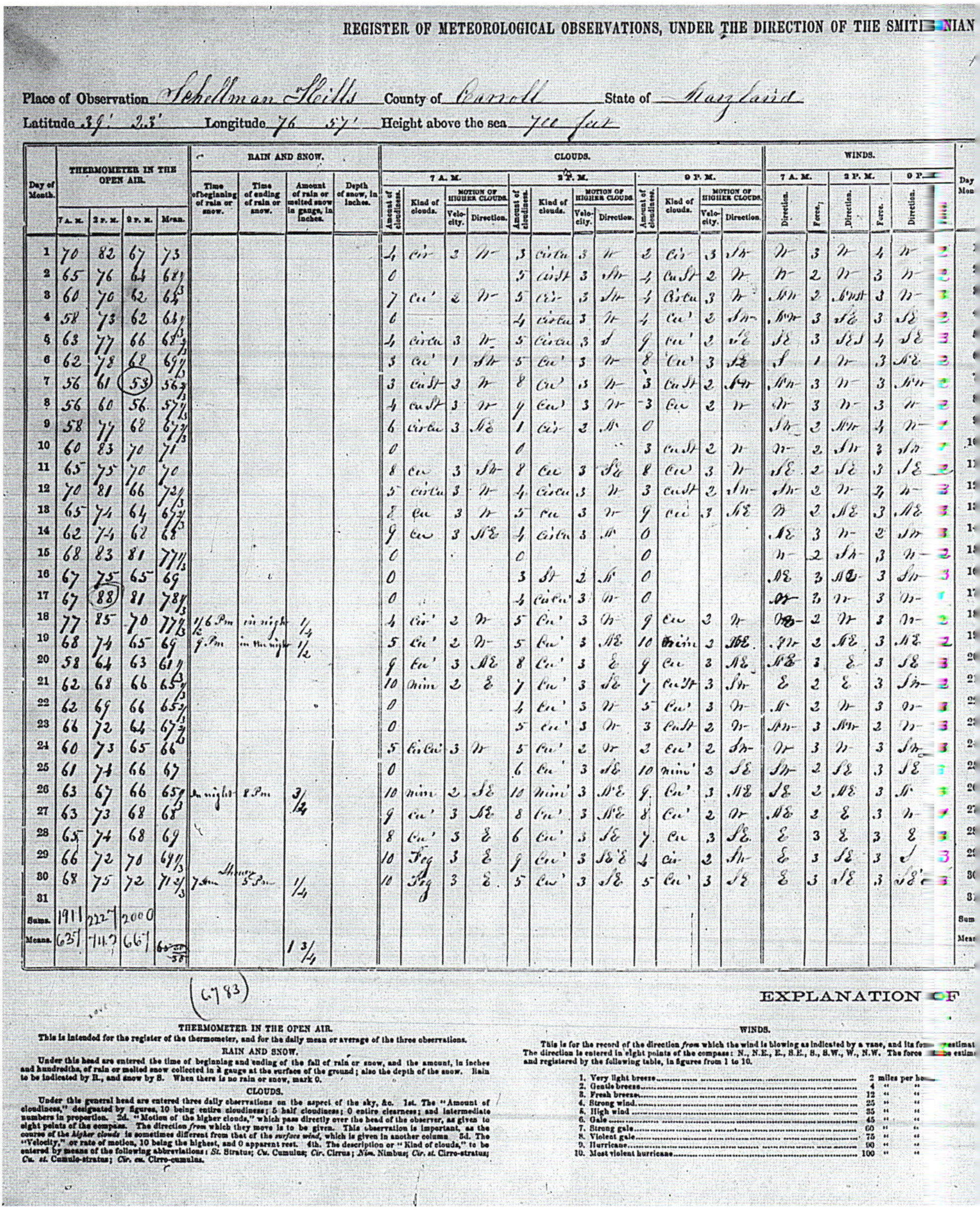

REGISTER OF METEOROLOGICAL OBSERVATIONS, UNDER THE DIRECTION OF THE SMIT[illegible]NIAN

Place of Observation Schellman Hills County of Carroll State of Maryland

Latitude 39' 23' Longitude 76 57' Height above the sea 700 feet

Day of Month	Thermometer 7 A.M.	2 P.M.	9 P.M.	Mean	Time of beginning of rain or snow	Time of ending of rain or snow	Amount of rain or melted snow in gauge, in inches	Depth of snow, in inches	Amount of cloudiness 7 A.M.	Amount of cloudiness 2 P.M.	Amount of cloudiness 9 P.M.
1	70	82	67	73					4	3	2
2	65	76	64	68⅓					0	5	4
3	60	70	62	64					7	5	4
4	58	73	62	64⅓					6	4	4
5	63	77	66	68⅔					4	5	9
6	62	78	68	69⅓					3	5	8
7	56	61	(53)	56⅔					3	8	3
8	56	60	56	57⅓					4	4	3
9	58	77	68	67⅔					6	1	0
10	60	83	70	71					0	0	3
11	65	75	70	70					8	8	8
12	70	81	66	72⅓					5	4	3
13	65	74	64	67⅔					8	5	9
14	62	74	68	68					9	4	0
15	68	83	81	77⅓					0	0	0
16	67	75	65	69					0	3	0
17	67	(88)	81	78⅔					0	4	0
18	77	85	70	77⅓	½ 6 Pm	in night	¼		4	5	9
19	68	74	65	69	9 Pm	in the night	½		5	5	10
20	58	64	63	61⅔					9	8	9
21	62	68	66	65⅓					10	7	7
22	62	69	66	65⅔					0	4	5
23	66	72	64	67⅓					0	5	3
24	60	73	65	66					5	5	2
25	61	74	66	67					0	6	10
26	63	67	66	65⅓	In night	8 Pm	¾		10	10	9
27	63	73	68	68					9	8	8
28	65	74	68	69					8	6	7
29	66	72	70	69⅓					10	7	4
30	68	75	72	71⅔	7 Am	Shower 5 Pm	¼		10	5	5
31											
Sums	1911	2227	2000								
Means	63.7	74.2	66.7	68 28/58			1¾				

(6783)

THERMOMETER IN THE OPEN AIR.

This is intended for the register of the thermometer, and for the daily mean or average of the three observations.

RAIN AND SNOW.

Under this head are entered the time of beginning and ending of the fall of rain or snow, and the amount, in inches and hundredths, of rain or melted snow collected in a gauge at the surface of the ground; also the depth of the snow. Rain to be indicated by R., and snow by S. When there is no rain or snow, mark 0.

CLOUDS.

Under this general head are entered three daily observations on the aspect of the sky, &c. 1st. The "Amount of cloudiness," designated by figures, 10 being entire cloudiness; 5 half cloudiness; 0 entire clearness; and intermediate numbers in proportion. 2d. "Motion of the higher clouds," which pass directly over the head of the observer, as given to eight points of the compass. The direction *from* which they move is to be given. This observation is important, as the course of the *higher clouds* is sometimes different from that of the *surface wind*, which is given in another column. 3d. The "Velocity," or rate of motion, 10 being the highest, and 0 apparent rest. 4th. The description or "Kind of clouds," to be entered by means of the following abbreviations: *St.* Stratus; *Cu.* Cumulus; *Cir.* Cirrus; *Nim.* Nimbus; *Cir. st.* Cirro-stratus; *Cu. st.* Cumulo-stratus; *Cir. cu.* Cirro-cumulus.

EXPLANATION OF

WINDS.

This is for the record of the direction *from* which the wind is blowing as indicated by a vane, and its fo[illegible] estimat[illegible] The direction is entered in eight points of the compass: N., N.E., E., S.E., S., S.W., W., N.W. The force [illegible] be estim[illegible] and registered by the following table, in figures from 1 to 10.

1. Very light breeze .... 2 miles per h[illegible]
2. Gentle breeze .... 4 " "
3. Fresh breeze .... 12 " "
4. Strong wind .... 25 " "
5. High wind .... 35 " "
6. Gale .... 45 " "
7. Strong gale .... 60 " "
8. Violent gale .... 75 " "
9. Hurricane .... 90 " "
10. Most violent hurricane .... 100 " "

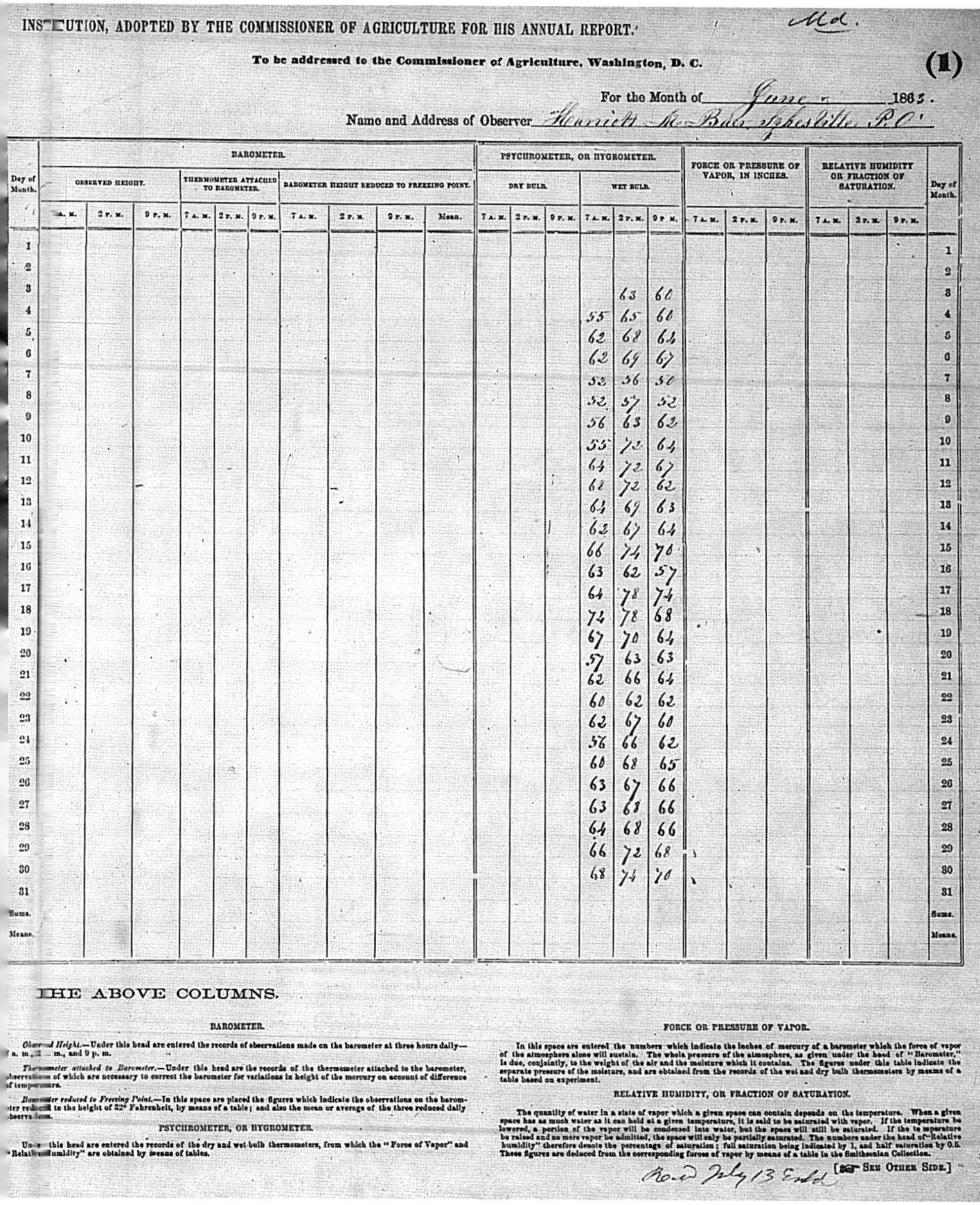

INS[illegible]UTION, ADOPTED BY THE COMMISSIONER OF AGRICULTURE FOR HIS ANNUAL REPORT. Md.

To be addressed to the Commissioner of Agriculture, Washington, D. C. (1)

For the Month of June 1863.

Name and Address of Observer Harriett M. Baer, Sykesville P.O.

Day of Month.	Barometer: Observed height.			Thermometer attached to barometer.			Barometer height reduced to freezing point.				Psychrometer, or hygrometer: Dry bulb.			Wet bulb.			Force or pressure of vapor, in inches.			Relative humidity or fraction of saturation.			Day of Month.
	7 A. M.	2 P. M.	9 P. M.	7 A. M.	2 P. M.	9 P. M.	7 A. M.	2 P. M.	9 P. M.	Mean.	7 A. M.	2 P. M.	9 P. M.	7 A. M.	2 P. M.	9 P. M.	7 A. M.	2 P. M.	9 P. M.	7 A. M.	2 P. M.	9 P. M.	
1																							1
2																							2
3															63	60							3
4														55	65	60							4
5														62	68	64							5
6														62	69	67							6
7														52	56	50							7
8														52	57	52							8
9														56	63	62							9
10														55	72	64							10
11														64	72	67							11
12														62	72	62							12
13														64	69	63							13
14														62	67	64							14
15														66	74	70							15
16														63	62	57							16
17														64	78	74							17
18														74	78	68							18
19														67	70	64							19
20														57	63	63							20
21														62	66	64							21
22														60	62	62							22
23														62	67	60							23
24														56	66	62							24
25														60	68	65							25
26														63	67	66							26
27														63	68	66							27
28														64	68	66							28
29														66	72	68							29
30														68	74	70							30
31																							31
Sums.																							Sums.
Means.																							Means.

[illegible]HE ABOVE COLUMNS.

BAROMETER.

Obs[illegible] Height.—Under this head are entered the records of observations made on the barometer at three hours daily—[illegible] a. m., [illegible] m., and 9 p. m.

Th[illegible]meter attached to Barometer.—Under this head are the records of the thermometer attached to the barometer, [illegible] of which are necessary to correct the barometer for variations in height of the mercury on account of difference of temp[illegible].

Baro[illegible] reduced to Freezing Point.—In this space are placed the figures which indicate the observations on the barometer red[illegible] to the height of 32° Fahrenheit, by means of a table; and also the mean or average of the three reduced daily [illegible].

PSYCHROMETER, OR HYGROMETER.

Un[illegible] this head are entered the records of the dry and wet-bulb thermometers, from which the "Force of Vapor" and "Relat[illegible]umidity" are obtained by means of tables.

FORCE OR PRESSURE OF VAPOR.

In this space are entered the numbers which indicate the inches of mercury of a barometer which the force of vapor of the atmosphere alone will sustain. The whole pressure of the atmosphere, as given under the head of "Barometer," is due, conjointly, to the weight of the air and the moisture which it contains. The figures under this table indicate the separate pressure of the moisture, and are obtained from the records of the wet and dry bulb thermometers by means of a table based on experiment.

RELATIVE HUMIDITY, OR FRACTION OF SATURATION.

The quantity of water in a state of vapor which a given space can contain depends on the temperature. When a given space has as much water as it can hold at a given temperature, it is said to be saturated with vapor. If the temperature be lowered, a portion of the vapor will be condensed into water, but the space will still be saturated. If the temperature be raised and no more vapor be admitted, the space will only be partially saturated. The numbers under the head of "Relative humidity" therefore denote the percentage of saturation; full saturation being indicated by 1, and half saturation by 0.5. These figures are deduced from the corresponding forces of vapor by means of a table in the Smithsonian Collection.

Rec'd July 13 Entd [See Other Side.]

Fig. 64 Sykesville, Maryland weather observer report for June 1863. Note Harriet Baer's signature. *NOAA FORTS.*

between 1855 and 1865.[180] NOAA's FORTS database contains copies of the Sykesville monthly weather reports from August 1853 to October 1865, and each lists Harriet Baer as the person responsible for recording data and forwarding the reports to the Smithsonian. Harriet diligently took weather observations such as temperature, cloud type, wind speed and wind direction three times per day.[181] In doing so, she became one of the earliest known women involved in an official capacity with observational meteorology, though she did so in relative anonymity.

William Baer predeceased his wife, dying in Frederick on June 7, 1866, at seventy-eight years of age.[182] Harriet outlived her beloved husband by five years, dying in Frederick on August 25, 1871, at the age of eighty-two.[183]

7
THE BATTLE

Hell on Earth, July 1–4, 1863

Great Battles of Gettysburg fought[184]
—*Reverend Dr. "Professor" Michael Jacobs, Smithsonian weather observer, Gettysburg, Pennsylvania*

Setting the Stage

Situation Report—A Brief Summary of Troop Movements and Dispositions

Military historians term it a "meeting engagement." Others simply say the opposing armies came to blows at Gettysburg "accidentally on purpose." Regardless, both immense armies had been on a collision course for nearly a month. And as dawn approached on July 1, the ten roads that came together at the burgeoning crossroads town of Gettysburg drew the opposing forces dangerously close to one another. With this, it seemed battle could not be avoided.

The three-day battle that followed proved to be the largest to ever occur on the North American continent. At Gettysburg, an estimated 163,000 troops collided in mortal combat that resulted in approximately 51,000 soldiers killed, wounded, captured or missing in action. As detailed in Tom Desjardin's fine work *These Honored Dead*, 1 out of every 200 people alive in the United States in 1863 took part in the Battle of Gettysburg. A battle of equivalent size today, relative to the current U.S. population, would include over 1.5 million souls.[185]

Troop Location Map

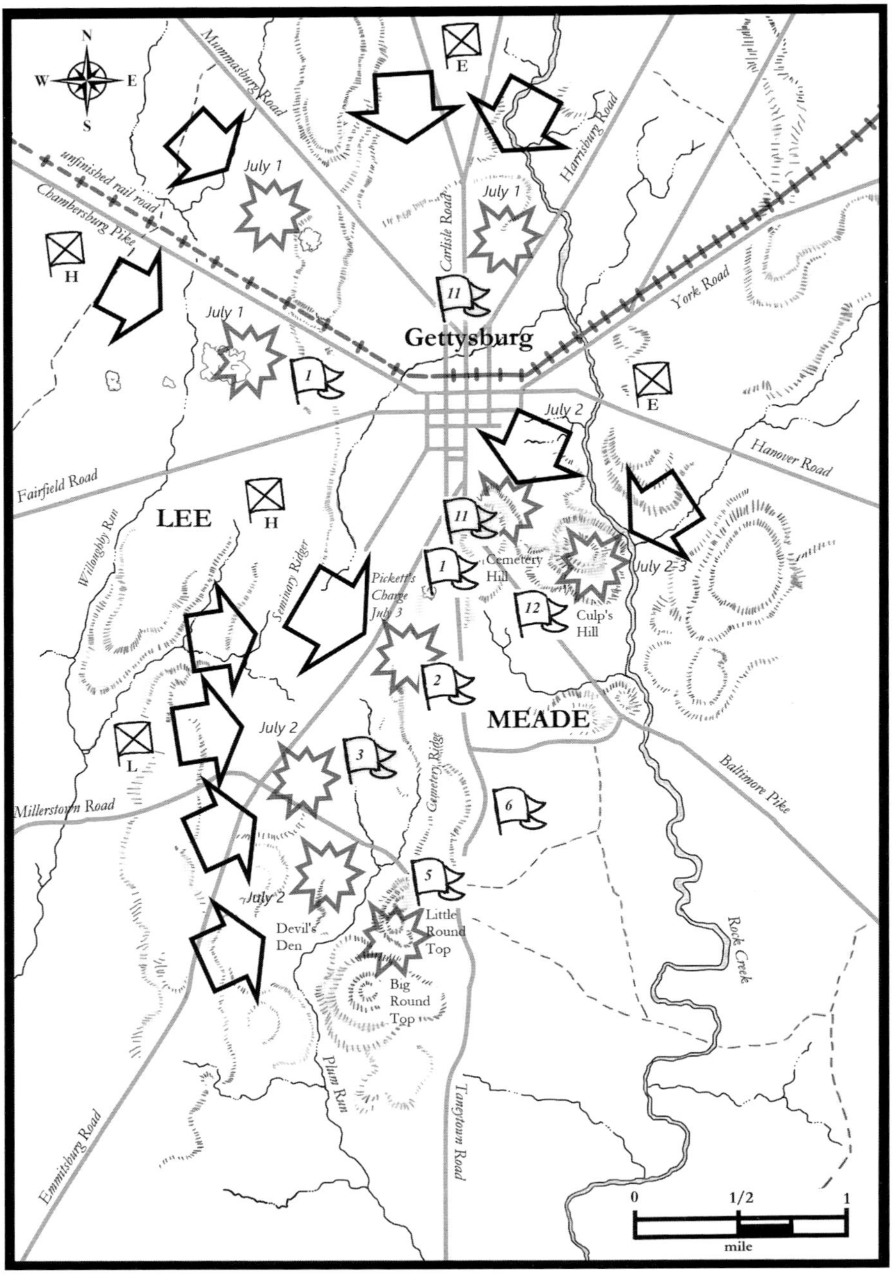

Fig. 65 Gettysburg Campaign, July 1–4, 1863. *Courtesy of J. Heiser.*

The Weather—Background

As the theater of action contracted in size and focused on Gettysburg in the period July 1–4, the most effective approach to reconstructing the weather conditions from official observers' data changes. Smithsonian observer Professor Michael Jacobs, posted literally just a few miles from the battlefield, faithfully continued his observations during and after the battle. Predictably, his data provide the primary official source for this period. Of course, as July 1 dawned, not all eventual participants in the battle had arrived on the field. A portion of Ewell's Corps was still en route from York and the Carlisle area, some in Longstreet's Corps remained on the far side of South Mountain, and Sedgwick's Sixth Corps spent the day in Manchester, Maryland. Thus, the official observations from Sykesville (south of Manchester) and Harrisburg (just northeast of Carlisle) will also be germane, as well as the finer resolution Naval Observatory data.

Figures 66 and 67 show a portion of Professor Jacobs's Smithsonian observation form for July 1863, covering the period July 1–17, while Figure 68 is a close-up of the temperature and precipitation columns for the first five days of the month. Two points are worth noting. First, Jacobs observed no rain on July 1–3, leading to the oft-made assertion that rain did not fall during the battle. But various diarists do mention rain in the area, particularly on July 1 and late in the day on July 3. Second—and central to quantifying what it really felt like during the battle—the columns on the right side of Figure 67 remain blank, indicating that Jacobs did not record wet-bulb temperature, a necessary ingredient in the computation of a discomfort measure such as the heat index.

Fortunately, nearby observers did measure wet-bulb temperature. In Harrisburg, thirty-five miles to the north-northeast of Gettysburg, Smithsonian observers John Heisely and William Hickok made independent observations at 7:00 a.m., 2:00 p.m. and 9:00 p.m., while Smithsonian observer Harriett Baer in Sykesville, Maryland, also observed the wet-bulb temperature. As a result, dewpoints can be computed in both locations. The question remains: How applicable are they to Gettysburg?

REGISTER OF METEOROLOGICAL (

Place of Observation Gettysburg County of A[illegible]

Latitude 39° 49½′ Longitude 77° 15′ Height above the

Day of Month.	THERMOMETER IN THE OPEN AIR. 7 A. M.	2 P. M.	9 P. M.	Mean.	RAIN AND SNOW. Time of beginning of rain or snow.	Time of ending of rain or snow.	Amount of rain or melted snow in gauge, in inches.	Depth of snow, in inches.	7 A. M. Amount of cloudiness.	Kind of clouds.	Motion of higher clouds: Velocity.	Dir
1	72	76	74	74					10	cu st	2	[illegible]
2	74	81	76	77					10	cu st	1	[illegible]
3	73	87	76	78 2/3					10	cu st	2	[illegible]
4	74	76	69	73	at 6 A.M. & at 2½ P.M. 4 P.M.	& at to 9 P.M.	0.390		10	cu st	2	[illegible]
5	69	72	70	70 1/3					10	cu st	2	[illegible]
6	69	76	73	72 2/3	x	x			10	cu st	2	[illegible]
7	69	73	78	70	x	x			10	cu st	1	[illegible]
8	67	72	69	69 1/3	3 A.M.	11½ A.M.	1.300		10	cu st	2	[illegible]
9	69	81	71	73 2/3					10	strat		
10	71	79	74	74 2/3					1	cu	1	[illegible]
11	74	84	75	77 2/3					10	cu st	1	
12	75	84	71	76 2/3	Thund at 3 & 6 P.M. & night P.M.		0.550		10	cu st	2	[illegible]
13	69	72	71	70 1/3	& day —				10	cu st	2	[illegible]
14	68	80	75	74 5/3					10	cu st	2	[illegible]
15	73	82	72	75 2/3					10	cir cu	2	[illegible]
16	71	80	67	72 2/3	at 4 3/4 P.M.				0			
17	61	62	60	61	—	4 P.M.	0.325		10	cu st	1	[illegible]

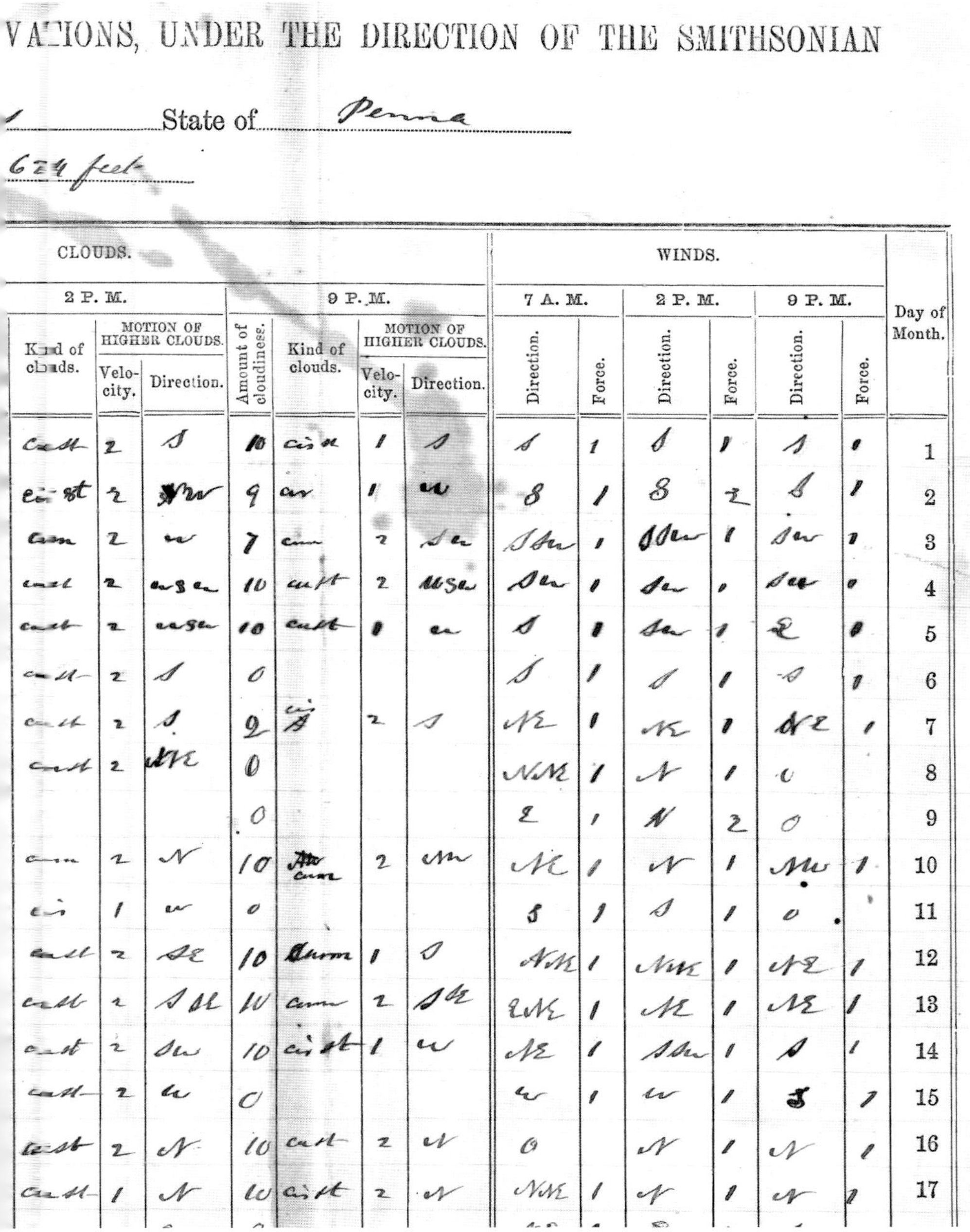

VATIONS, UNDER THE DIRECTION OF THE SMITHSONIAN

State of Penna

624 feet

CLOUDS.							WINDS.						
2 P. M.			9 P. M.				7 A. M.		2 P. M.		9 P. M.		
Kind of clouds.	Motion of higher clouds. Velocity.	Motion of higher clouds. Direction.	Amount of cloudiness.	Kind of clouds.	Motion of higher clouds. Velocity.	Motion of higher clouds. Direction.	Direction.	Force.	Direction.	Force.	Direction.	Force.	Day of Month.
cu st	2	S	10	ci st	1	S	S	1	S	1	S	0	1
ci st	2	NW	9	cu	1	W	S	1	S	2	S	1	2
cum	2	W	7	cum	2	SE	SW	1	SW	1	SW	1	3
cu st	2	WSE	10	cu st	2	WSW	SW	1	SW	0	SW	0	4
cu st	2	WSW	10	cu st	0	W	S	0	SW	1	E	0	5
cu st	2	S	0				S	1	S	1	S	0	6
cu st	2	S	9	ci S	2	S	NE	0	NE	0	NE	1	7
cu st	2	NE	0				NE	1	N	1	0		8
			0				E	1	N	2	0		9
cum	2	N	10	St cum	2	NW	NE	1	N	1	NW	1	10
ci	1	W	0				S	1	S	1	0		11
cu st	2	SE	10	[illegible]	1	S	NE	1	NE	1	NE	1	12
cu st	2	SE	10	cum	2	SE	ENE	1	NE	1	NE	1	13
cu st	2	SW	10	ci st	1	W	NE	1	SW	1	S	1	14
cu st	2	W	0				W	1	W	1	S	1	15
cu st	2	N	10	cu st	2	N	0		N	1	N	1	16
cu st	1	N	10	ci st	2	N	NE	1	N	1	N	1	17

Fig. 66 Jacobs's Gettysburg observations for July 1–17, 1863, showing temperature, rainfall, clouds and wind. *Courtesy of American Philosophical Society.*

INSTITUTION, ADOPTED BY THE COMMISSIONER OF PATE

Name and Address

Day of Month.	BAROMETER.									
	OBSERVED HEIGHT.			THERMOMETER ATTACHED TO BAROMETER.			BAROMETER HEIGHT REDUCED TO FREEZING POI			
	7 A. M.	2 P. M.	9 P. M.	7 A. M.	2 P. M.	9 P. M.	7 A. M.	2 P. M.	9 P. M.	Mean.
1	29.60	.60	.59	72	73	75	29.499	29.496	29 ~~.522~~ .481	[illegible]
2	.65	.67	64	73	75	76	.546	.561	.529	[illegible]
3	.67	67	.66	75	76	78	.561	.559	544	[illegible]
4	.66	.64	.61	75	76	73	.551	.529	.506	[illegible]
5	.57	.55	.52	72	73	73	.469	.444	.416	[illegible]
6	.53	.53	.52	72	72	73	.429	.429	.416	[illegible]
7	.54	.52	.52	70	72	72	.444	.419	.419	[illegible]
8	.43	.38	.36	71	71	73	.331 ~~.326~~	.281	.256	[illegible]
9	.30	.31	.30	70	73	73	.204	.206	.196	[illegible]
10	.33	.34	.40	71	75	74	.231	.231	.294	[illegible]
11	.44	.45	.50	74	77	77	.334	.336	.386	[illegible]
12	.56	.56	.61	75	78	74	.451	.444	.504	[illegible]
13	.60	.58	.53	72	73	73	.499	.476	.426	[illegible]
14	.46	.42	.46	72	74	75	.359	.314	.301	[illegible]
15	.55	.54	.56	74	76	75	.444	.424	.451	[illegible]
16	.64	.62	.65	73	75	72	.536	.511	.549	[illegible]
17	.66	.69	.71	68	67	67	.569	.602	.622	[illegible]

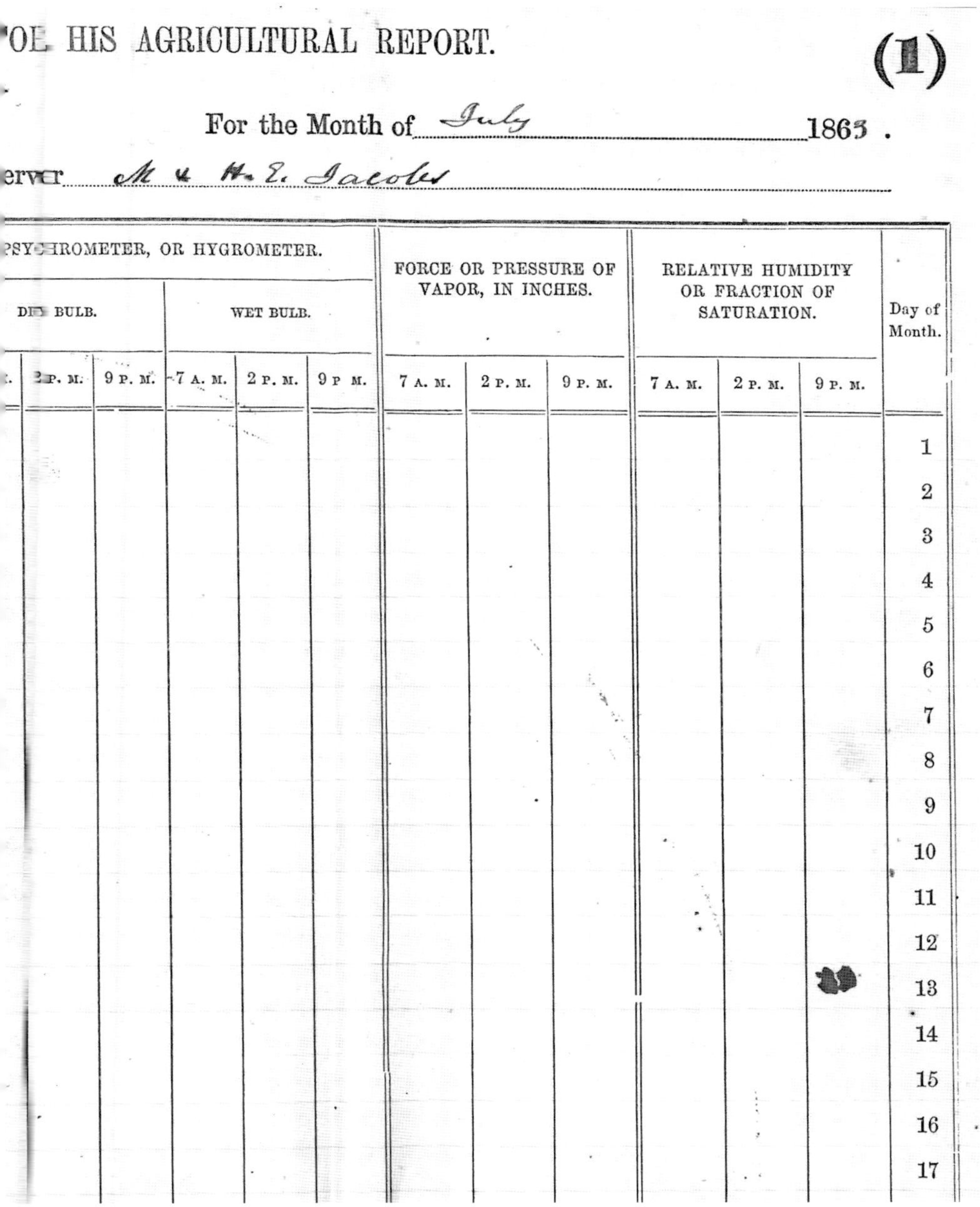

'OL HIS AGRICULTURAL REPORT. (1)

For the Month of July 1863.

erver M & H. E. Jacobs

PSYCHROMETER, OR HYGROMETER.					FORCE OR PRESSURE OF VAPOR, IN INCHES.			RELATIVE HUMIDITY OR FRACTION OF SATURATION.			Day of Month.
DRY BULB.		WET BULB.									
2 P. M.	9 P. M.	7 A. M.	2 P. M.	9 P M.	7 A. M.	2 P. M.	9 P. M.	7 A. M.	2 P. M.	9 P. M.	
											1
											2
											3
											4
											5
											6
											7
											8
											9
											10
											11
											12
											13
											14
											15
											16
											17

Fig. 67 Jacobs's Gettysburg observations for July 1–17, 1863, showing pressure, but missing key moisture data. *Courtesy of American Philosophical Society.*

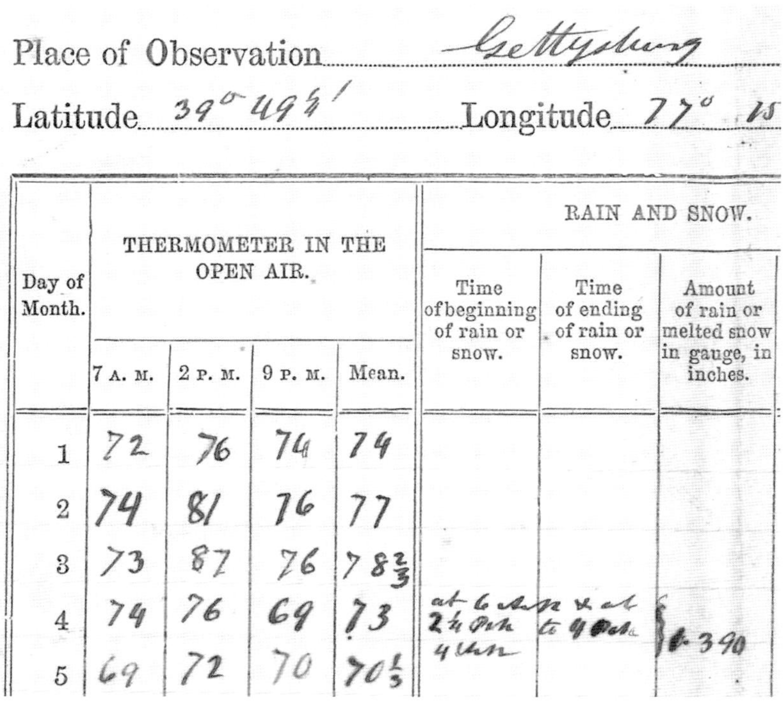

Place of Observation Gettysburg

Latitude 39° 49½′ Longitude 77° 15

Day of Month.	THERMOMETER IN THE OPEN AIR.				RAIN AND SNOW.		
	7 A. M.	2 P. M.	9 P. M.	Mean.	Time of beginning of rain or snow.	Time of ending of rain or snow.	Amount of rain or melted snow in gauge, in inches.
1	72	76	74	74			
2	74	81	76	77			
3	73	87	76	78⅔			
4	74	76	69	73	at 6 A.M. 2¼ P.M. 4 P.M.	& at to 9 P.M.	0.390
5	69	72	70	70⅓			

Fig. 68 Close-up of Jacobs's temperature and rainfall observations for July 1–5, 1863. *Courtesy of American Philosophical Society.*

The Primary Source Data—Gettysburg, Harrisburg and the Dewpoint

The short answer: very applicable, particularly the Harrisburg observations, given that the modern-day climates of Gettysburg and Harrisburg are similar. A comparison of temperature data from Eisenhower National Historical Site—about three miles from where Jacobs made his observations—with an average of observations from three official observing sites near Harrisburg reflects a difference of only about one degree in summer temperatures.[186] Moreover, typical summer precipitation at the Eisenhower observing site is nearly identical to an average from the three Harrisburg sites.

Unfortunately, dewpoints are not observed at the Eisenhower National Historical site. The nearest modern-day observing location to Gettysburg with consistent, high-quality measurements of dewpoint is York, about twenty-eight miles to the east-northeast. On average, the dewpoint there differs from that of the average of the Harrisburg observing sites by less than one degree in summer, strengthening the argument that Gettysburg's climate strongly resembles that of Harrisburg.

The parallels are not surprising because in terms of Pennsylvania's geographic regions, both Harrisburg and Gettysburg sit on the western edge of the Piedmont Plateau, in the shadow of the Appalachians. In addition to being only thirty-five miles apart, the cities differ in elevation by only about two hundred feet.[187] These geographic similarities often lead to similar weather conditions, particularly in summer when large-scale warm and humid air masses frequently envelop the entire mid-Atlantic.[188]

In a 1960 article in *Weatherwise Magazine*, weather historian David Ludlum first noted that such a weather pattern was in place during the battle. He wrote: "The general weather map on the opening days of July 1863 presented a picture of typical stagnant, summertime conditions. A Bermuda high situation prevailed."[189] This claim can now be substantiated with the NOAA reanalysis system. Figure 7A (see color section) shows a reconstruction of the average pressure pattern for the period July 1–3, 1863. The *H* marks the center of the Bermuda High referenced by Ludlum, while a front across the Great Lakes stalled out. This stagnant weather pattern essentially carried over from the June 25–30 period. The shape of the isobars over the mid-Atlantic favors a broad southerly wind flow, in agreement with Jacobs's observations in Gettysburg and those of the observers in Harrisburg and Sykesville. This pattern is consistent with an increasingly warm and moist period in south-central Pennsylvania.

This evidence leads to the following conclusion: dewpoints from Harrisburg will be used as proxies for those in Gettysburg. In essence, any quantitative difference between the dewpoints at these locations on these days would fall within the margin of observational error and local variations. In practical terms, soldiers would have perceived the combination of heat and humidity essentially the same way had the battle been fought in Harrisburg instead of Gettysburg. Observations from Sykesville, Washington and Philadelphia are also useful, though distance and less geographical similarity constrain their use as direct proxies.[190]

Table 6 compiles the observed values of temperature (T) and computed values of dewpoint (Td) and heat index (HI, when applicable) for Harrisburg (two observers, John Heisely and William Hickok), the Naval Observatory, Sykesville, Annapolis and Philadelphia at the three daily observing times. Dewpoint and heat index values are rounded to the nearest degree F. Professor Jacobs's temperature observations are also shown, as well as the estimated dewpoint and heat index in Gettysburg. The specific values in

Table 6. Temperature (T), Dewpoint (Td) and Heat Index (HI, in Degrees F) at Harrisburg (two observers), the Naval Observatory, Sykesville, Annapolis, Philadelphia and Gettysburg for the Period July 1–4, 1863

Harrisburg

	Heisely			Hickok			Naval Observatory*		
	T	Td	HI	T	Td	HI	T	Td	HI
July 1									
7:00 a.m.	71	70					71	69	
2:00 p.m.	78	74					83	77	92
9:00 p.m.	77	73					73	72	
July 2									
7:00 a.m.	74	73		75	68		72	71	
2:00 p.m.	82	77	90	84	68	87	82	73	87
9:00 p.m.	79	75		79	72		75	68	
July 3									
7:00 a.m.	75	74		76	67		72	71	
2:00 p.m.	85	78	97	89	74	98	87	78	100
9:00 p.m.	80	77	86	86	72	91	76	73	
July 4									
7:00 a.m.	75	72		76	69		71	71	
2:00 p.m.	76	73		72	68		81	75	87
9:00 p.m.	73	72		70	66		72	71	

All observations were made at 7:00 a.m., 2:00 p.m. and 9:00 p.m. except at the Naval Observatory, where observations were taken every three hours starting at midnight. There, we have used the nearest (in time) observation.

Heat index is provided only for temperatures of 80 degrees F and above.

**The closest observation times at the Naval Observatory were 6:00 a.m., 3:00 p.m. and 9:00 p.m.*
***The dewpoints at Gettysburg are estimated as the average of the two dewpoints in Harrisburg.*

Sykesville			**Annapolis**			**Philadelphia**			**Gettysburg****		
T	**Td**	**HI**	**T**	**Td**	**HI**	**T**	**Td**	**HI**	**T**	**Td**	**HI**
70	70		74	71		70	66		72	70	
76	73		82	74	88	76	67		76	74	
75	71		77	73		75	65		74	73	
73	73		76	73		74	67		74	70	
77	76		82	72	87	82	63	83	81	72	85
74	68		77	71		77	65		76	73	
73	72		78	74		75	65		73	70	
80	77	87	86	75	95	84	70	88	87	76	98
76	73		79	72		81	68	83	76	74	
74	74		76	72		76	67		74	70	
78	75		83	67	86	84	67	87	76	70	
70	70		78	71		76	66		69	69	

the table for dewpoint and heat index should be considered best estimates, essentially the centers of ranges of order perhaps ±2 degrees F given the uncertainties mentioned in chapter 1.[191]

Before delving into day-by-day details, understand several nuances about these observations. As mentioned, dewpoints from Harrisburg serve as proxies for those in Gettysburg, but Harrisburg had <u>two</u> observers, John Heisely and William Hickok. In June and July 1863, on average, their temperatures were similar, but Heisely's wet-bulb measurements were two to six degrees higher than Hickok's much of the time. As a result, the dewpoints derived from Heisely's observations averaged a few degrees higher than those computed from Hickok's data. With no a priori reason to weigh one more than the other, an average of the two dewpoints will be used for our Harrisburg value, except on July 1, when Hickok's observations are missing (his observations for June 27–30 are also missing). In his notes, he explained the reason for the omissions: "On account of the great excitement here, the observation has not been taken for the last four days."[192]

JULY 1

The first day of July broke clear and bright, and the sun as it moved toward the zenith, had an angry look and sent down upon us blistering rays.[193]
—Captain Charles H. Weygant, 124th New York Infantry

Situation Report

As Confederate cavalry commander General Jeb Stuart's ill-fated foray continued to deprive General Lee of his "eyes and ears" when he needed them the most, Lee found himself moving blindly in enemy territory. These circumstances forced Lee to use Confederate infantry to perform reconnaissance duties normally conducted by cavalry. This was a recipe for disaster. And sure enough, as two brigades of Major General Henry Heth's Division from A.P. Hill's Third Corps pressed forward from the west on the morning of July 1, 1863, the odds for battle increased dramatically.

At approximately 7:30 a.m., lead elements of this force took fire from a Union cavalry outpost situated just a few miles west of Gettysburg, along the Chambersburg Pike. That initial contact spurred a growing morning clash between a portion of Hill's infantry and General Buford's cavalry. Soon after, the lead elements of the First Corps, under the personal supervision of Major General John F. Reynolds, confronted Hill's men. Drawn into the fray west of town, Reynolds fell dead, killed by enemy fire, the highest-ranking officer to fall in the entire battle. After a late morning lull in the action, additional forces from both armies arrived. This prompted an extension of the battle north of town in the afternoon. Before the day's end, nearly 50,000 troops had engaged each other in ferocious fighting that resulted in nearly 16,000 casualties.

Ultimately, the Union forces retreated. And as the sun set on July 1, Lee had gained what most considered to be a tactical victory. However, the resultant Army of the Potomac withdrawal to a strong defensive position on the high ground of Cemetery Hill portended difficulties for Lee. Union forces strengthened their position as reinforcements arrived throughout the night and into July 2.

July 1—The Weather

The weather on July 1, 1863, was not particularly warm by typical early July standards in south-central Pennsylvania, where the modern-day average high temperature in early July is around 85 degrees F. Based on Jacobs's observations, the temperature may not have reached 80 degrees F in Gettysburg, so the midday heat index was not excessively high. Still, the dewpoint, likely in the 72–74–degree F range in the afternoon, made the day uncomfortable, with only a light breeze to take the edge off. Many soldiers acknowledged their discomfort. Lieutenant Colonel Rufus Dawes of the 6th Wisconsin wrote: "The weather was sultry. The sweat streamed from the faces of the men."[194] Captain Theodore Dodge of the 119th New York commented, "The marching is wretched and the atmosphere is so oppressively close that the men scarcely make any way at all."[195] Meanwhile, on the Confederate side, Private Samuel Pickens of the 5th Alabama Battalion said it was "an excessively hot day....I was perfectly exhausted & never suffered so from heat & fatigue in my life."[196] Figures 69, 70 and 71 show the temperature, dewpoint and heat index (if 80 degrees F or higher) at the relevant observing sites at 2:00 p.m. on July 1.

Jacobs reported cloudy skies at all three observation times, but no rain. Smithsonian observers in Harrisburg and Sykesville also did not record rain. However, July 1 likely illustrated a classic summer day when three observations

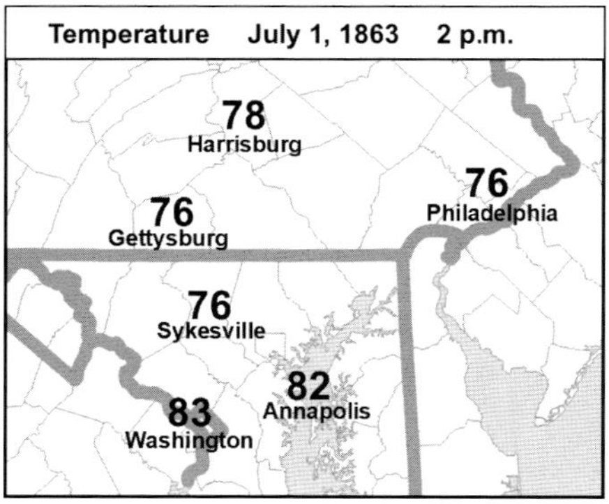

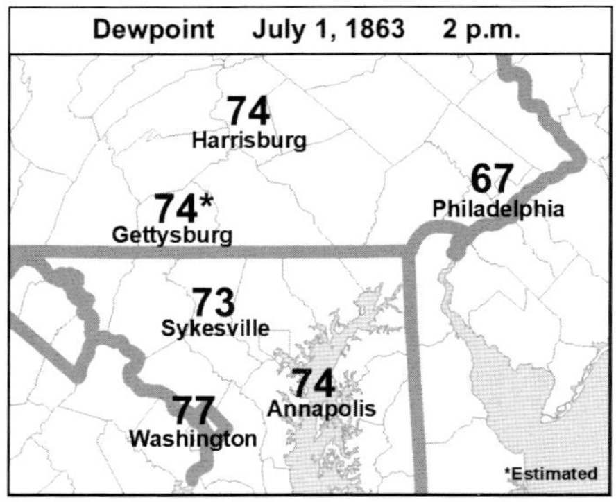

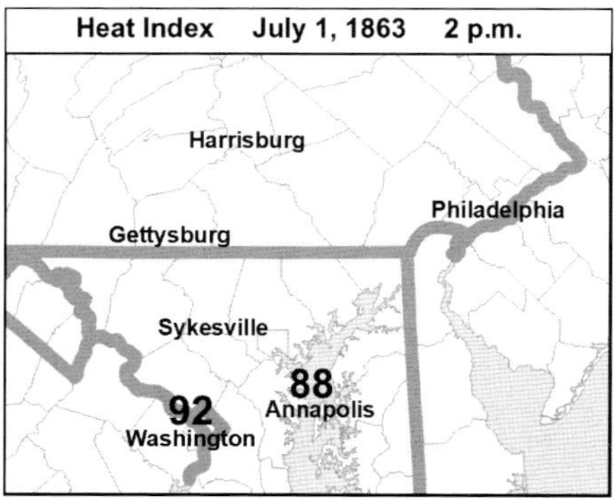

Clockwise from top left:

Fig. 69 Temperature (in degrees F) at 2:00 p.m. on July 1, 1863. *Data from NOAA FORTS.*

Fig. 70 Dewpoint (in degrees F) at 2:00 p.m. on July 1, 1863. *Data from NOAA FORTS.*

Fig. 71 Heat index (when 80 degrees F or higher) at 2:00 p.m. on July 1, 1863. *Data from NOAA FORTS.*

taken seven hours apart did not capture the full picture of sky conditions, and a few widely spaced rain gauges could not represent the entirety of the local atmosphere. Several soldiers mentioned rain in the morning, particularly among the Union ranks still moving toward Gettysburg from the south. The report from Chaplain David Craft with the Third Corps' 141st Pennsylvania near Emmitsburg is typical: "The forenoon of Wednesday, July 1st, is rainy....Soon after noon the bugle sounded and the men started off in the midst of a drenching rain." He also added, "The roads were muddy and slippery from the rain in the morning, and the marching hard."[197] But others mentioned afternoon sun, including Colonel Robert McAllister of the 11th New Jersey, who observed, "The sun poured down a torrid heat."[198] And a few miles farther north, just across the Pennsylvania state line, the First Corps' Major Thomas Chamberlin of the 150th Pennsylvania Infantry remarked, "The air, moist and sultry, and pierced by a broiling sun, soon started the perspiration in cascades, and made each pound of arms and accoutrements seem a ton."[199]

The observations of Lieutenant George K. Collins of the 149th New York, on the march from Littlestown to Gettysburg on July 1, introduce a new element that may have played a role in creating discomfort that day and beyond. He wrote that the men marched "through a wheat field, nearly ready to cut and emitting an almost insufferable heat."[200] In fact, plants take moisture from the soil and evaporate it into the air, increasing the dewpoint. Modern research suggests this phenomenon, commonly called "corn sweat" (because the crop is often, but not always, corn), is most significant in the afternoon and could locally increase the dewpoint by as much as 9 degrees F.[201] Although the effect tends to be greatest later in the summer, the Battle of Gettysburg took place in an area surrounded by fields of maturing crops. As a result, this phenomenon may well have played at least a minor role in increasing the soldiers' discomfort.

Fig. 72 Major Thomas Chamberlin (shown as a lieutenant colonel). *From Chamberlin,* History of the One Hundred and Fiftieth Regiment Pennsylvania Volunteers.

July 2

After lying all day under a July sun, suffering with intense heat, and continually annoyed by the enemy's sharpshooters from the heights, from sheer desperation, we hailed with delight the order to again meet the veteran foe.[202]
—Major James F. Beall, 21st North Carolina Infantry

Situation Report

As more troops from both armies closed on Gettysburg during the night of July 1 into July 2, Meade established his line of defense. Here he positioned troops on Cemetery Ridge, to the south of Cemetery Hill, and anchored his flanks on Culp's Hill, just to the southeast of Cemetery Hill, and Little Round Top at the southern terminus of Cemetery Ridge. The resultant line of defense formed a fishhook-shaped line, as viewed from above (see map on page 132). This formidable defensive position proved the bane of Lee's existence for the remainder of the battle.

Most of Meade's and Lee's armies had arrived by midmorning on July 2. Notable among the exceptions for the Army of the Potomac was the Sixth Corps under Major General John Sedgwick, which faced a thirty-plus-mile march to reach the field late that day. For the Army of Northern Virginia, Brigadier General Evander M. Law's Brigade of Alabamians and Major General George E. Pickett's Division of Virginians both faced twenty-plus-mile marches to reach the battlefield. Amazingly, despite their long march, Law's men would open the attack on Meade's left flank that afternoon. Pickett's men arrived late in the afternoon and did not join the fray until July 3.

Meade's strong line of defense featured topographical advantages and interior lines that allowed for easier communications and troop movements along the length of the three-mile-long fishhook. The one great vulnerability of Meade's line of defense came in its limited road network. Only two roads led in and out of the fishhook: the Baltimore Pike (adjacent to Culp's Hill and Cemetery Hill) and the Taneytown Road (adjacent to Little Round Top). This situation limited the routes by which Meade could receive incoming support, such as troops, ammunition and other supplies. Equally, if not more importantly, access to both roads remained critical to Meade because each provided an avenue of escape. With an army estimated at over seventy miles in length if placed on one road, Meade could ill afford to lose either of his would-be "lifelines."[203]

After an early morning Confederate reconnaissance indicated a possible vulnerability on the left flank of General Meade's line of defense, General Lee met with subordinate officers to formulate battle plans for the day. Lee aimed to threaten both flanks of the Union line simultaneously, with Longstreet attacking Meade's left flank while Ewell "demonstrated" on Meade's right flank with the option to convert his demonstration to an actual attack if the opportunity arose. Lee's plan stood to not only pressure both flanks of Meade's army but also cause confusion within the fishhook line of defense. Moreover, if such confusion resulted in a breach in Meade's line, Lee might possibly gain the victory on Northern soil he so desperately sought—a victory he believed would bring an end to the war.

Be that as it may, several factors foiled Lee's plans. Longstreet's attack on the Army of the Potomac's left flank occurred much later in the day than Lee had originally planned. As Longstreet's Corps attempted to move into position to assault Meade's left flank, his avenue of approach exposed his troops to discovery by men of the U.S. Army Signal Corps, positioned on Little Round Top. This necessitated a countermarch to secure a better route, and the resulting delay threatened the veracity of Lee's plans. As it turned out, a fluid situation on the Union's fishhook line of defense, namely General Daniel E. Sickles's unauthorized movement, changed everything. Here, Sickles repositioned his entire Third Corps, locating some of his men as far as three-quarters of a mile to the west of the fishhook position. And in doing so, he left Little Round Top unoccupied. This movement severely corrupted the integrity of Meade's previously established line of defense. Meanwhile, Lee's plan was predicated on the aforementioned early morning reconnaissance. But the content of the intelligence gained on that foray proved outdated by the time Longstreet's men completed their redeployment and Sickles moved his corps. As a result, much frustration resulted between Longstreet and the subordinate officers assigned to lead his forces into action that afternoon based on what was now an obsolete plan.

In any event, the battle finally opened at approximately 4:30 p.m. as Confederate artillery commenced firing on both flanks of the Army of the Potomac. After a spirited exchange of fire on the Union right, Meade's artillery repulsed Ewell's artillery barrage that had sought to soften the position of the troops assigned to defend Culp's Hill, the barb of the fishhook position. With this, any possible infantry movement of Ewell's forces against Meade's right flank was delayed. Meanwhile, Longstreet's attack on the Union left flank began in earnest. Soon the fighting there erupted into a sanguinary series of brutal actions all along, and adjacent to, Meade's fishhook line of defense. These epic struggles occurred at places that would forever after remain etched in the minds of those who fought in these maelstroms of death: "Devil's Den," "Slaughter Pen," "Little Round Top," "The Peach Orchard," "The Wheatfield," "The Valley of Death" and "Plum Run." Only Meade's adept use of reserve forces and the timely redeployment of various brigades to particularly vulnerable locations prevented a Confederate breakthrough of the fishhook position.

However, as Longstreet's ferocious assault continued to pressure the Union army's line of defense to the near breaking point, General Meade sought to further buttress his beleaguered forces. He did so by redeploying nearly all of the 10,000 soldiers that had occupied Culp's Hill to his left and center. But here, this action proved nearly catastrophic, as only a mere cadre of 1,500 soldiers of Brigadier General George S. Greene's Brigade remained to defend Culp's Hill. Moreover, this movement afforded General Ewell just the opportunity he needed to convert his stymied demonstration into a full-fledged attack. As it happened, during the late evening, an estimated 5,000 Confederates fell upon Greene's men in a desperate attempt to seize the barb of the fishhook, Culp's Hill. Though

Ewell's forces claimed valuable ground near the base of the hill and upward of the hill's midpoint, Greene's men held firm near the hill's peak. Here Greene's initiative in having his troops build light field fortifications known as breastworks (dirt, wood, rocks piled chest high) proved critical in helping his heavily outnumbered men thwart the Confederate onslaught. Soon aided by timely reinforcements, Greene and his stalwart forces secured the Union right. Meanwhile, additional forces from Ewell's Corps attacked up the steep slopes of nearby Cemetery Hill, nearly seizing that key position. Once again, only the tenacious efforts of some of the forces defending the hill and the timely aid of redeployed Union regiments prevented the Confederates from claiming the linchpin to Meade's fishhook line of defense. By day's end, the desperate fighting all along Meade's fishhook resulted in some 18,000 casualties. Despite this calamity, the fate of the battle remained anything but certain.

July 2—The Weather

The moon was nearly full as July 1 turned to July 2. Around 1:00 a.m., Sergeant James Wright of the 1st Minnesota noted, "There seemed to be a bit of mist or fog resting on the ground, but the moon was shining. The grass was wet, and the leaves on the trees and bushes were loaded with drops of moisture."[204] Such a heavy dew is consistent with high dewpoints and skies clearing, at least for a time. When morning dawned, Colonel McAllister noted, "A heavy fog hung over the town. We could see but little."[205] Professor Jacobs, in his book written immediately after the battle, remarked, "The morning was pleasant, the air was calm, the sun shone mildly through a smoky atmosphere."[206]

As on July 1, Jacobs reported no precipitation on July 2, but several participants mentioned rain, with descriptions running the gamut from "an intermittent pelting rain" in the morning at Marsh Creek, about five miles from Gettysburg,[207] to "a fine day, some little rain," just west of town.[208] Most likely, drizzle associated with the morning fog and dew was the culprit early in the day, but high dewpoints and at least some sunshine could have contributed to a few random showers. Regardless, by far, the heat and humidity were Mother Nature's most notable weapons on July 2.

Officially, July 2 was warmer than July 1 by 2–5 degrees F at all three observation times in Gettysburg (see Table 6 on pages 140–41). The biggest difference came at 2:00 p.m., a jump from 76 degrees F to 81 degrees F,

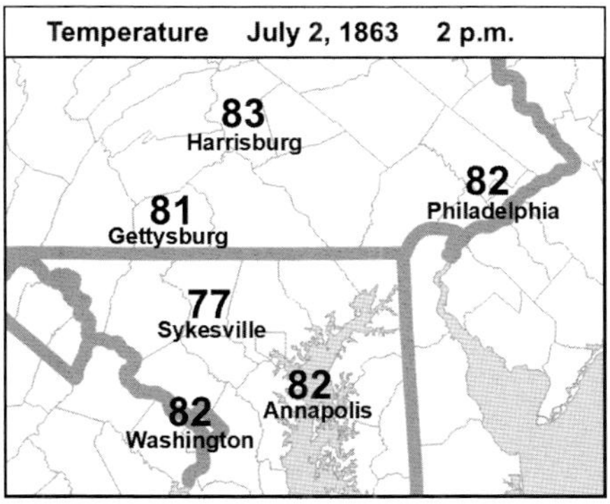

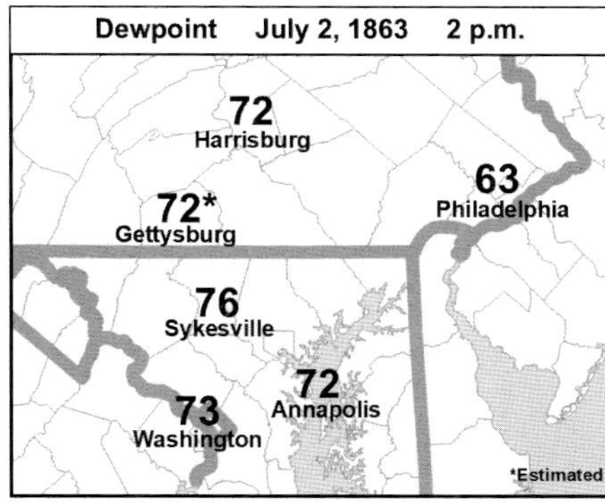

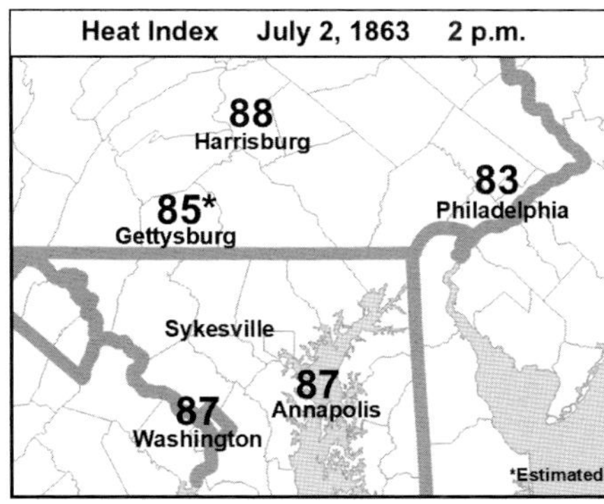

***Clockwise from top left*:**

Fig. 73 Temperature (in degrees F) at 2:00 p.m. on July 2, 1863. *Data from NOAA FORTS.*

Fig. 74 Dewpoint (in degrees F) at 2:00 p.m. on July 2, 1863. *Data from NOAA FORTS.*

Fig. 75 Heat index (when 80 degrees F or higher) at 2:00 p.m. on July 2, 1863. *Data from NOAA FORTS.*

likely owing to more sunshine and fewer clouds—Jacobs recorded 7/10 cloud cover at the time. Figures 73, 74 and 75 show the regional view of temperature, dewpoint and heat index at 2:00 p.m. on July 2. The afternoon dewpoint fell by a few degrees from the previous day, not unusual when the sun comes out on a summer afternoon and creates up and down motions in the lower atmosphere, mixing drier air just above the surface with more humid air near the ground. Still, dewpoints in the corridor from Harrisburg to Washington remained in the "sultry and tropical" range, and the higher temperatures sent the maximum heat index in Gettysburg into at least the mid- to upper 80s, given that temperatures may have been higher after 2:00 p.m. And remember, heat index is a shade measurement; in the sun, it could have felt 10 to 15 degrees hotter. Almost certainly, soldiers would have perceived July 2 as more uncomfortable than July 1, especially in the heat of the afternoon.

Men who marched long distances that day, such as the soldiers in General Pickett's Division, became particularly vulnerable. One suffering soul, Private Randolph Shotwell of the 8th Virginia Infantry, recorded a particularly descriptive account:

> *As the day advanced the sun took effect on the overladen men (carrying three days' rations, and extra ammunition), and quite a number were prostrated, while all of us suffered most severely. As we approached the Cashtown Gap about noon the vertical rays of the sun seemed like real lances of steel tipped with fire! The broken rock of the McAdamized* [sic] *turnpike and the broad flat flagstones of mountain slate reflected the heat until a perfect steam arose in our faces as we trudged along and the chocking dust gathered in throats and eyes causing infinite annoyance.*[209]

However, perhaps the plight of General John Sedgwick's Sixth Corps and Brigadier General Evander Law's Brigade of Alabamians best represents the impact, and ultimate cost, of the heat and humidity on July 2, 1863.

When Weather Mattered the Most: Sedgwick and Law Go "Rolling Along"

In 1908, West Point graduate Brigadier General Edmund Louis "Snitz" Gruber first drew inspiration for a tune he would later compose with the assistance of his lieutenants, "The Caissons Go Rolling Along."[210] Armies have marched to Gruber's inspirational tune ever since. But long before Gruber's timeless lyrics came to the fore, his score could easily have applied to the epic marches of the Sixth Corps of the Army of the Potomac and Law's Brigade of Alabamians of the Army of Northern Virginia to reach the battlefield at Gettysburg.

The march of General "Uncle John" Sedgwick's Sixth Corps on July 1–2 and that of Evander Law's Brigade (Hood's Division, Longstreet's Corps) on July 2 remain among the most compelling stories from the Battle of Gettysburg. Numerous detailed accounts have chronicled these grand marches. What follows here is neither meant to supplant such works nor to offer yet another in-depth account of the subject. Rather, this analysis examines these marches, and the subsequent battlefield actions of Law's Brigade, through the lens of previously unused primary source accounts of the weather on July 2, 1863.

Ordered to the theater of action by their respective commanding officers, both groups marched for some thirty-plus miles to reach the battlefield. Sedgwick's men, starting at 9:00 p.m. on July 1, trudged along for about

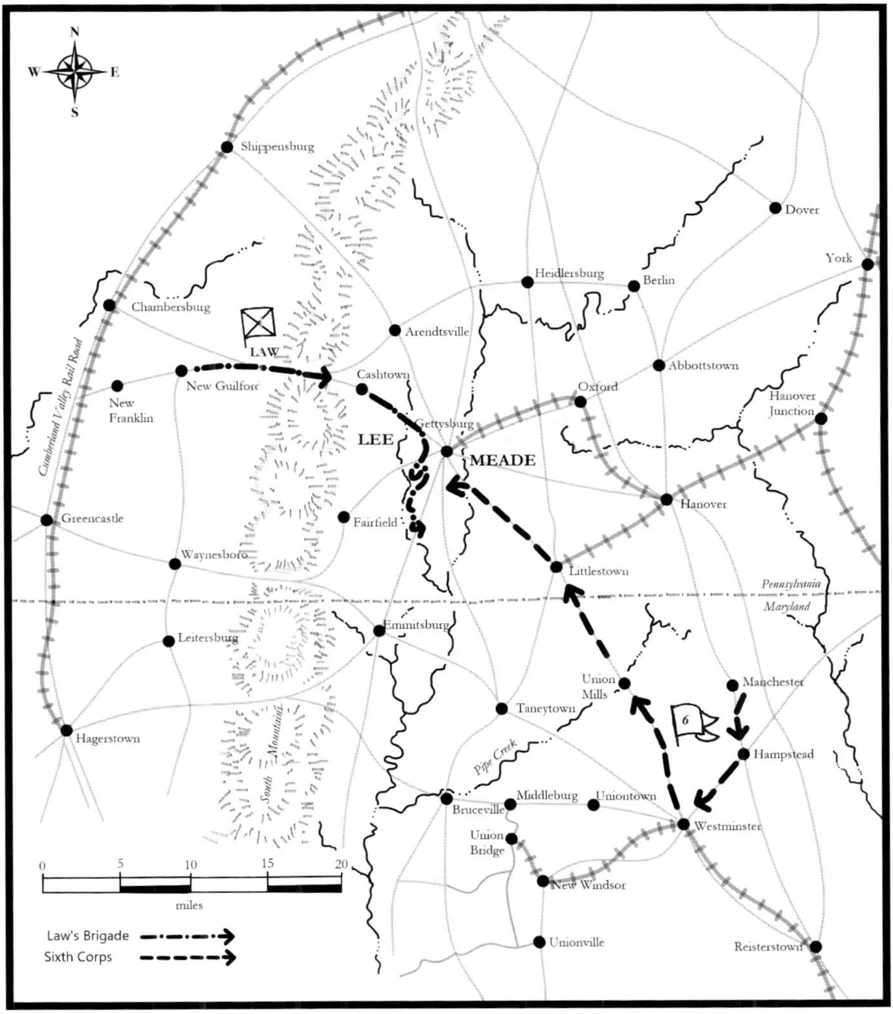

Fig. 76 The routes of Sedgwick's Corps (Army of the Potomac), July 1–2, 1863, and Law's Brigade (Army of Northern Virginia) on July 2. *Courtesy of J. Heiser.*

nineteen hours and upward of thirty-four miles. Law's men, stepping off in the wee hours of the morning of July 2, marched for nearly twelve hours and covered approximately twenty-eight miles. Law's Brigade first arrived west of Gettysburg at midday and finally settled into their assigned battlefield position on the late afternoon of July 2. Here they served as the tip of Robert E. Lee's "spear" in the Confederate attack on the Union left flank. In leading the subsequent attack, the entire brigade advanced

***Left*: Fig. 77** Brigadier General Evander M. Law. *LOC.*

***Right*: Fig. 78** Major General John Sedgwick. *From Dawes,* Service with the Sixth Wisconsin Volunteers.

another one to two miles to include some of the most difficult terrain imaginable. As it happened, Colonel David Nevin's brigade of Sedgwick's Sixth Corps saw significant action before July 2 ended. But unlike Law's Brigade, the rest of Sedgwick's men enjoyed a brief rest before joining the fray in a support role.

Over the years, both veterans and historians have considered various aspects of these marches, including their sheer length and the types of roads used. Many also highlighted the agony experienced by both groups of soldiers due to the weather. Yet until now, any understanding of this situation relied on incomplete meteorological data. The numerous soldiers' accounts of extreme suffering seemed to belie Professor Jacobs's records indicating temperatures may have reached into only the lower 80s. Yet soldier after soldier, Union and Confederate alike, documented the intense heat on July 2. As Chaplain J.S. Lame of the 93rd Pennsylvania Infantry wrote, "Again the weary march was taken up in the heat and dust. Many fell fainting in their tracks."[211] Likewise, Corporal W.C. Ward of the 4th Alabama Infantry indicated, "The day was hot, and we were thirsty and had not stopped to rest or drink."[212] But now, a better understanding of the weather circumstances brings clarity to this matter.

General Sedgwick's Sixth Corps, numbering some 15,000 men, received word from Meade's headquarters during the evening of July 1 that a battle had been joined at Gettysburg, and they were sorely needed.[213] Initial orders called them to report to Meade's headquarters at Taneytown, Maryland.[214] Bivouacked at Manchester, some twenty miles from Taneytown, "Uncle John's" boys faced a long and hard march.

Meanwhile, in the Army of Northern Virginia, orders went out far and wide for all elements of Lee's army to make haste for the battlefield. Left to guard the army's rear, Evander Law's Brigade was one of the last to receive word that it was time to join the fray. Orders came just a few hours past midnight on July 2, and by 4:00 a.m. Law's Brigade had begun their hard-pressed march to Gettysburg.

Sedgwick's Corps began their march in earnest during the late evening of July 1. At that time, temperatures hovered in the mid-70s with the dewpoint in the sticky low 70s. After working their way southwestward from Manchester, the Sixth Corps passed Westminster, about ten miles southeast of Meade's headquarters in Taneytown. But the situation was fluid, and by then Meade had moved north, toward Gettysburg. As a result, Sedgwick received revised orders to move north from Westminster toward Hanover, Pennsylvania, and from there west to Gettysburg. However, many of his men had already passed a key crossroads on the route, at Westminster. So, Sedgwick had to order those troops to backtrack to locate the road north from Westminster.[215] Although much confusion and frustration ensued, the men who proudly donned the Sixth Corps' Greek Cross were fortunate in that they endured all of this at night, when temperatures reached their minimum for July 2, likely in the 70–72–degree F range.

But the overnight march also meant loss of sleep. As a result, fatigue certainly became a factor. However, the delays caused by the countermarch of some troops inadvertently created an opportunity for those not involved to gain an invaluable respite, albeit a brief one. Such opportunities for rest proved to be one of two key elixirs—the other hydration—for those forced to march during such extreme heat as that facing Sedgwick's men. Be that as it may, Sedgwick's men were fortunate in that on at least two (and perhaps three) occasions, they received respites. Brigadier General A.T.A. Torbert mentioned one such break in his official report, "only stopping an hour, about 1 p.m.…to make coffee."[216]

Interestingly, as Law's battle-hardened Alabamians left the South Mountain hamlet of New Guilford, Pennsylvania (today, the town of Duffield), bound for Gettysburg, they likely never fathomed a countermarch lay in their futures. Nevertheless, before their countermarch became necessary, Law's men marched some twenty miles en route to Gettysburg, all of it at a hurried pace with no stops for rest and water.[217] As one might expect, the lack of both took its toll. Here it seemed that operating in enemy territory proved quite a "game changer" for the boys from the Yellowhammer State, given that most of the Pennsylvania farmers they encountered were not nearly as interested in offering a cool drink of water to the Southern invaders as had been their counterparts south of the Mason-Dixon line.

In contrast, as Sedgwick's men made their way to the Pennsylvania state line, many farmers offered the careworn soldiers a cool drink. In fact, at the outer edges of Hanover, family after family set out pails of water for the desperately parched Union soldiers. Numerous accounts echoed that of the 77th New York's regimental surgeon, James T. Stevens, who indicated, "At the houses on the roadsides, the citizens, their wives and daughters, were bringing water, from which the soldiers filled their canteens as they passed."[218] At least in Pennsylvania, the "home field" advantage that Lee's troops had enjoyed for most of the war swung decisively in favor of the boys in blue. Here, as they made their way closer to Gettysburg, many of Sedgwick's battle-hardened veterans received the essential hydration they needed just as the sun's rays intensified. Ultimately, the combination of hydration and periodic breaks served Sedgwick's men well. Undeniably, these two factors proved critical in allowing them to accomplish their storied march to the field.

As Sedgwick's men approached Hanover, Law's Alabamians began to reach the vicinity of Gettysburg at approximately high noon. It had been a grueling march. By then, the temperatures likely reached into the 78–80–degree F range as the heat index climbed into the low to mid-80s. After reaching the Gettysburg area, Law's hardened veterans fell out for a timely break. Unfortunately for the exhausted troops, water continued to be scarce. And their break proved all too short. Within moments, orders arrived to fall in for yet another march. This trudge sent Law's men toward the front in preparation for battle.

Meanwhile, by mid- to late afternoon, lead elements of Sedgwick's Corps had begun to arrive near Gettysburg. It seemed like a miracle. Drenched with sweat, they had marched some thirty-four miles in nineteen hours. Of the marching, Sergeant A.T. Brewer of the 61st Pennsylvania Infantry wrote, "The sun, warm at the beginning, grew hotter and more piercing every hour and his rays gathered fresh force as they were reflected from the hard road. Toward noon the radiating heat could be observed in waves, like colorless clouds, floating from the earth."[219] The 37th Massachusetts regimental historian James Lorenzo Bowen added that July 2 "was a hot, breathless July day. The sun poured down with merciless, unbroken heat." Bowen reasoned, "What wonder that the sun-stroke was omnipresent along the line."[220] Yet despite all of this, the bulk of Sedgwick's Corps arrived before day's end, and their presence proved critical. By late afternoon, the left flank of the Army of the Potomac was extremely hard-pressed by attacking foes. Worse yet, Meade had already used the Fifth Corps, his previously existing reserves. Here, Nevin's Brigade actively entered the fray while several other Sixth Corps brigades stood ready in support. Fortunately, those who saw action that day did so after gaining a timely respite and some much-needed water.

Law's Alabamians experienced far less good fortune. As Law's men rejoined Hood's Division of Longstreet's Corps, they slogged toward the Union left flank. But in the process, Longstreet's column soon found itself in sight of the enemy. To maintain an element of surprise, the entire column retraced its steps to find another approach to their assigned position, further exhausting Law's men. After the men marched twenty miles in the growing heat that morning, the afternoon tramp and countermarch required them to journey another five to eight miles in the mid- to late afternoon heat. Indeed, based on the dewpoints at Harrisburg, Sykesville and the Naval Observatory that afternoon, the heat index in Gettysburg likely peaked around 90 degrees F.[221] Thus, July 2 became a much warmer and stressful day on the human body than would have been suggested by Jacobs's 2:00 p.m. temperature reading of 81 degrees F.[222] Here it is crucial to remember that temperature and heat index are shade readings. Direct sunlight can increase the perceived temperature by 10–15 degrees. *In essence, accounting for humidity and sunshine, that afternoon in Gettysburg likely would have felt like at least 90 degrees F and possibly as high as 105 degrees F.*[223]

We note that Professor Jacobs indicated 7/10 cloud cover at 2:00 p.m. on July 2. However, the cirrostratus clouds he identified are relatively thin and would only have blocked a small part of incoming sunlight.[224] Additionally, July 2 fell just eleven days after the summer solstice, so the sun's rays shone nearly as intensely as on the first day of summer. Moreover, when the sun emerged, it did so largely in the afternoon, at the very time the Alabamians faced the cumulative effects of their extremely long morning march and their circuitous afternoon trek to get into position on the battlefield. Jacobs also noted the lack of cooling winds on July 2, describing them as "Force 2," representing a breeze of only about four mph, with even weaker winds in the morning and evening. Such light breezes offered little to no relief to the suffering Alabamians.

Arriving in their assigned position, some of Law's men reached the point of collapse. By this time, their combined marches of some twenty-five to twenty-eight miles in approximately twelve hours resulted in a desperate need for significant amounts of water and rest. They found neither. In one particularly painful episode, officers from Colonel William C. Oates's 15th Alabama ordered a cadre of men to collect armfuls of canteens from their comrades to seek water for their entire group. Unfortunately for the parched troops, the regiment advanced into battle before the canteen bearers returned. And in the cruelest of ironies, despite all their trials this dreadful day, the men of Law's Brigade led the attack against the Union left. Thus, it seems the most exhausted and dehydrated troops available in the Army of Northern Virginia spearheaded the attack on this crucial second day of the battle.

During the initial portion of the attack, Major General Hood, Law's division commander, went down with a disabling injury. As a result, Law immediately assumed command of the division. Yet the situation remained fluid, and much confusion ensued. While some of the regiments from Law's Brigade moved to the left toward the front of Little Round Top (LRT), others veered to the right toward Big Round Top (BRT).

Five hundred yards to the southwest of LRT a huge outcropping of elephantine boulders, dubbed "Devil's Den," acted as a barrier to LRT. The valley-like cockpit between Devil's Den and the western face of LRT formed a morass of briars, brush, wetlands and scattered boulders. The portion of Law's Brigade that moved to the left saw heavy action in and around Devil's Den and the valley, later dubbed "The Valley of Death." Although the exhausted Alabamians helped seize Devil's Den and a portion of The Valley of Death, they and other Confederate forces proved unable to contribute significantly to the attack on LRT. Meanwhile, the regiments of Law's Brigade that veered to the right found trouble of an altogether different sort.

As the 15th and 47th Alabama of Law's Brigade veered to their right (the Union left), they ran into Major Homer Stoughton's 2nd U.S. Sharpshooters. At that moment, these elite troops represented the only forces guarding the far left flank of the Army of the Potomac. If facing sharpshooters did not challenge them enough, the exhausted Alabamians now advanced up

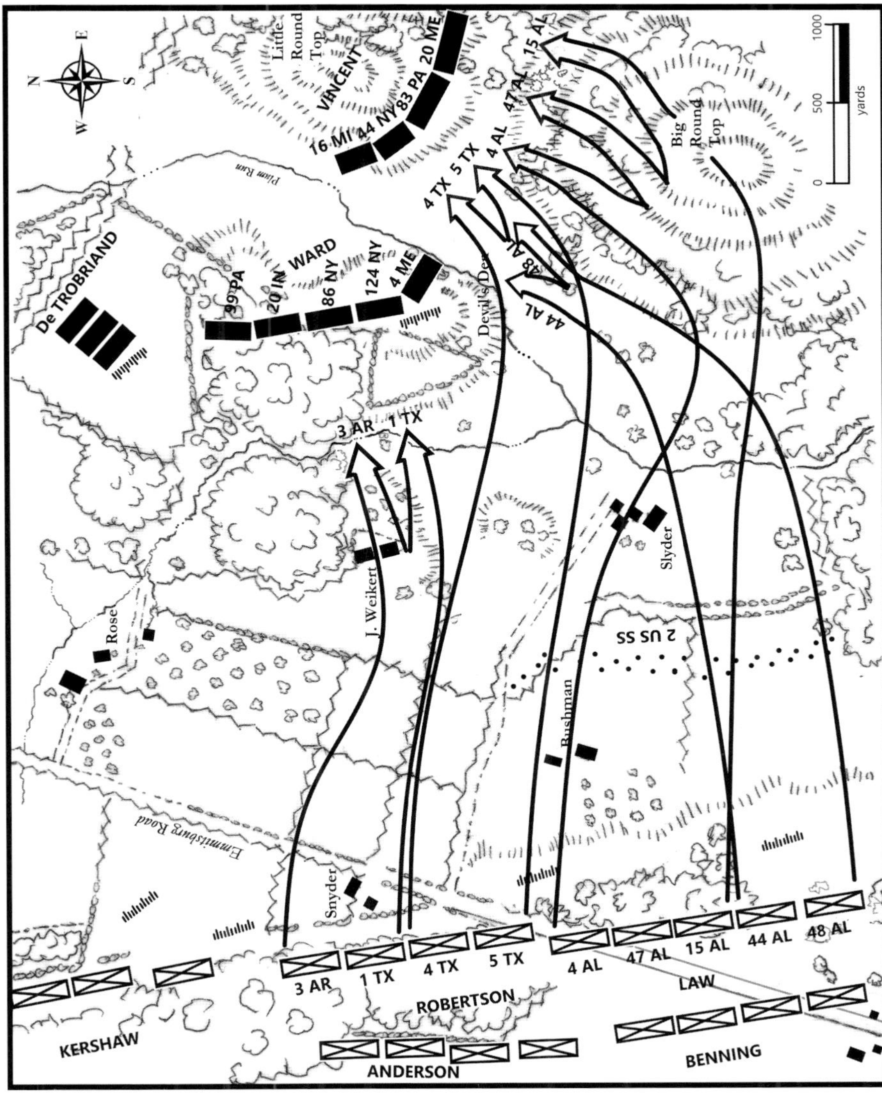

Fig. 79 Law's Brigade July 2 attack. *Courtesy of J. Heiser.*

the highest prominence of the battlefield, 250-foot-high BRT (785 feet above sea level). Covered with trees, thick underbrush and briars, the hill was also strewn with enormous boulders. Pushed to the limit of human endurance, the Alabamians scaled the hill while simultaneously forcing back the sharpshooters. In the process, the men of the 15th Alabama found themselves at the hill's summit while the 47th Alabama remained to their left, just downslope of the 15th. Then, and only then, did they receive a sorely needed break. Still without water, many fatigued members of the regiment collapsed. The commanding officer of the 15th, Colonel William C. Oates, later recalled, "Some of my men fainted from heat, exhaustion, and thirst. I halted and let them lie down and rest a few minutes." He explained, "I knew that my men were too much exhausted to make a good fight without a few minutes' rest."[225]

Unfortunately for the weary men of the 15th, after about ten minutes they returned to action. Here they advanced down the northern slope of BRT as the 47th Alabama, to their left, moved toward neighboring LRT. Upon reaching the deep swale between the two hills, the beleaguered Alabamians ran into a virtual buzzsaw in the form of Colonel Joshua L. Chamberlain's 20th Maine Infantry and the 83rd Pennsylvania. Ironically, the men from Maine had arrived in their assigned position just moments earlier, likely doing so while the exhausted Alabamians took their fateful break at the top of BRT. Thus, the combination of their arduous trek in terribly uncomfortable weather, poor hydration and the demands of

***Left*: Fig. 80** Colonel William C. Oates, circa 1864. *From Oates,* The War Between the Union and the Confederacy.

***Right*: Fig. 81** Colonel Joshua L. Chamberlain (shown as a brigadier general). *Courtesy of Maine State Archives.*

armed conflict had not only sapped the strength of Law's Brigade but also helped rob the Alabamians of the opportunity to seize a key position on the southern slopes of LRT.[226]

As described in the July 2 sitrep, extensive and brutal fighting occurred all along the Union fishhook. These actions played out across a previously benign landscape, a line replete with gigantic boulders, meandering streams, ripening wheat and flourishing peach trees—areas destined to become infamous for bloodshed.[227] Cemetery Hill and Culp's Hill saw fierce fighting that day as well. By day's end, these places were etched into the memories of those soldiers who somehow survived. Over 160 years later, these stories still resonate with historians and all those who appreciate history. Undeniably, they should, as each of these actions offers more than ample evidence of the heroism, tragedy and sacrifice that occurred on the battlefield at Gettysburg on that horrific day. Meanwhile, the effect of the weather, as we now understand it, likely took its greatest toll that day on the men of Sedgwick's Corps and Law's Alabama Brigade during both their respective marches to the battlefield and their ensuing combat actions.

Historians continue to differ on how the outcome of the fighting on the Army of the Potomac's left flank might have been different had Sedgwick's Corps not arrived by the afternoon of July 2. And they also debate how the course of the battle might have changed had the 15th Alabama and their comrades seized a portion of LRT. That said, there can be no denying that the weather on the second day of the battle, hotter and more uncomfortable than previously known, played a pivotal role in trying the endurance of Sedgwick's men during their march to the battlefield, while also contributing more than had been previously understood to the inability of Law's Alabamians to seize a portion of the Union left flank at LRT (see color section, Figure 13A).

JULY 3

The sun was shining in all its glory, giving forth a heat almost stifling and not a breath of air came to cause the slightest quiver to the most delicate leaf, or blade of grass.[228]
—Private Anthony W. McDermott, 69th Pennsylvania Infantry.

Situation Report

Believing he had come close to crushing the flanks of General Meade's defensive line on July 2, Lee planned to finish the job on July 3. Surely, he likely thought, a renewed attack along the same lines, augmented by fresh troops, would finally "break the camel's back." But before Lee attacked, General Meade's army seized the initiative and struck first at Culp's Hill during the early morning hours of July 3, thereby disrupting Lee's plans for the day. The fighting that ensued proved to be the longest sustained engagement of the entire three-day battle. During seven hours of ferocious fighting, from 4:00 a.m. until 11:00 a.m., the fate of the Union's right flank remained uncertain. Ultimately, Meade's men prevailed.

Meanwhile, Lee had also planned for Longstreet's corps to resume its July 2 attack on the Union's left flank on the morning of July 3. Here, he expected Longstreet to employ General Pickett's fresh division along with the remainder of his corps that had survived the fight on July 2. However, those plans went awry when Longstreet did not attack. The repulse of the Confederate forces on Culp's Hill and Longstreet's failure to assault the Union left flank forced Lee to turn to an alternative plan.

Fig. 82 Lieutenant General James Longstreet. *From Longstreet,* From Manassas to Appomattox.

Reasoning that Meade had strengthened his flanks at the expense of his center, Lee planned a massive attack designed to penetrate the middle of the Union line. Again, Lee put his faith in his most trusted subordinate, General Longstreet, placing him in overall command of the afternoon assault. Nearly half the total

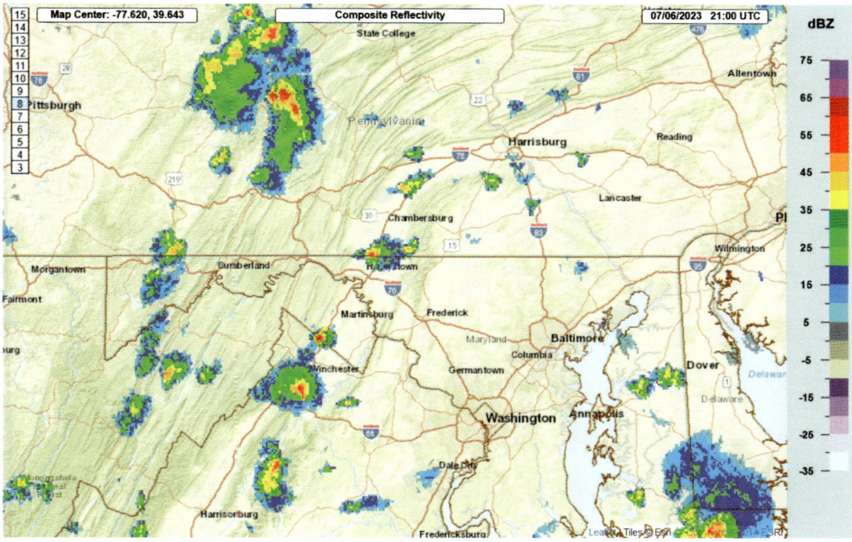

Fig. 1A Radar image at 5:00 p.m. ET on July 6, 2023. *NOAA*.

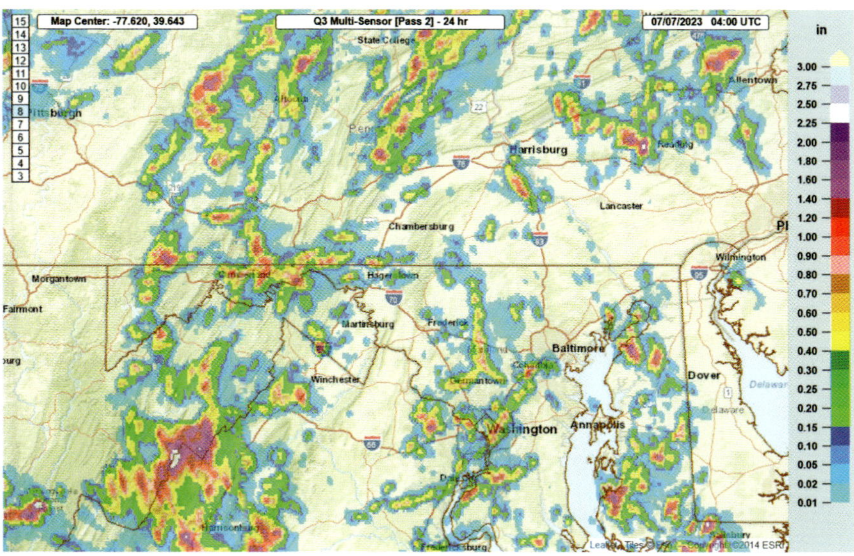

Fig. 1B Estimated total rainfall (in inches) on July 6, 2023, using a blend of surface observations and radar estimates. *NOAA*.

DATE	HIGH	LOW	MAX HI	RAIN
1-Jun	90	57	90	
2-Jun	85.5	64	86	
3-Jun	81	52.5	82	0.09
4-Jun	78.5	54		
5-Jun	82	58	83	
6-Jun	85.5	61	84	Trace
7-Jun	76	53.5		
8-Jun	72	49		
9-Jun	85	52	86	
10-Jun	89	55	92	
11-Jun	82	64	85	Trace
12-Jun	86.5	67	91	
13-Jun	85.5	60	90	0.22
14-Jun	79	60		
15-Jun	96	59	100	
16-Jun	93.5	69	96	
17-Jun	99	60	118	
18-Jun	97.5	68	108	Rain
19-Jun	84	66.4	88	0.27
20-Jun	72	59		
21-Jun	79	62.5		0.12
22-Jun	79	60		
23-Jun	79.5	58.5		
24-Jun	78.5	56		
25-Jun	78	56.5		0.11
26-Jun	73.5	62.4		0.30
27-Jun	75	62		
28-Jun	78.5	62.5		
29-Jun	82	66	87	0.04
30-Jun	81.5	68	87	Trace
1-Jul	86	70.5	96	0.06
2-Jul	88.5	68.5	99	
3-Jul	90.5	71	107	0.06
4-Jul	88	70	99	0.32
5-Jul	82	70	89	Trace
6-Jul	79	66.5		0.92
7-Jul	85	68.5	94	0.06
8-Jul	81	66.5	85	0.55
9-Jul	84	61	89	
10-Jul	88	67	100	
11-Jul	87.5	65	99	
12-Jul	87.5	67.5	98	0.80
13-Jul	76	64.5		1.80
14-Jul	86.5	71.5	98	0.24

8+ above
8+ below

3-7 above
3-7 below

Averages computed from 1872-1921

Fig. 2A High and low temperature and maximum heat index (all in degrees F) and daily rainfall (in inches) at the Naval Observatory from June 1 to July 14, 1863. Purple shading indicates temperatures above average, while blue shading indicates below average. Averages were computed from the period 1872–1921. The word "Trace" indicates that rain occurred but measured less than 0.01 inches. On June 18, the word "Rain" indicates that rain fell, but no amount was given. *NOAA FORTS.*

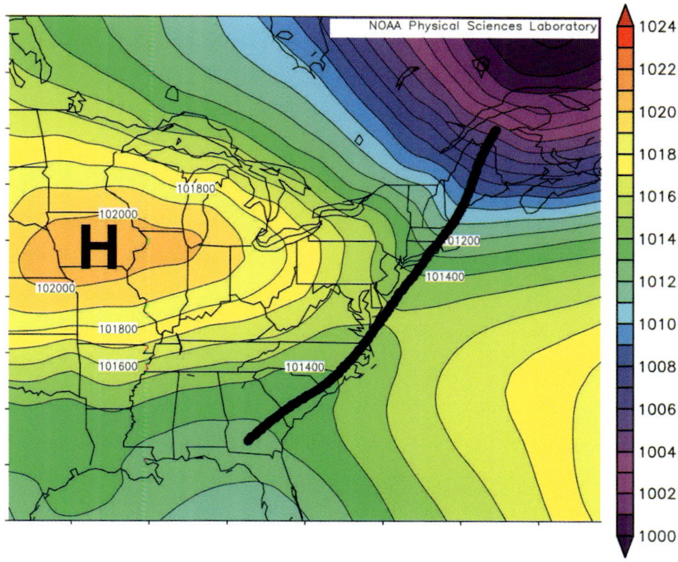

Fig. 3A Average sea-level pressure on June 3, 1863. *Image provided by the NOAA Physical Sciences Laboratory (PSL), Boulder, CO, from their website at https://psl.noaa.gov/data/gridded/data.20thC_ReanV3.html. Support for the Twentieth Century Reanalysis Project version 3 dataset is provided by the U.S. DOE, Office of Science Biological and Environmental Research (BER), by the NOAA Climate Program Office, and by the NOAA Physical Sciences Laboratory.*

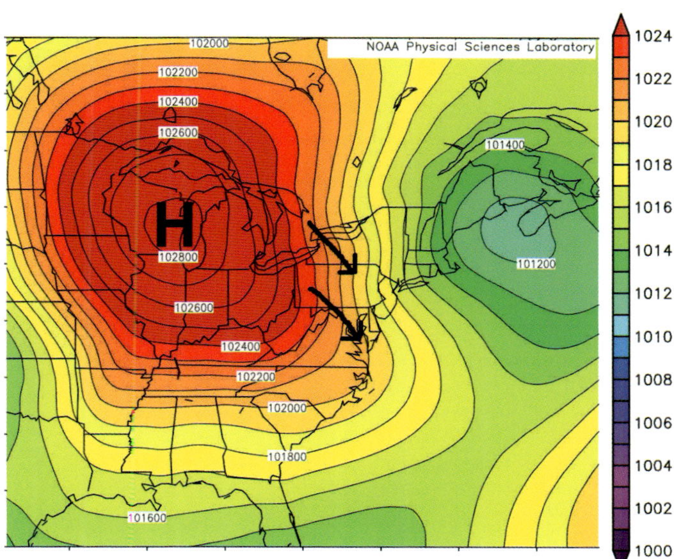

Fig. 3B Average sea-level pressure on June 7–8, 1863. *NOAA PSL.*

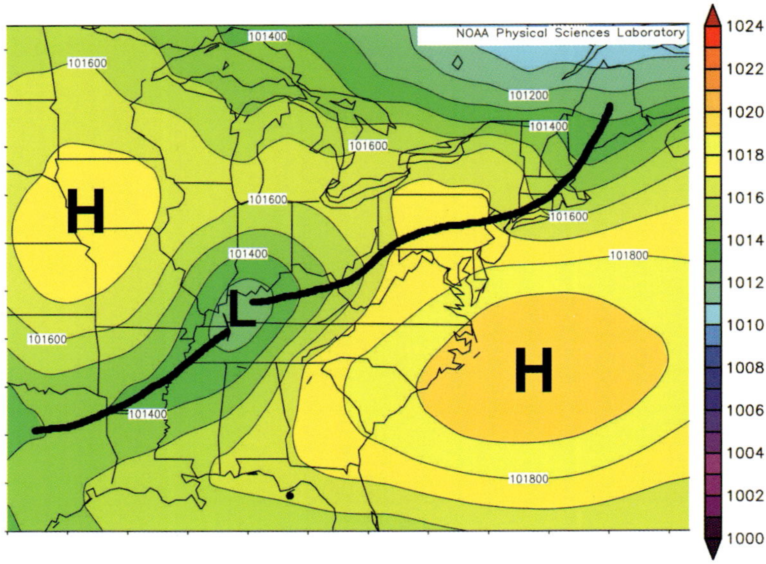

Fig. 4A Sea-level pressure the morning of June 11, 1863. *NOAA PSL.*

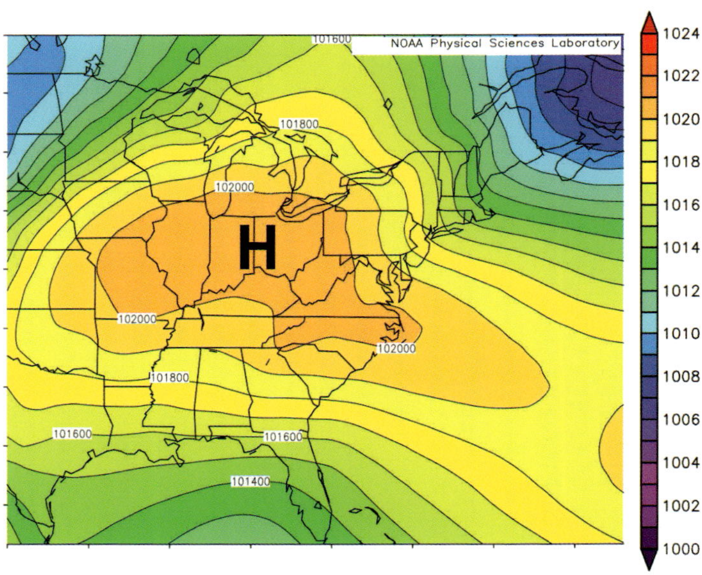

Fig. 4B Average sea-level pressure on June 15–16, 1863. *NOAA PSL.*

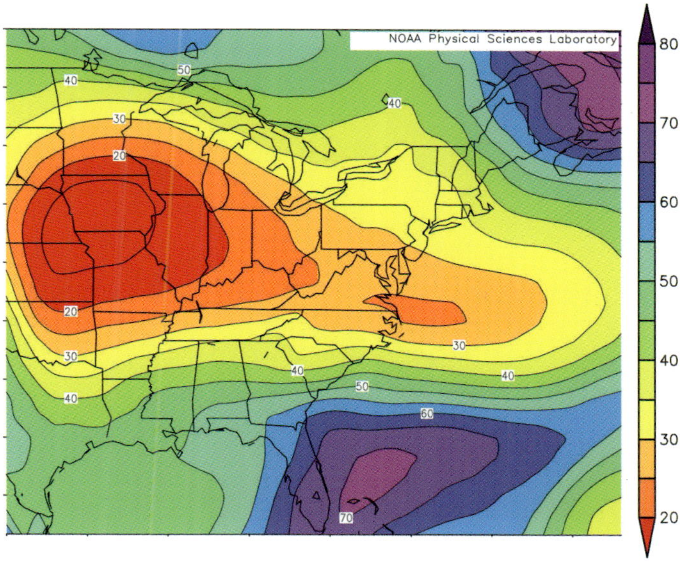

Fig. 5A Average relative humidity around 10,000 feet altitude on June 15–16, 1863. *NOAA PSL.*

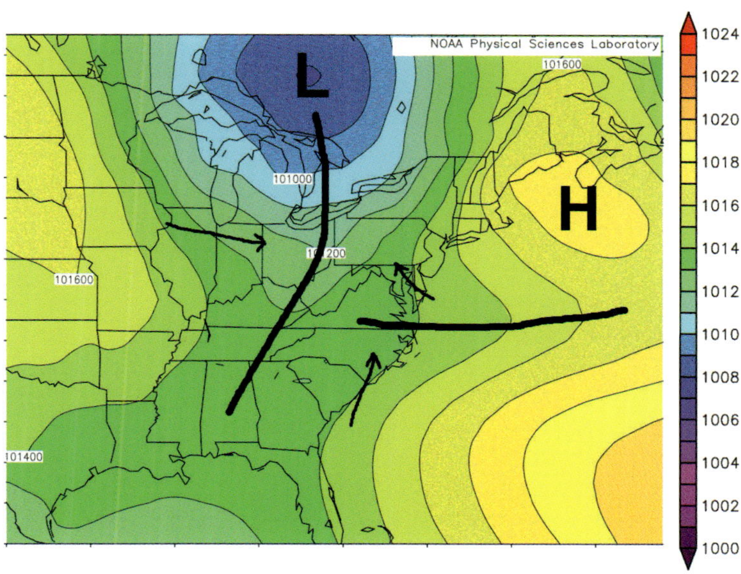

Fig. 5B Average sea-level pressure from the evening of June 18 to the morning of June 21, 1863. *NOAA PSL.*

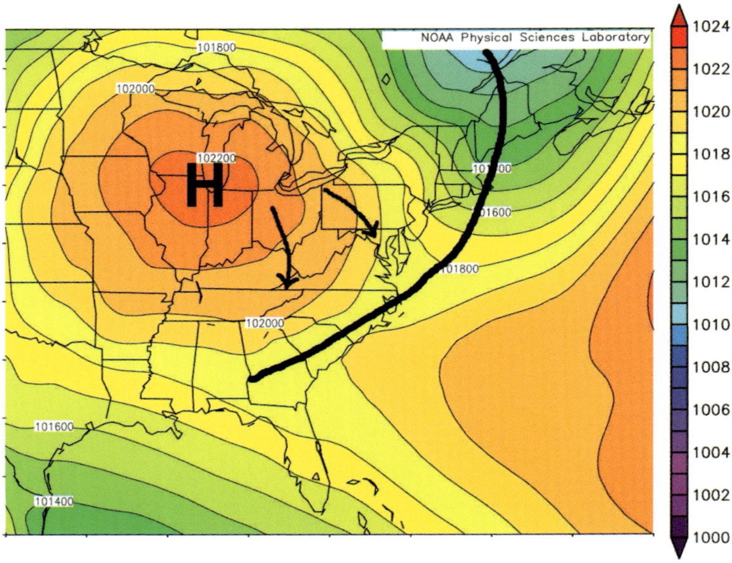

Fig. 6A Sea-level pressure the morning of June 23, 1863. *NOAA PSL.*

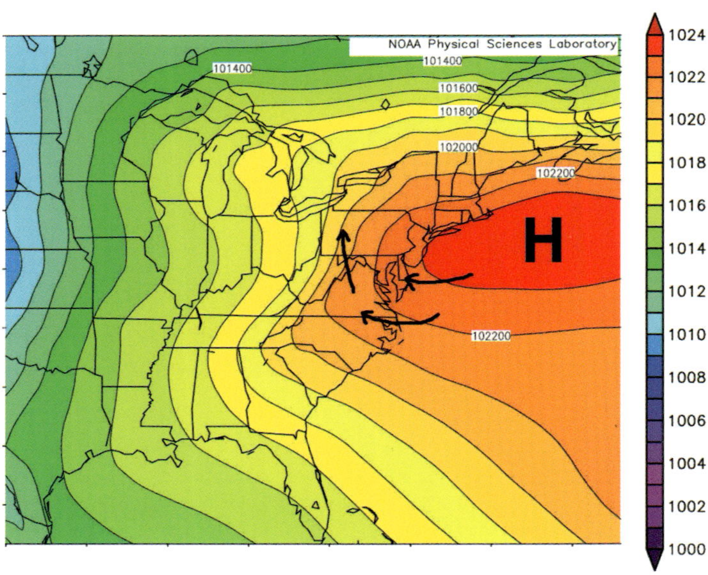

Fig. 6B Average sea-level pressure for the period June 25–30, 1863. *NOAA PSL.*

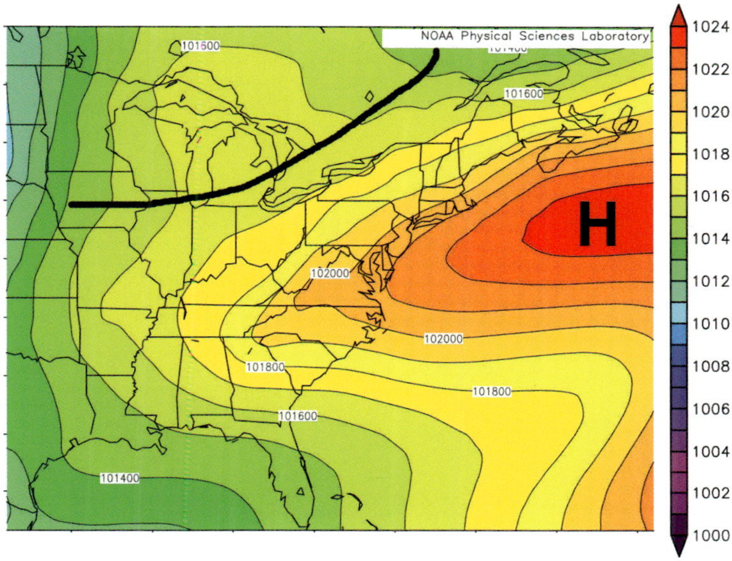

Fig. 7A Average sea-level pressure for the period July 1–3, 1863. *NOAA PSL.*

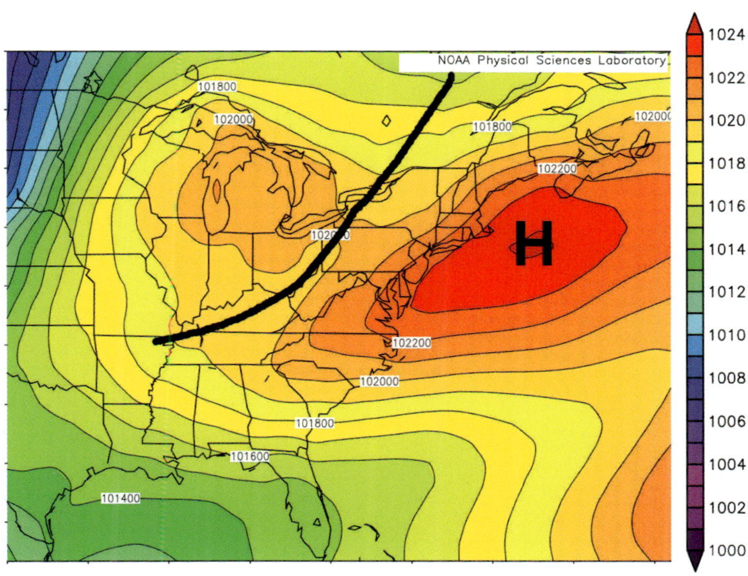

Fig. 7B Sea-level pressure in the early afternoon of July 4, 1863. *NOAA PSL.*

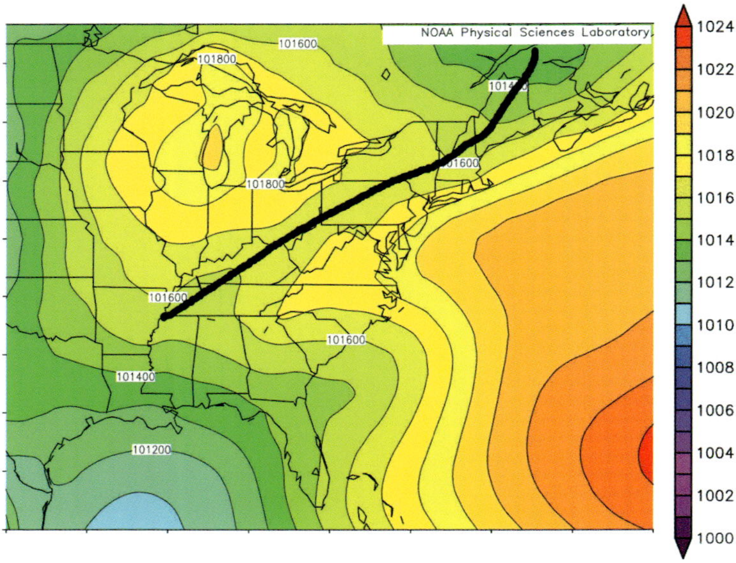

Fig. 8A Sea-level pressure in the early afternoon of July 6, 1863. *NOAA PSL.*

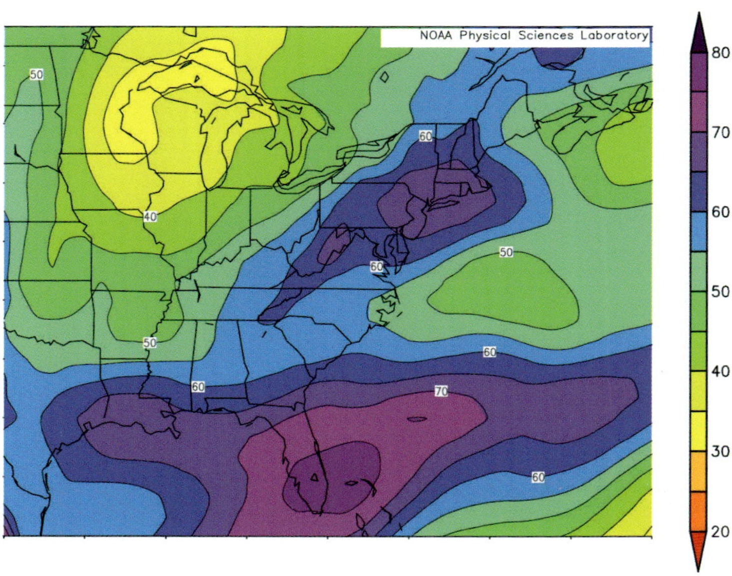

Fig. 8B Average relative humidity around 10,000 feet altitude from the early afternoon of July 4 to the early afternoon of July 6, 1863. *NOAA PSL.*

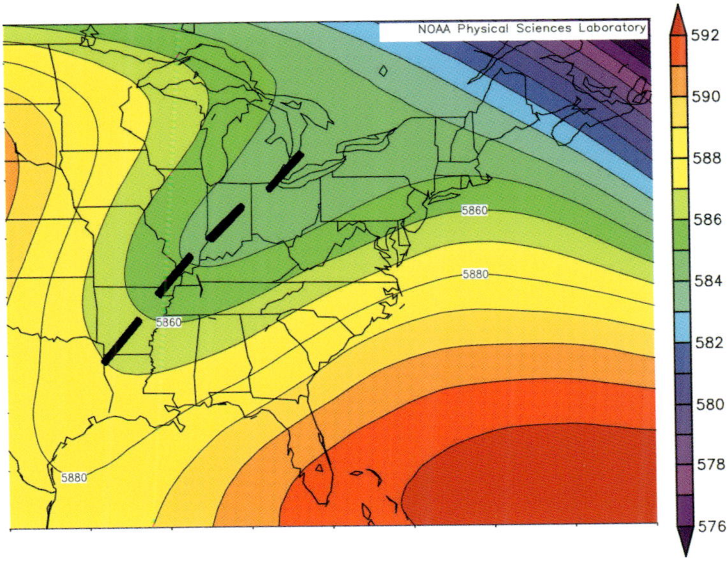

Fig. 9A The 500-millibar "height," a proxy for pressure around 20,000 feet, the morning of July 8, 1863. *NOAA PSL.*

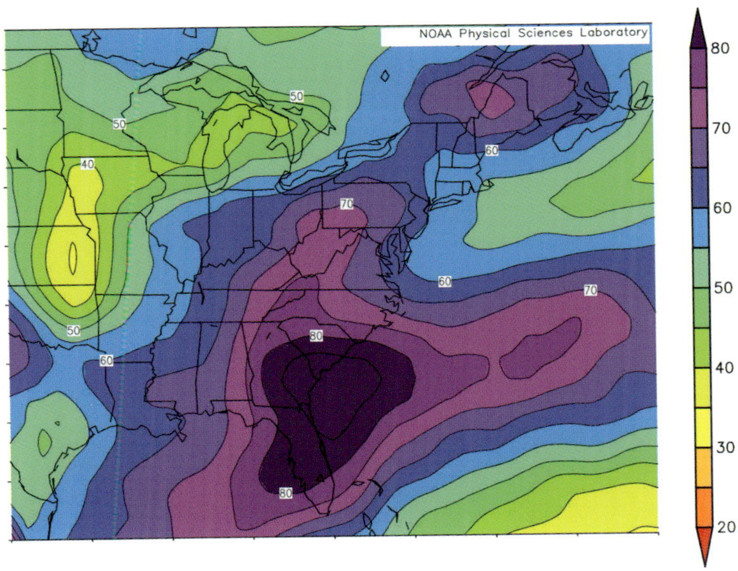

Fig. 9B Relative humidity around 10,000 feet altitude on the morning of July 8, 1863. *NOAA PSL.*

Fig. 10A Standard-issue U.S. Army sack coat, circa 1863. *Courtesy of National Park Service, Gettysburg National Military Park, Museum Collection, GETT # 31189.*

***Right*: Fig. 11A**
Confederate States Army first sergeant shell jacket, Richmond Clothing Bureau, circa 1863. *Courtesy of NPS, GNMP, Museum Collection, GETT # 29207.*

***Below*: Fig. 11B**
Confederate States Army shell jacket, Richmond Clothing Bureau, circa 1863. *Courtesy of Louisiana State Museum.*

Fig. 12A General Lee arriving at Williamsport, Maryland, on June 25, via Light's Ford, watercolor by Garnet W. Jex. *Courtesy of Sharpsburg, Maryland Historical Society.*

Fig. 12B Major General Stuart's forces crossing the Potomac via Rowser's Ford, just below Seneca Creek, Maryland, on June 28, 1863, watercolor by Garnet W. Jex. *Courtesy of Sharpsburg, Maryland Historical Society.*

Fig. 12C Major General Hooker watches his Army of the Potomac enter Maryland via two pontoon bridges spanning the Potomac River at Edward's Ferry, watercolor by Garnet W. Jex. *Courtesy of Sharpsburg, Maryland Historical Society.*

***Top*: Fig 13A** The 20th Maine and 15th Alabama. *Courtesy of Dale Gallon, www.gallon.com.*

***Middle*: Fig. 13B** Pickett's Charge, by E. Forbes. *LOC.*

***Bottom*: Fig. 13C** The Army of the Potomac's pursuit of the Army of Northern Virginia near Emmitsburg, marching through the rain, by E. Forbes. *LOC.*

***Above*: Figs. 14A, 14B** The modern-day Williamsport, Maryland riverfront, in late November 2024 on a day when the river is in the normal range (two to three feet) and in April 2024, when the river crested between fifteen and twenty feet. *Courtesy of Sandy Izer and Tom Freeman.*

***Opposite*: Figs. 15A, 15B** The Williamsport, Maryland riverfront (*to the left of above images*) in early December 2024, on a day when the river is in the normal range, and in April 2024, when the river crested between fifteen and twenty feet. *Courtesy of Sandy Izer and Tom Freeman.*

Fig. 16A Ewell's Corps make a perilous crossing at the Williamsport ford, watercolor by Garnet W. Jex. *Courtesy of the Sharpsburg Historical Society.*

Fig. 16B Confederate forces crossing at Williamsport. Note the ferry cable tower located in the middle foreground and the wagons crossing via the river ford, by E. Forbes. *LOC.*

Fig. 83 Major General George E. Pickett. *LOC.*

attacking force of approximately 12,000 men, Pickett's 5,500-man division from Longstreet's own First Corps, had yet to see action.[229] The other attacking force would come from brigades in A.P. Hill's Third Corps, many of whom had seen heavy fighting and suffered significant casualties on July 1. As a prelude to this assault, Lee ordered a colossal artillery bombardment involving some 150 cannon. Here he intended to disrupt and demoralize Meade's forces defending the center of the Union line and to disable the artillery defending the position. If the bombardment proved successful, Lee's infantry *might* have a fighting chance. Little did Lee know that Meade had recognized the vulnerability of his center and acted to remedy the situation, drawing on numerous reserve forces and artillery batteries. These men and guns were nearby and available should the forces defending his center falter. Thus, the stage was set for a clash of arms that would live in infamy.[230]

With this as a backdrop, we now consider how the weather likely affected the armies on July 3, particularly during the central event, best recognized as Pickett's Charge. The story of this attack has been told countless times. In fact, Pickett's Charge may be the most frequently studied and chronicled event from the entire Battle of Gettysburg. So, one might ask: What more can be written about it? As far as the prevailing weather that day, and its likely effect on the men who were there, much remains to be said.

Professor Jacobs observed 87 degrees F in the shade in Gettysburg at 2:00 p.m. on July 3. Surely it was humid, or was it? If so, how hot did it feel to the soldiers? In modern terms, what was the heat index? Moreover, because heat index, like temperature, is a shade measurement, what did it truly feel like for Confederate soldiers who languished on Gettysburg's sun-drenched fields, waiting for orders to advance, and for Union soldiers who awaited their foe's next move? Jacobs made his afternoon observation at 2:00 p.m., but Pickett's Charge took place perhaps an hour later. What did it feel like then? Finally, did other previously unrecognized weather-related factors influence the soldiers in any quantifiable way?[231] Modern science offers some insight.

July 3—The Weather

In contrast to some aspects of the weather on the first two days of the battle, both official and unofficial observations generally agree about the weather on July 3: hot and oppressive, with morning clouds giving way to some sunshine and eventually a late-day heavy thunderstorm. As David Ludlum said qualitatively in his original weather history of the Battle of Gettysburg, July 3 was the most uncomfortable day of the battle and likely the entire month in Gettysburg.[232] Lieutenant Frank A. Haskell, Union Second Corps staff officer, described the start of the day: "As the sun arose to-day, the clouds became broken, and we had once more glimpses of sky, and fits of sunshine." He added, "Eleven o'clock came....The sky is bright, with only the white fleecy clouds floating over from the West. The July sun streams down its fire....The army lolls, and longs for the shade....The silence and sultriness of a July noon are supreme."[233]

Figures 84, 85 and 86 show that regionally, both temperature and dewpoint increased three to six degrees from the afternoon of July 2. Jacobs observed 87 degrees F at 2:00 p.m. in the shade, his highest temperature for the entire month of July, while the dewpoint as estimated from the Harrisburg observers was 76 degrees F. This combination yields a heat index of 98 degrees F, within the "Extreme Caution" category of the heat index in which heatstroke, heat cramps or heat exhaustion are possible with prolonged exposure. Given the prevailing weather pattern; the 100 degrees F heat index in Washington at 2:00 p.m.; and the Harrisburg observers' independent heat index values of 97 degrees F and 98 degrees F, this estimated heat index of 98 degrees F in Gettysburg is robust. Even if the dewpoint in Gettysburg registered a few degrees lower at 2:00 p.m. (for example, 74 degrees F), the heat index still would have been 95 degrees F.

At the other extreme, on many summer days the temperature reaches its maximum an hour or two after 2:00 p.m. An analysis of similar days in five recent Julys in Harrisburg shows that, on average, the daily maximum temperature is usually one to three degrees higher than the temperature at 2:00 p.m. In addition, the aforementioned corn sweat effect may have added several degrees to the heat index. Taken together, one can easily project heat indices during Pickett's Charge exceeding 100 degrees F and perhaps as high as 105 degrees F. And as mentioned previously, all of this assumes "in the shade."

While the early morning fighting of July 3 took place on the shaded slopes of Culp's Hill, the afternoon cannonade and ensuing attack took place,

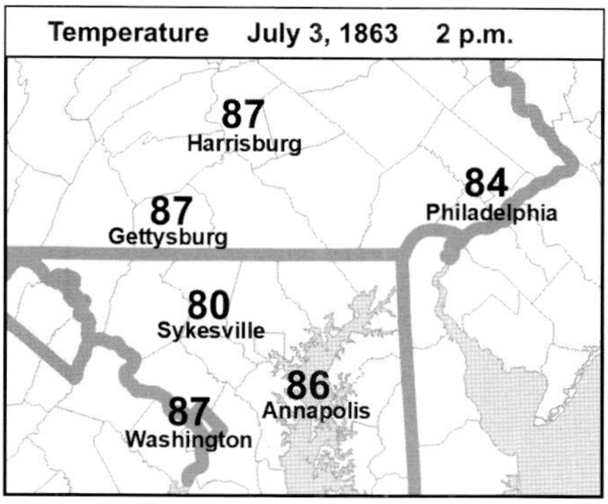

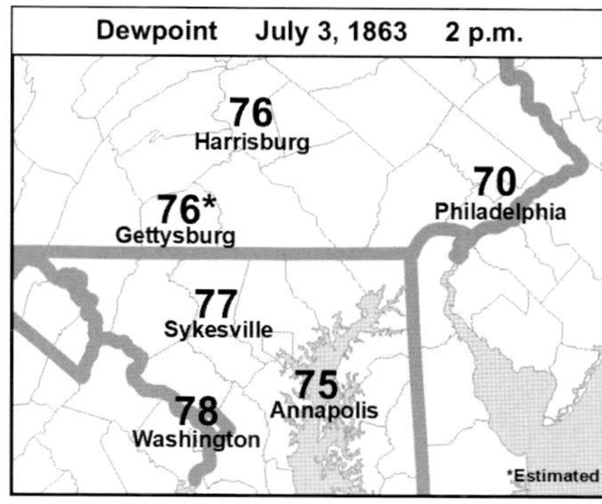

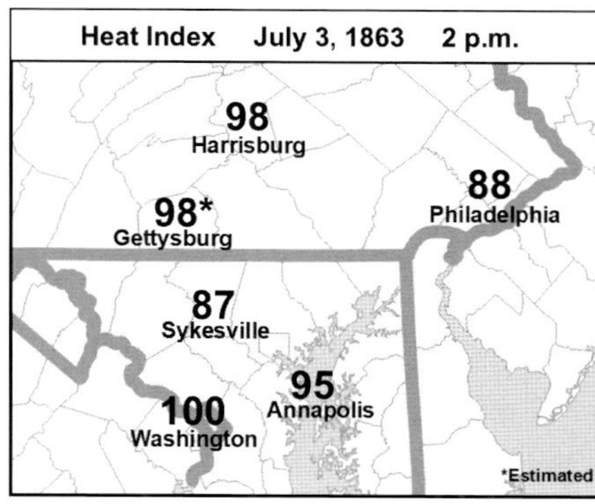

Clockwise from top left:

Fig. 84 Temperature (in degrees F) at 2:00 p.m. on July 3, 1863. *Data from NOAA FORTS.*

Fig. 85 Dewpoint (in degrees F) at 2:00 p.m. on July 3, 1863. *Data from NOAA FORTS.*

Fig. 86 Heat index (when 80 degrees F or higher) at 2:00 p.m. on July 3, 1863. *Data from NOAA FORTS.*

for the most part, in open fields under partly cloudy skies. Indeed, Jacobs reported 4/10 cloud cover at 2:00 p.m. As such, soldiers on open areas of the battlefield lay exposed to the sun much of the time, heating up their skin and clothes, exacerbating the already dangerous weather conditions.

The "solar thermometer" at the Naval Observatory in Washington provides insight into what this sun-exposed position may have felt like to soldiers. This special thermometer was placed in a non-shaded location a few inches above the ground. On the afternoon of July 3, cloud cover and temperature at the Naval Observatory mimicked that in Gettysburg—in fact, the 3:00 p.m. shade temperature there was 87 degrees F, the same as in Gettysburg at 2:00 p.m. Remarkably, the sun thermometer at the Observatory read 136 degrees F at 3:00 p.m. Though extrapolating this value sixty-five miles to Gettysburg is fraught with uncertainty, it provides a reasonable estimate of how much hotter it could have felt for soldiers on the battlefield close to the ground in the sun.

Because Jacobs observed wind speed (Force 1, a very light breeze) and cloud cover (4/10 sky cover), it is possible to get a different quantitative assessment of the combined impact of the heat, humidity and sunshine by estimating the wet-bulb globe temperature (WBGT). The WBGT estimated range is 85–87 degrees F. At those values, the human body is stressed after thirty minutes, and heat cramps are likely (see Figure 10, page 41). Recommended actions include at least a thirty-minute break each hour if working or exercising in direct sunlight and drinking one half to one quart of water per hour. It is inconceivable that soldiers on July 3 met both criteria.

Regardless of which measure of the true heat quotient applies best, the soldiers left to suffer from the searing heat offer ample evidence of its ultimate consequences. First Lieutenant John Dooley of the 1st Virginia Infantry recalled: "The midday sun strikes unmercifully upon the necks and heads of our prostrate men."[234] Similarly, Lieutenant John T. James of the 11th Virginia recalled the effect on the soldiers of Kemper's Brigade during the artillery bombardment that preceded Pickett's Charge: "Whilst this artillery duel was in progress we were lying in a field with a very heavy growth of grass, so thick in fact, it was impossible for any wind to get through it, and this, with the intense heat of the sun, produced several cases of sunstroke among our men."[235] Lieutenant William Wood of the 19th Virginia Infantry, Garnett's Brigade, amplified James's account: "All along the line men were falling from seeming sunstroke with dreadful contortions of the body, foaming at the mouth, and almost lifeless. Some were possibly shamming but much, real, downright suffering from the sun's hot rays was experienced"[236] (see color section, Figure 13B).

As one might expect, Mother Nature did not discriminate between the armies. Union soldiers positioned in the center of Meade's line who could not escape the direct sunlight suffered similarly to their Confederate counterparts. Private Anthony W. McDermott of the 69th Pennsylvania Infantry set the scene:

> *The sun was shining in all its glory, giving forth a heat almost stifling and not a breath of air came to cause the slightest quiver to the most delicate leaf, or blade of grass. Of that stillness you have often heard, no language of mine could cause you to imagine its reality, such a stillness I had never before experienced, nor since, and I have borne part in every engagement of the Army of the Potomac.*[237]

Major St. Clair A. Mulholland of the 116th Pennsylvania related, "During the day's fighting the heat was very great, and the men, being exposed and having neither shelter nor water, suffered intensely."[238] Brigadier General

George J. Stannard recalled the suffering of his men: "The weather was hot through the day, and some men nearly fainted from the effects of the heat. Notwithstanding they laid flat upon the ground, I had to move some portions of my command to shelter them from the rays of the sun, before the fight on our front actually commenced."[239]

Fortunately, the afternoon was not completely sunny, given that Jacobs reported 4/10 sky cover at 2:00 p.m. His observation indicated clouds of the "cumulus" variety, the puffy type that often develop vertically into showers and thunderstorms, especially in summer. Jacobs's son Henry, eighteen years old at the time, noted that following Pickett's Charge "a heavy thunderstorm, such a thunderstorm as we never knew at Gettysburg came roaring over us and it sounded extremely tame"[240] (as compared to the cannon fire earlier in the day). Despite this observation, Jacobs recorded no rain on July 3 on the official observation sheet. Perhaps it thundered at Jacobs's residence but rained little there, or maybe the activity of the day simply prevented him from making an official recording of rain amount. Regardless, numerous participants reported rain late on July 3. The 15th Alabama's Colonel Oates noted that "late in the evening…a hard rain set in & continued until dark."[241] And Chaplain Ezra D. Simons of the 125th New York offered this poignant observation: "As the battle closed a shower came up, and on the eastern sky was painted by the hand of God a beautiful rainbow." Simons also reflected, "The shower alluded to was succeeded by a rain which fell freely, as if to wash the blood-stains from the earth."[242]

JULY 4

Of all the nights I spent during the war, I think that was the saddest. We were already sad and disheartened by our misfortune, and this mental condition was made worse by the thunder and lightning and great torrents of rain which came down, augmented by the horrible groans of the wounded and dying.[243]

—Private W.A. Popkins, 18th Virginia Cavalry

Situation Report

Combatants with the two armies glared at one another like wounded animals. And why wouldn't they? Over 51,000 soldiers had been killed, wounded, captured or were missing in action as a result of the three days of fighting. The scenes were frightful beyond description. Sometime during the early morning hours of July 4, Lee ordered subordinate officers to prepare for retreat. Two columns—one made up mostly of supply wagons, the other a seventeen-mile wagon train of wounded—led the way. Then, over the course of the next twenty-four hours, the remaining infantry and artillery followed. Meanwhile, the Confederate cavalry provided protective escorts.

Within Union lines, Meade prepared for all possible contingencies while also looking to recover from the shock of the last three days. Wisely, he continued to strengthen his line of defense in preparation for whatever Lee might throw his way next. But it was all for naught. By nightfall, Lee's retreat was well underway.

In Gettysburg itself, the residents tried to come to grips with the never-ending flow of wounded carried into their churches, schools and homes. Over 21,000 wounded remained in the town of 2,400 after the armies departed.

July 4—The Weather

As the retreat began, the weather's most significant impact shifted from heat and humidity to rain. Although reports differ in the details, nearly all agree that July 4 and the ensuing night were cloudy and rainy much of the time. These conditions suppressed daytime temperatures; Jacobs's 2:00 p.m. observation of 76 degrees F was eleven degrees lower than the temperature at the same time on July 3. However, based on the Harrisburg proxies and readings from nearby Sykesville to the south, the dewpoint in Gettysburg on July 4 likely remained in the low 70s. Thus, the air still felt quite humid.

The reconstructed pressure pattern from the NOAA reanalysis system in the early afternoon of July 4, shown in Figure 7B (see color section), reveals a subtle weakness in the pressure field from Lake Ontario to Kentucky, likely housing a cold front that had ever so slowly progressed over the last few days into northwestern Pennsylvania. Two Smithsonian observers in Cincinnati reported that winds had shifted to west or northwest, while the dewpoint in northern Michigan was in the 50s, supporting the presence of a different air mass to the north and west of that front. This boundary, coupled with a mature warm and humid air mass still in place across the Gettysburg area, likely conspired to produce the cloudy and rainy pattern that had set in.

Regarding the start and end times of the precipitation in Gettysburg on July 4, Jacobs wrote "at 6 A.M." and later "at 2¼ P.M. to 4 P.M.," suggesting both morning and afternoon rain. For July 5, he added "at 4 A.M.," indicating rain began again the night of July 4. His aggregate rainfall total for those two days was 1.39 inches. In general, and perhaps not surprising given the nightmarish post-battle scenes in their midst, the unofficial weather reports paint a rainier picture. From a field hospital in Gettysburg, Private Jacob Carter of the 148th Pennsylvania wrote of July 4: "It was very disagreeable today. It was raining nearly all day, but it is so much better for the wounded."[244] Captain Asa Bartlett of the 12th New Hampshire reported that "during the afternoon and night the rain descended in torrents, filling the burial trenches that had been dug before the rain commenced."[245]

Confederate reports during the start of the retreat typically expressed similarly dire circumstances. Brigadier General John D. Imboden, in command of the anaconda-like seventeen-mile-long wagon train of wounded soldiers retreating via Cashtown Road, wrote of July 4:

> *Shortly after noon the very windows of heaven seemed to have been opened. Rain fell in dashing torrents, and in a little while the whole face of the earth was covered with water. The meadows became small lakes; raging streams ran across the road in every depression of the ground; wagons, ambulances, and artillery carriages filled the roads and fields in all directions. The storm increased in fury every moment. Canvas was no protection against it, and the poor wounded, lying upon the hard, naked boards of the wagon-bodies were drenched by the cold rain. Horses and mules were blinded and maddened by the storm.... The roar of the winds and waters made it almost impossible to communicate orders.*[246]

Sergeant Norval Baker of the 18th Virginia Cavalry, assigned to help this train of misery, described that night this way: "Twas an awful night, it rained all night, one thunder storm after another. The rain fell in sheets and vivid flashes of lightning and so dark we could not see our hands an inch from our eyes when there was no lightning."[247]

Those Confederates retreating through the Fairfield Pass suffered, too. Hard-pressing Union cavalry made their troubles all the worse. To a man, all of those who saw action in the resultant skirmish of Monterey Pass attested to the dreadful circumstances. Trooper William W. Glazier of the 2nd New York Cavalry provided this vivid description, "To add to the horrors of the scene and position, the rain fell in floods, accompanied with groaning thunders, while lightnings flashed from cloud to cloud over our heads, and cleft the darkness only to leave friend and foe enveloped in greater darkness in the interval of light."[248]

These rains also contributed to quick rises on local streams and creeks and, more importantly, on the Potomac River. In *Retreat from Gettysburg*, historian Kent Masterson Brown wrote that "where Longstreet's Corps had forded the river less than two weeks before and where wagons had been fording the river, it was almost five feet deep. The river was dangerous."[249] And it was about to get worse.

One final note on the weather of July 1–4: According to Jacobs, the temperature in Gettysburg fell to 69 degrees F at 9:00 p.m. on July 4, the first time since his 7:00 a.m. observation on June 30 that the temperature dropped below 70 degrees F at an observation time. Overnight low temperatures typically occur in the 5:00–6:00 a.m. time frame in summer in south-central Pennsylvania and are, on average, two to three degrees F lower than the 7:00 a.m. value, so temperatures may have dropped just below 70 degrees F the morning of July 1, when Jacobs observed 72 degrees F at 7:00 a.m. Regardless, given the high dewpoints, we can say confidently that the period July 1–4, 1863, also saw warm and uncomfortable nights that allowed little relief, even after sunset.

The last of the Army of Northern Virginia did not depart Gettysburg until the early morning hours of July 5. By that time, lead elements of the retreating column had arrived in the vicinity of Williamsport, Maryland. There they discovered a whole series of new weather-related problems that threatened their very survival.

People, Stories and Matters to Remember: The Observers

Professor Michael Jacobs, Gettysburg, Pennsylvania

In many ways, the Reverend Dr. "Professor" Michael Jacobs could be considered a Renaissance man. Born in Franklin County, Pennsylvania, in 1808, Jacobs attended Jefferson College, now Washington and Jefferson College. He went to Gettysburg in 1828 to assist his brother David with the newly founded school known as the Gettysburg Gymnasium. By 1832, the school had received its state charter as a college, and Michael Jacobs became

Fig. 87 Reverend Dr. "Professor" Michael Jacobs. *Courtesy of Gettysburg College, Musselman Library, Special Collections and College Archives.*

one of the founding instructors at what was known then as Pennsylvania College, later Gettysburg College. Jacobs first served as a professor in mathematics, chemistry and natural philosophy, and by 1841, he was also teaching meteorology.[250] His lessons in that fledgling science reportedly became the second such college-based program in the United States.[251]

Professor Jacobs was perhaps best known, at least during his lifetime, for writing one of the first published histories of the battle, titled *Notes on the Rebel Invasion of Maryland and Pennsylvania and the Battle of Gettysburg, July 1st, 2nd, and 3rd, 1863*. This book became so well known that requests for copies came from far and wide, from ordinary citizens to prominent veterans of the battle.[252] The book grew to be so wildly popular that Jacobs even felt compelled to send a copy to President Abraham Lincoln.[253]

By all accounts, Professor Jacobs was an astute lecturer, but his true strong suit as a teacher rested in lessons taught outside the formal classroom. Known for regularly leading sessions outdoors during which students tramped the terra firma of both the campus and the town, Jacobs left a lasting impression on his students and earned the admiration of his family and colleagues.[254] These lessons covered all matters of science and nature, including the weather and the flora and fauna of the area, subjects that thoroughly interested him. "A practical botanist and geologist, my father knew every inch of the territory for miles around," wrote Jacobs's son Henry years later.[255] In addition to his duties at the college, Jacobs helped establish Gettysburg Gasworks, the company that first gave the town light on its streets.[256] Jacobs also became a self-taught theologian and received a license as a Lutheran minister, serving for a time at Gettysburg's Christ Lutheran Church. Although health issues forced him to retire from his duties with the college in 1866, he remained a professor emeritus until his death in 1871.[257]

During the mid-1830s, James Espy of Philadelphia's Franklin Institute set out to establish a statewide weather observer network in Pennsylvania, and Professor Jacobs served as Adams County's observer as part of this program.[258]

Beginning in April 1840, he began thrice-daily weather observations at 7:00 a.m., 2:00 p.m. and 9:00 p.m., keeping records in a journal expressly dedicated to this purpose.[259] His observations included temperature, cloud cover and cloud type, wind speed, precipitation and pressure.[260] When Espy moved to Washington to work with Joseph Henry, the Smithsonian's first secretary, on the Smithsonian Meteorological Project, Professor Jacobs joined that network as the observer for Adams County.[261] From this point forward, Jacobs recorded his observations on a special form provided to him by the Smithsonian.[262] He continued his weather observations on behalf of the Smithsonian through February 1865.[263]

Most of Professor Jacobs's nearly three decades of weather observations took place under far less trying circumstances than those he faced during the battle. His diligence, especially considering that the Confederate army's line of battle rested close on his doorstep on Middle Street much of the time, is truly remarkable.[264] Indeed, much like a nineteenth-century version of modern-day meteorologists who report from the field during dangerous storms, Jacobs continued to take his weather observations despite the "storm" swirling immediately around him. But this storm was not a hurricane or blizzard but rather the largest battle to ever take place in the Western Hemisphere.[265]

Years later, Jacobs's classroom lessons on meteorology served as a template for training government weather forecasters in the U.S. Signal Corps as part of the development of a fledging American weather service.[266] As a result, Professor Michael Jacobs truly could be considered a "plank holder" in what we know today as NOAA's National Weather Service.

William O. Hickok, Harrisburg, Pennsylvania

William Orville Hickok met formidable challenges in his life starting at a very young age. Born on October 6, 1815, near Warsaw, in Wyoming County, New York, he survived a horrible accident at age five when he was trampled by a horse. Despite lasting injuries and limitations, he lived quite an accomplished life.

Hickok's family eventually relocated to Pennsylvania, and after some delay, William followed his family. He later joined his father in the book publishing business, where he showed quite a penchant for "inventive faculties." He went on to establish his own bookbinding service in Harrisburg, a business that grew to become Eagle Works; according to the *Biographical*

Fig. 88 William O. Hickok. *Courtesy of Peter Hickok.*

Encyclopedia of Dauphin County, the business served, at the time, as the "most extensive and most complete of the kind in the world." Officially founded in 1853, Eagle Works later became known as the Hickok Manufacturing Company and operated under its first president, William Orville Hickok.

Today, Hickok Manufacturing Company stands as the oldest continuously operating business in Harrisburg. Although his business activities often resulted in financial difficulties, Hickok developed many innovative processes that established him as one of the pioneers in his trade. Here he earned the respect and admiration of peers and underlings alike. Hickok remained civic-minded throughout his life and donated much time to the betterment of the community in which he lived. Fortunately, for the purposes of this study, he remained as dedicated to his activities as a weather observer for the Smithsonian as he did to his career, community, wife and five children. Hickok lived a full life, passing away on May 25, 1891, at the age of seventy-five.[267]

John Heisely, Harrisburg, Pennsylvania

Born in Frederick, Maryland, on November 30, 1794, Dr. John Heisely served during the War of 1812. He later studied medicine, graduating in 1820 from the Maryland Medical College in Baltimore. He then moved to Carlisle, Pennsylvania, where he opened a practice, eventually settling in Harrisburg by 1835. There, he established his residence and a drugstore at the corner of Second and Chestnut Streets, not far from the Susquehanna River.

Like Michael Jacobs in Gettysburg, Heisely served as a weather observer on behalf of the Franklin Institute and the Smithsonian for many years, including 1863. His efforts to keep detailed information on Harrisburg weather led to the moniker "the clerk of the weather." He became a leader in the temperance movement and well known for his good disposition and kindness. Heisely passed away on September 18, 1869.[268]

8

THE RETREAT

The Rain and the River, July 5–12, 1863

You know this country well enough to tell me whether it ever quits raining about here? If so, I should like to see a clear day soon.[269]
—*General Robert E. Lee*

Setting the Stage

Situation Report—A Brief Summary of Troop Movements and Dispositions

The epic struggle experienced by the Army of Northern Virginia on the retreat from Gettysburg represents one of the most significant weather-related events of the entire campaign. Historians and students of the battle know all too well that drenching rains haunted the armies during the initial phase of the retreat and again days later. Still, modern research methods offer new and interesting weather findings. This summary of troop movements, actions and dispositions provides context to the weather analysis that follows.

The Army of Northern Virginia was in trouble. And rain was the culprit. Lots of it. Rain on the march creates miserable conditions. In the extreme, deep mud can mire man and beast, even wagons. After a battle, particularly after a loss, relentless rainfall saps the soul, especially when the defeated army finds itself far from home. The Confederates retreated in two extremely long columns, one moving through the Fairfield Pass under the direction of Major John A. Harman and the other moving through the Cashtown Pass with Brigadier General John D. Imboden in command. Depending on their assigned routes, they had forty to forty-five miles to go before reaching their destination, Williamsport, Maryland. Imboden's wagon train, some seventeen miles long, carried primarily wounded soldiers through horrible weather as this train of misery relentlessly snaked its way through South Mountain. Of course, elements of General Meade's victorious force dealt with the same meteorological elements as they began to pursue Lee's army.

As Lee's retreating forces headed toward Williamsport, where they planned to cross the Potomac and return to Virginia, they clashed frequently with pursuing Union cavalry. This resulted in a running series of brief but ferocious fights at various locations, including an especially haunting nighttime clash at Monterey Pass. This action, replete with pyrotechnic-like flashes of lightning and thunder, took place the night of July 4 near the peak of South Mountain. Additional actions between opposing cavalry

Fig. 89 The wagon train of wounded, by A.C. Redwood. *From Johnson and Buel, eds.,* Battles and Leaders of the Civil War, *vol. 3.*

forces occurred at Smithsburg, Hagerstown and Boonsboro along the route to Williamsport.[270]

All the while, heavy post-battle deluges continued to swell the Potomac River. Thus, as lead elements of Lee's army arrived at Williamsport, they soon found that they could not ford the river as planned. Worse yet, they also learned that Union cavalry had destroyed the pontoon bridge that Lee's army left in place at Falling Waters, a few miles downriver from Williamsport. With this, Lee's men found themselves trapped. Colonel Imboden's description captured the scene: "The tremendous rains had raised the river more than ten feet above the fording stage of water, and we could not possibly cross then. There were two small ferry-boats, or 'flats' there, which I immediately put into requisition to carry across those of the wounded, who, after being fed and having their wounds dressed, thought they could walk to Winchester."[271]

Then on July 6, General Imboden faced a perilous situation. This came as Union cavalry threatened the safety of his infirm forces before the bulk of Lee's surviving infantry and artillery arrived. Here, in a remarkable action, a portion of Lee's cavalry and a few batteries under Imboden's command joined with a cobbled-together group of wounded soldiers, teamsters, commissaries and quartermasters to fend off a large force of Union cavalry. In a clash known as the "Wagoners' Fight," Imboden's desperate and isolated forces, outgunned nearly ten to one, held their ground. When lead elements of Lee's infantry arrived late that evening, the Union troopers broke off any further actions.[272]

Fig. 90 Brigadier General John D. Imboden. *Courtesy of Ben Ritter.*

Once he reconcentrated his army, Lee was determined to make a stand at Williamsport. Down but not out, he planned to cross the Potomac after it subsided enough to allow a portion of his army to cross via the Williamsport fords and the pontoon bridge his engineers feverishly worked to reconstruct at Falling Waters. To buy time, outgunned and trapped, Lee's army dug in.

General Meade and most of his army remained at Gettysburg until July 7. Uncertain of Lee's plans, Meade let caution rule, taking time to rest and refit his army. On moving out, the Army of the Potomac faced the same obstacles as the Army of Northern Virginia, namely rain and muddy roads. Nonetheless, the bulk of Meade's infantry corps arrived near Williamsport by July 11. But Meade's delayed pursuit, his deliberate assessment of the situation once he approached Lee's army, and his hesitancy to attack gave Lee time to establish a formidable line of defense. Thus, the stage was set for another major battle. With this, weather, not the rival generals, dictated future events.

Troop Location Map

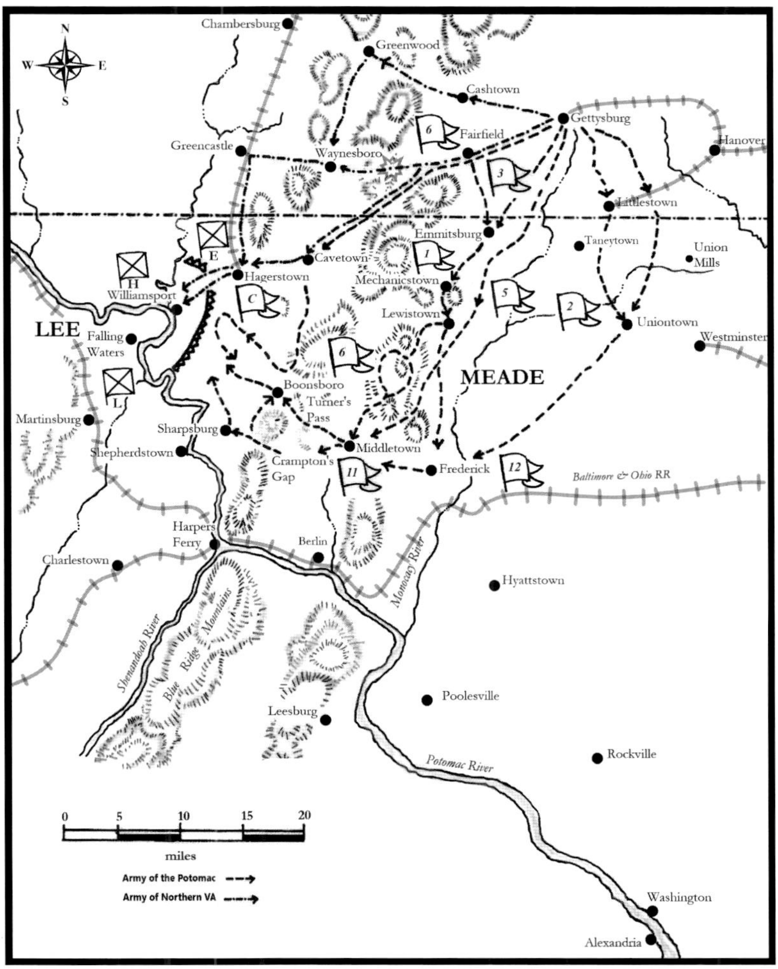

Fig. 91 Gettysburg Campaign, July 5–12, 1863. *Courtesy of J. Heiser.*

The Primary Source Data

To this point in the campaign, the armies had operated close enough to official weather observing sites such as the Naval Observatory and Gettysburg to allow data from those locations to steer the weather narrative. As the retreat began and the Army of Northern Virginia moved west and south toward Williamsport, active maneuvering shifted into an area that lacked any official in situ weather records, even though official observers did reside in the area. Henry Hanshew in Frederick reported in June 1863, but no record of his observations exists from July. Smithsonian observer Jacob Bell in Leitersburg, about four miles northeast of Hagerstown, last reported in June 1862.[273] Ironically, Bell later published annual rainfall statistics for 1863 and 1864, so he did measure rainfall in those years, but no record of a daily or monthly breakdown exists for 1863.

Thus, during the retreat, Professor Jacobs in Gettysburg remained the closest official weather observer. However, observations from Harrisburg, Sykesville and the Naval Observatory also contribute valuable information for inferring conditions in the region the armies covered, largely because winds frequently blew from an easterly direction during the period. Such a flow of air, particularly wind directions from east through south, tends to upslope as the air moved from the lower elevations of eastern Maryland and Virginia westward toward the mountains, enhancing the chances of clouds and precipitation.

The Weather—Background

Most students of the Gettysburg Campaign already appreciate the weather-related human-interest aspects of the retreat phase of the campaign. Therefore, this narrative shifts largely to the prevailing weather in the July 4–14 period in a detailed analysis unlike any previously offered. In the end, this forensic weather analysis greatly enhances historians' understanding of the meteorological dynamics in play. In turn, this improved understanding provides all students of the campaign with an unappreciated yet invaluable piece of the history of the retreat.

Although excessive heat and humidity remain part of the weather story during the retreat, the focus certainly shifted to rainfall. Yes, showers had shadowed the armies during previous portions of the campaign, especially during the latter part of June. But that precipitation paled in comparison to the rain and periodic torrential downpours during the retreat. Never one to mince words, Lee may have put it best, when he, according to General Imboden, laughingly quipped, "You know this country well enough to tell me whether it ever quits raining about here? If so, I should like to see a clear day soon."[274] The shift in emphasis to precipitation adds a layer of complexity to any weather analysis because during the summer, rain is more often "convective" in nature, taking the form of scattered showers and thunderstorms. The rain falls here, there, but not everywhere, with just a few miles often separating flooding downpours from barely a drop. As a result, extrapolating information about rainfall from the available official observations comes with caveats and enhanced uncertainty.

The humid air mass that had matured in the Gettysburg area during the battle was in no hurry to exit. The front that likely played a prominent role in the rain late on July 3 and into July 4 did not clear the region, probably stalling just to the north, setting up the rainy period of weather that marked the start of the retreat.

The pressure traces from Gettysburg and the Naval Observatory during the period July 4–14 are shown in Figures 92 and 93. The overall patterns

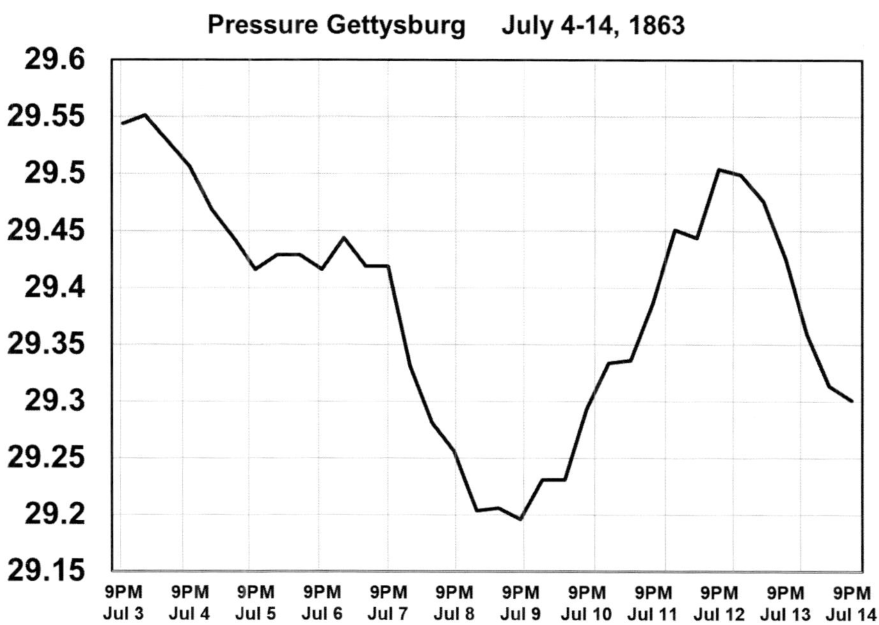

Fig. 92 Pressure (in inches of mercury) at Gettysburg, July 4–14, 1863. *Data from NOAA FORTS.*

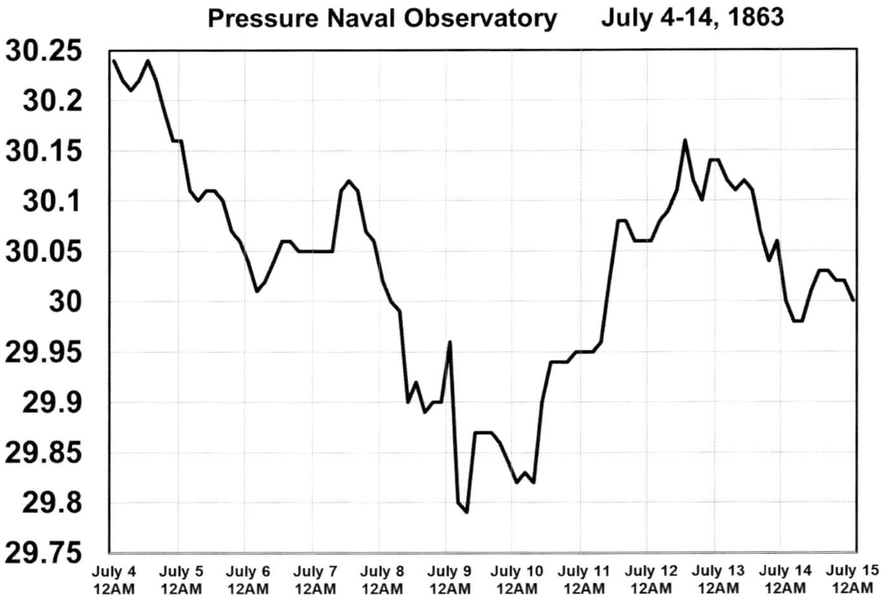

Fig. 93 Pressure (in inches of mercury) at the Naval Observatory, July 4–14, 1863. *Data from NOAA FORTS.*

match well, though the greater frequency of observations at the Naval Observatory, eight observations per day versus three per day in Gettysburg, provides more granularity. These pressure traces suggest a reasonable sequencing of weather systems to explain conditions during the retreat. Initially, pressure generally fell until about midnight on July 6, coinciding with the first rainy period. Then pressure steadied for about a day, in concert with a relative respite in the weather on July 7. Pressure then began a steady fall that correlates well with the arrival of the next rainstorm centered on July 8. A steady rise in pressure then aligns with a three-day break in the weather during the period July 9–11. After peaking on July 12, the barometer began to fall again, signaling the next storm, which brought widespread rain from late that day through the time when Lee's forces finally crossed the Potomac to safety.

Table 7 shows daily rainfall amounts from July 4 to July 14 for observing sites within about a seventy-five-mile radius of the retreat zone. Pittsburgh is included to represent the west side of the Appalachians. Daily totals of an inch or more appear in bold, while vertical lines identify periods when the amount likely was spread over two or more calendar days (observers sometimes accumulated rain over multiple days). Rainfall totals for the period for each location appear in the last row.

Jacobs recorded at least 1 inch of rain on two days, but the extreme amounts in Harrisburg stand out immediately. In fact, had only one observer reported there, these values and their frequency—including four 1-inch-plus rainfalls in such a short period of time—would likely generate great skepticism, particularly considering the much smaller rainfall totals in nearby Gettysburg. However, having *two* independent observers (William Hickok and John Heisely) in Harrisburg lends credibility to the reports. For modern-day context, Gettysburg averages about three days per summer with 1 inch or more of rain, so having two within a week, though unusual, is certainly plausible. In contrast, the 3-inch-plus totals in Harrisburg are exceptional; since 1888, that much rain has fallen there on only six July days. In addition, Heisely totaled 13.58 inches in his rain gauge for July 1863 and Hickok 11.49 inches. The modern-day record, going back to 1888, for the rainiest July in Harrisburg is 12.09 inches, demonstrating how unusually rainy the first half of July 1863 was in that area.

Despite the more modest rainfall totals measured by Jacobs in Gettysburg, the extremes in Harrisburg, and, to some extent, those in Sykesville, provide evidence that frequent but scattered tropical downpours roamed the Gettysburg region in the first two weeks of July 1863. Given the nature of showers and thunderstorms in the summer, it is certainly possible, and perhaps likely, that the retreating Confederates and their Union pursuers bound for Hagerstown and eventually Williamsport experienced rainfall amounts greater than what Jacobs tallied in Gettysburg. Having said that, days of very heavy rain in summer occur twice as often in Harrisburg as in Hagerstown, so odds favor less rain on the retreat route than what fell in Harrisburg.[275]

Day-to-Day Analysis

Previous analyses of the weather during the retreat, culled primarily from soldiers' accounts and Jacobs's observations, have clearly established that July 5–8 was exceptionally cloudy and rainy across the Gettysburg theater. Data from other locations, plus the NOAA reanalysis system, offer additional clues as to the nature of this unsettled period.

Table 7. Daily Rainfall (in Inches) for the Period July 4–14, 1863

Double vertical lines indicate that rain fell on that day, but it was not officially recorded until a subsequent day or that the amount was included in a previous day's total.

	Harrisburg Hickok	Heisely	Sykesville	Gettysburg
July 4	**1.08**	**2.79**	**1.50**	||
July 5	**2.48**	**1.33**	0.10	**1.39**
July 6	0.29	0.35	0.50	||
July 7	-	-	||	||
July 8	**2.04**	**3.31**	**3.00**	**1.30**
July 9	-	-	-	-
July 10	||	-	-	-
July 11	0.38	0.39	-	-
July 12	||	**3.47**	-	||
July 13	||	0.21	||	0.55
July 14	**2.63**	||	**1.50**	-
Total	8.90	11.85	6.60	3.24

Naval Observatory	Georgetown	Annapolis	Pittsburgh
0.32	0.68	-	0.05
| |	-	0.02	-
0.92	Trace	**1.57**	-
0.06	| |	0.02	-
0.55	**1.36**	0.35	-
-	-	-	-
-	-	0.08	-
-	-	-	-
0.80	| |	0.01	-
1.80	**1.56**	0.32	0.15
0.24	-	0.75	0.10
4.69	3.60	3.12	0.30

Over that four-day span, thirty-one of the thirty-two observations from the Naval Observatory reported at least 8/10 cloud coverage, with twenty-four of the thirty-one observations completely (10/10) cloudy. In both Gettysburg and Sykesville, every observation taken during the daylight hours of July 5–8 claimed at least 8/10 sky cover, with all observations in Gettysburg fully overcast. Including July 4, Jacobs reported 2.39 inches of rain during the period, the two Harrisburg observers 6.09 inches and 7.98 inches, and 5.10 inches was measured in Sykesville.

A reconstruction of sea-level pressure on the early afternoon of July 6 from the NOAA reanalysis system in Figure 8A (color section) shows the aforementioned front splayed from eastern New England into eastern Kentucky, providing a focusing mechanism for the showers and thunderstorms. Figure 8B (see color section) shows the relative humidity pattern at 10,000 feet, a critical altitude for precipitation-producing clouds, averaged from the early afternoon of July 4 to that of July 6. A zone of relatively high values is oriented along and around that front (the even deeper moisture lurking farther south will play a role a few days later). All sixteen wind observations from the Naval Observatory during the period July 5–6 and all six made at Sykesville had an easterly component to the wind, indicating a funnel of low-level Atlantic moisture toward this front. With such an easterly flow, locations west of the mountains experienced "downsloping" as air descends the western side of the Appalachians, which is unfavorable for precipitation. In support of this assertion, Pittsburgh reported a meager 0.05 inches of rain during this time.

The official observers and the soldiers in both armies who recorded their observations generally agree that some of the heaviest rain fell during the wee hours of July 5 and, to a lesser extent, July 6. Of that first night on the retreat westward toward Fairfield, Captain J.F.J. Caldwell of the 1st South Carolina Infantry wrote, "A heavy rain fell during the greater part of the night, and the roads were a universal quagmire."[276] About their march from Littlestown to Frederick on July 6, Sergeant Samuel Toombs of the 13th New York Infantry noted, "The morning of the 6th of July was rainy and disagreeable." He also noted, "The rain came down in torrents during the day."[277] After approximately midday on July 5, the Potomac River at Williamsport could no longer be forded, a state that would persist for about a week (see color insert, Figure 13C).

The river level as Lee's forces approached the Potomac on July 5 represents one of the most prominent, and indeed key, weather-related

Fig. 94 Union soldiers, with heavy guns, marching toward Frederick after the Battle of Gettysburg, by E. Forbes. *LOC.*

factors of the entire Gettysburg Campaign. Lee's problems were further exacerbated by additional bouts of rain that occurred between July 5 and July 14.

Most official observers reported a respite in precipitation on July 7, although some soldiers reported occasional rain during the day. By this time, "the Potomac was a raging torrent," according to Second Lieutenant William Alexander Gordon, 1st Regiment Confederate Engineers (temporarily assigned to Pickett's Division, Longstreet's Corps),[278] and more rain was on the way. Air pressure at Gettysburg and the Naval Observatory began to fall that afternoon, and rain began anew in Gettysburg and Harrisburg at 3:00 a.m. on July 8. By the time the rain ended at 11:30 a.m. in Gettysburg, 1.30 inches had accumulated in Jacobs's rain gauge, while 3 inches fell in Sykesville and as much as 3.51 inches in Harrisburg, where the rain lasted until around 5:00 p.m.

The NOAA reanalysis system provides evidence of the elements that led to this heavy burst of rain. A prominent disturbance in the mid-levels of the atmosphere the morning of July 8, marked with a dashed line in Figure 9A (see color section), generated to its east a concentrated zone of upward motion in the atmosphere, largely superimposed on the remnants of the stalled front. In addition, Figure 9B (see color section) shows that a plume of higher relative humidity that originated in the Southeast moved northward toward the Gettysburg theater. This combination of weather elements favors heavy rain any time of the year, let alone in the middle of summer when low-level air is already laden with moisture. The pocket of rain continued to progress to the north and east; rain did not end in New York City until 3:00 a.m. on July 9, and rain was still falling in Providence at 9:00 p.m.

This disturbance dislodged the stagnant weather pattern. In its wake, winds at Harrisburg, Gettysburg, Sykesville and Washington turned to a drier northerly and westerly direction, at least briefly. For two days, and in some places three, the rain stopped and some sun returned, although dewpoints remained near 70 degrees F much of the time. By the afternoon of July 11, temperatures in Gettysburg once again reached the mid-80s and the heat index at least the low 90s, while at the Naval Observatory the heat index approached 100 degrees F. For the first time in a week, descriptions of "hot," "hazy" and "sultry" appeared in soldiers' notes, a spike in discomfort also felt by those left behind in Gettysburg. On July 9, the Potomac at Williamsport, by all accounts, still ran very full and swift, but it had begun to fall by July 11.

One more round of rain was on the way, however. Signs of an atmosphere once again primed to produce precipitation first appeared on July 11, when both Harrisburg observers reported nearly four-tenths of an inch of rain. As on July 5–6, winds in Gettysburg, Sykesville and Washington took on a moist easterly component, particularly by July 12. Rain began in Gettysburg and the Naval Observatory that day around dinnertime, with similar timing reported by Abner Hard, surgeon with the 8th Illinois Cavalry positioned south of Hagerstown near the Potomac, who wrote, "Sunday, the 12th, was one of the warmest days of the season, and as our dinner was spread upon the ground, there came up one of the hardest rain-storms I ever witnessed. In five minutes the water came down the hills, carrying away some tent-flies we had put up, and stood over a foot deep in camp." And he emphasized the feeling that "the artillery of Heaven had supplanted that of man."[279] Indeed, the next wave of rain had arrived. With this, the operative question remained: Could Lee get his army across the Potomac before the river rose again?

PEOPLE, STORIES AND MATTERS TO REMEMBER: A METEOROLOGICAL "MOST WANTED"—BELL, HEYSER AND MARVIN

Most Smithsonian observers in the South ceased their activity during the Civil War. In contrast, in the North recordkeeping continued as usual for most weather observers. Unaffected by the war, they carried on with their duties. That said, some such as Gettysburg's Michael Jacobs and Harrisburg's Heisely and Hickok, located near active military operations, certainly felt the effects of the war. Meanwhile, in the border states, all bets were off. For instance, the Frederick observer, Henry Hanshew, recorded observations in June 1863, but that was his final extant monthly report.[280]

Interestingly, three Smithsonian observers located within the geographic confines of the Gettysburg Campaign stood to greatly enhance our understanding of the weather during the retreat: Jacob E. Bell[281] in Leitersburg, Maryland, near Hagerstown; John W. Marvin in Winchester, Virginia; and William Heyser in Chambersburg, Pennsylvania. These men not only recorded weather data for the Smithsonian but served their local communities as well. Marvin toiled as a school headmaster, Heyser was an influential farmer and Bell cofounded the Planter's Insurance Company. Unfortunately, either these men did not record observations for the Smithsonian during the war or their records were lost to history.[282] Those missing records would have helped immensely, providing a much fuller regional weather picture, especially during the period of heavy rain that began just after the battle and continued through July 14. Thus, Bell, Heyser and Marvin—or, more specifically, their missing weather observations for June and July 1863—do indeed constitute a meteorological "Most Wanted."

9

THE RETREAT

The Weather Gods' Last Dance, July 13–14, 1863

The fording of the Potomac in the dim starlight of that 13th of July night, and early morning of the 14th, was a spectacular phase of war so quaint and impressive as to leave itself lastingly daguerreotyped on the memory.[283]
—Brigadier General John Brown Gordon

Setting the Stage

Situation Report—A Brief Summary of Troop Movements and Dispositions

As General Robert E. Lee looked for the soonest opportunity to cross the Potomac to the safe confines of Virginia, he also deployed his forces for battle. With his back against the swollen Potomac River, Lee ordered his army to construct substantial earthworks for protection from any assault the Union army might launch. In the meantime, engineers of the Army of Northern Virginia worked to complete the reconstruction of the pontoon bridge at Falling Waters. Once finished, this bridge and usable fords at nearby Williamsport offered an escape route for his army's safe return to Virginia. But Lee could only wait, as the weather would dictate the timing of his army's salvation.

Meanwhile, General Meade wrestled with a difficult decision. Should he attack Lee's army with the hope of destroying it once and for all? Or should he act more cautiously? Here, Meade may have been mindful of Napoleon's maxim of never doing what the enemy wishes you to do. Lee's army had built formidable defensive lines. Any attack most certainly would result in huge casualties, and Meade knew full well the dangers inherent in tangling with a desperate and defeated foe, especially one led by Robert E. Lee. As Meade vacillated, the weather took center stage for the last time in the Gettysburg Campaign.

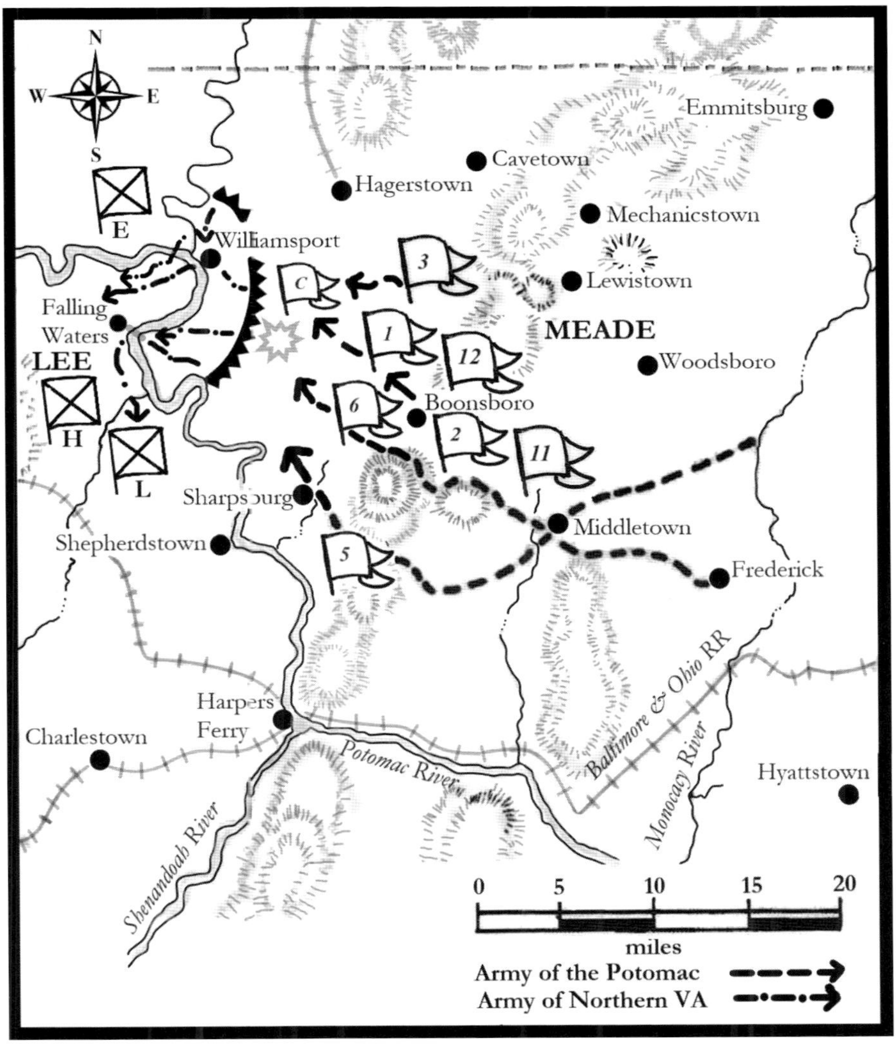

Fig. 95 Gettysburg Campaign, July 13–15, 1863. (This map includes July 15 to demonstrate troop positions as of that date.) *Courtesy of J. Heiser.*

Then, as fate would have it, rain on the night of July 13 that extended into the early morning hours of July 14 threatened, yet again, to raise the river to a level that would make the river fords impassable and pontoon crossing extremely precarious. Nevertheless, Lee's forces successfully crossed the Potomac River via both the fords and the bridge on that harrowing night. Ironically, the Confederates completed their movement just as Meade finally decided to attack. But he was too late. Many criticized Meade at the time, and for many years thereafter, for his hesitancy to potentially bring an immediate end to the war. However, recent scholarship suggests that had he attacked Lee's formidable line of defense, Meade might have suffered an ignominious defeat, negating his great success at Gettysburg. There can be no debating that the weather weighed heavily in his decision.

The Weather—Background

The atmosphere's last deluge of rain on the armies of the Gettysburg Campaign began late on July 12 and carried over into the wee hours of the morning of July 14. In fact, July 13 was the only day during the retreat when all observing sites included in Table 7 (see chapter 8, pages 180–81) reported rain. Even Pittsburgh, west of the mountains, experienced about six hours of light rain that day. Other diarists and unofficial observers almost unanimously agree that July 13, particularly at night, was rainy. The precipitation stretched at least from Chambersburg in the north to Front Royal in the south and from Hancock on the west to Baltimore on the east.

General Lee described the night of July 13 as "one of the most inclement nights I have ever known at this season of the year. It rained w/out cessation, rendering the road by which our troops marched to the bridge at Falling Waters very difficult to pass."[284] Longstreet, while helping oversee the crossing at that bridge just downstream from Williamsport, wrote, "And such a night is seldom experienced even in the rough life of the soldier. The rain fell in showers, sometimes in blinding sheets....The best standing points were ankle deep in mud, and the roads half-way to the knee."[285]

Meteorologically speaking, what explains this final deluge before the Army of Northern Virginia's crossing to relative safety? Clues emerge from the winds that consistently blew from an easterly direction at all eight observation times at the Naval Observatory on July 13 and at all three times at most other official observing sites in the area. Lifting of this moist flow that originated largely over the ocean would have been slightly aided by higher terrain to the west. In addition, air pressure had started to fall at Gettysburg, the Naval Observatory and other locations such as Annapolis and Harrisburg late on July 12 (see Figures 92 and 93 on pages 177 and 178). That pressure decline continued until midday on July 14, symptomatic of the approach and passage of an area of lower pressure. Interestingly, the NOAA reanalysis system does not capture the falling pressures or the easterly flow that characterized this period. Nor does it reproduce the high relative humidities in the mid-levels of the atmosphere that typically accompany heavy rain events. This failure may indicate that a smaller-scale weather system, or perhaps one originating in a relatively data sparse area such as over the ocean, was responsible.

Observations along the East Coast, from the Carolinas to southern New England, suggest a possible answer: a storm moving up the coast and strengthening, perhaps resembling a cold-season nor'easter. Such a storm is preceded by east and northeast winds and often carries a large shield of precipitation on its northern and western flanks. The initial signs of such a system appear in the Charleston, South Carolina observations, as air pressure there bottomed out at 7:00 a.m. on July 13 at a modest 30.12 inches of mercury. Rain ended that morning, leaving 1.4 inches in the gauge, but no easterly winds were observed there. Farther north, at Annapolis (effectively at sea level), the minimum observed pressure dipped noticeably lower, at 29.85 inches, and occurred on the afternoon of July 14. At that latitude, easterly winds blew all day on July 13 and into the morning of July 14. Meanwhile, up the coast at both New York City and Providence, similar easterly winds and minimum pressures were reported. Rain fell from 9:15 p.m. on July 13 until 8:00 a.m. on July 14 in New York City, and from 1:00 a.m. to around noon on July 14 in Providence, totaling 2.1 inches in the gauge. This sequence of observations is consistent with a coastal storm moving northeast and generally parallel to the coast, an atypical event in July.

To close, it is useful to take a broad look at the period of the retreat and review the impact of the rains of July 4–14, 1863, on the Potomac River to uncover yet another unusual weather-related aspect of the campaign.

THE RAIN AND THE RIVER

The Potomac River at Williamsport, Maryland, could be forded with relative ease when the Army of Northern Virginia crossed in late June.

At the time, by most reports, the water measured three feet or so, perhaps knee to waist deep. During the retreat, however, the river ran too high to ford from July 5 until late on July 13 due to runoff from heavy rains in the river basin in the period July 4–8. By all accounts, the river at Williamsport appears to have reached a peak between fifteen and twenty feet deep, at a place where the normal depth is around three feet. According to the National Weather Service, minor flood stage at Williamsport was twenty-three feet (Williamsport is no longer an official forecast point for the NWS on the Potomac, thus the "was").[286] By modern standards, then, the rise on the river in July 1863, despite its obvious disruptiveness, would not be considered a flood. Given its profound effect on Lee's army, however, was the rise unusual, nonetheless?

Based on modern-day river data at Williamsport, the answer is a resounding "yes." River-level data available at least once per day since August 1996 reveal that during this nearly thirty-year span, the highest reported level in any July was 6.8 feet, well below the minimum estimated level of 15 feet from July 1863. In fact, the Potomac crested above 5 feet on only two July days since 1996. Even in the adjacent summer months of June and August, crests of 15 feet or higher occurred on only two days in the nearly thirty years of observations. The bottom line: in recent decades, the Potomac River at Williamsport in July has not come close to reaching the level that delayed Lee's crossing for a week in July 1863, and even in the other summer months, rarely has it crested that high.[287] To support further the relative rarity of high-water levels on the Potomac at Williamsport in July, consider that the list of the dozen highest water levels there since 1932, which includes all crests of 22.9 feet or higher, contains no events from the month of July.[288]

How much rain fell in the drainage basin of the Potomac (shown in Figure 96) to produce the river levels encountered by the Army of Northern Virginia in July 1863? The rain totals shown in Table 7 (see chapter 8, page 180–81) come from downriver (that is, to the east) of Williamsport, but no quantitative information from locations upriver survives. One approach is to "reverse engineer" the problem by identifying days in the modern record when the Potomac at Williamsport reached a level similar to the July 1863 level and then determine how much rain fell to produce those modern-day crests. No July comparables appear in the previously analyzed data since 1996, so proxies must come from other months in the warm season.

One such proxy occurred in May 2022. Between May 3 and May 4, the water level at Williamsport hovered in the three-to-four-foot range

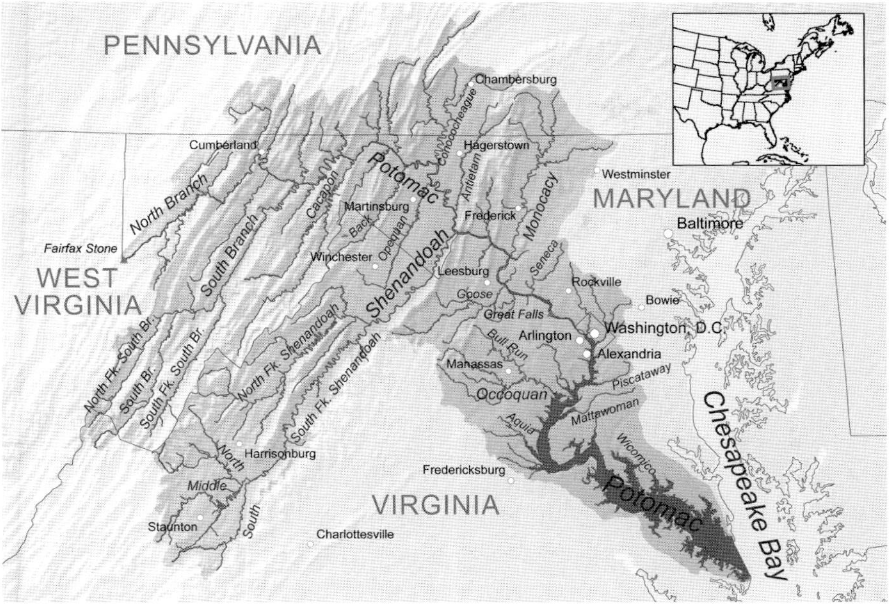

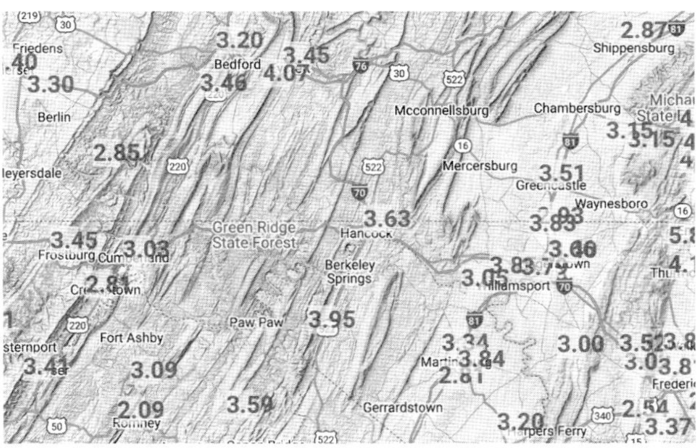

***Above*: Fig. 96** Watershed map of the Potomac. *Wikimedia Commons.*

***Right*: Fig. 97** Rainfall (in inches), May 4–8, 2022. *NOAA/NRCC/ACIS.*

but by May 8 had reached nearly twenty feet. The intervening period featured two rain events, one centered on May 4 and another primarily May 6–7, not dissimilar to the multiple rain events in the July 4–8, 1863 period. Figure 97 shows observed rainfall from May 4 to May 8, 2022, in the Potomac basin and some observing sites just outside the basin.[289] Notice that from Williamsport upriver, generally three to four inches of rain fell in that period.

A second comparable hails from early June 2018. In this case, the previous April and May had been rainy, and the river level at Williamsport had exceeded 10 feet on several days during each of those months. By late May, however, the river level had settled into the 4–5–foot range. Then, heavy rains in the period June 1–4 led to a crest of 24.1 feet on June 4, several feet higher than the estimated crest in July 1863. Figure 98 shows observed rainfall in that four-day period.[290] Notable here are the 4-inch-plus values near Hancock, upriver of Williamsport, where the river also rose about 20 feet as a result of the rain.

A third, relatively recent proxy—and one that arguably offers the best match to July 1863—occurred in early April 2024. The river level at Williamsport during the last two weeks of March 2024 primarily remained in the 3–4–foot range. Rainfall from April 1 to April 3, shown in Figure 99, pushed the river to a crest of 17.85 feet on April 4.[291] In this case, a general 3–4–inch rainfall in the basin sufficed to create a river rise at Williamsport to a height that compares favorably with what likely occurred in July 1863. Interestingly, the river at Hancock also rose about 14 feet in this event, mimicking the rise at Williamsport.

In summary, to get a sense for how much rain might have fallen across the Potomac basin upriver of Williamsport to create the river rise observed there in July 1863, we identified three occasions during the warm season in the last ten years when the river peaked at or above the height likely reached to prevent Lee from crossing. Those proxies suggest, broadly, that three to four inches of rain across much of the basin would have caused such a rise. Figure 100 combines what we know (the actual observations) and what we can now estimate about the rain in the period July 4–8.

Admittedly, a true apples-to-apples comparison is challenging for several reasons. Two dams present in 1863, one approximately seven miles upriver of Williamsport and the other about fourteen miles downriver, have since been raised several feet. In addition, a new, smaller dam was constructed in the 1930s just downstream from where Lee forded the river. Other uncertainties include matching the antecedent conditions, such as soil moisture and the exact distribution of rain in the basin in July 1863, to the modern proxies. Despite these cautions, this analysis provides some quantitative sense for the magnitude of rainfall that likely fell in the area during that multiday rainy period in early July 1863.[292]

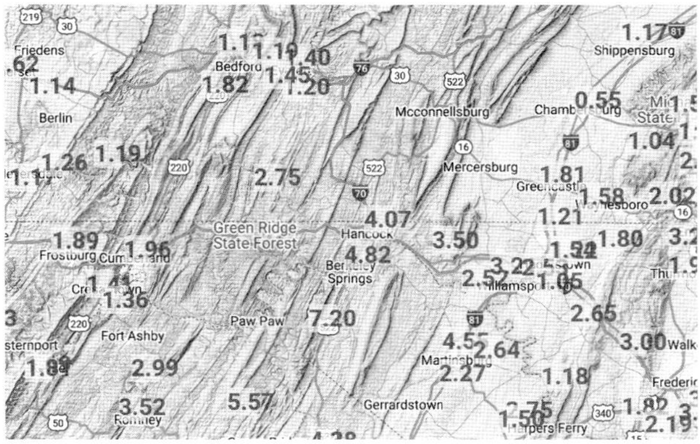

Fig. 98 Rainfall (in inches), June 1–4, 2018. *NOAA/NRCC/ACIS.*

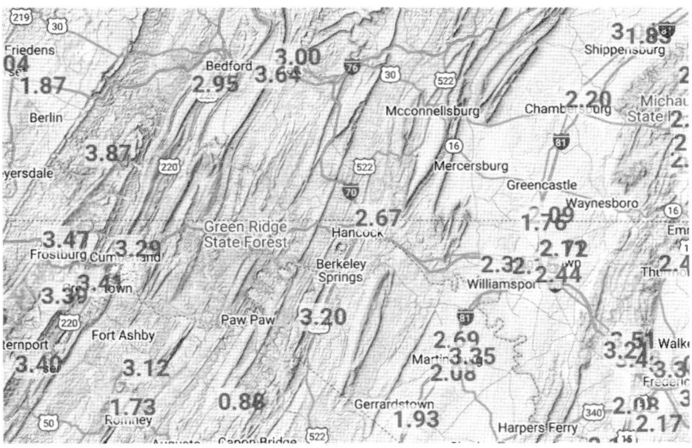

Fig. 99 Rainfall (in inches), April 1–3, 2024. *NOAA/NRCC/ACIS.*

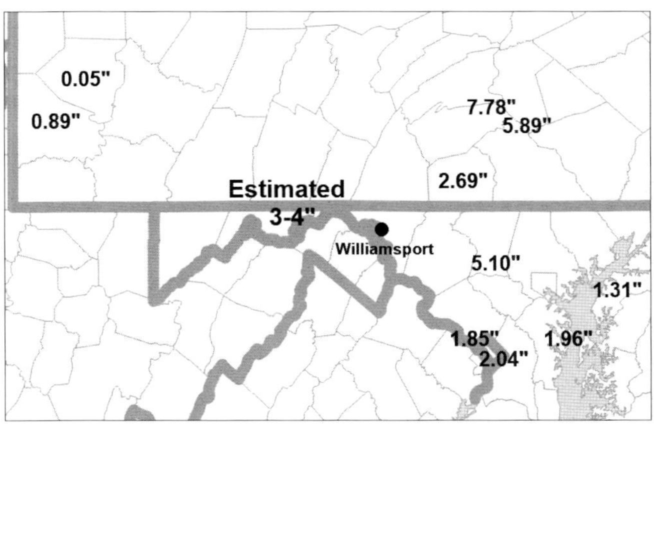

Fig. 100 Rainfall (in inches), July 4–8, 1863, both observed and estimated. *Data from NOAA FORTS.*

People, Stories and Matters to Remember: Time Travel

Many period artists attempted to depict the situation on the Potomac River during those fateful July days at Williamsport in 1863 as Lee waited to cross. Despite their collective efforts, the actual visual circumstances remained a mystery. While extreme crests on the Potomac at Williamsport such as the record-setting 1936 St. Patrick's Day flood, when the river reached 48.6 feet, have been well documented, modest rises similar to the 15–20–foot level in July 1863 remained largely ignored. However, for the purposes of an analysis of the July 1863 river rise and rainfall amounts that prompted that rise, these lesser "cousins" of true floods prove very useful. Moreover, the April 2024 event mentioned previously appears to be an excellent comparable to the Potomac River rise of July 1863.

Quite fortuitously, a Williamsport resident captured several photographs of the river near its peak on April 4–5. Also, a local historian provided images of the river later in 2024, from similar vantage points, when the river returned to its "normal" depth of approximately two to three feet.[293] Thus, with a reasonable degree of confidence, it is possible to see an approximation of what the Potomac River in the area of the Williamsport fords, and along the adjacent floodplain, likely looked like to Robert E. Lee and his army near its high-water mark in early July 1863. In turn, it is also possible to compare (and contrast) the high-water images with those showing the river at its normal level.

Figures 14A–15B (see color section) compare the Potomac River at Williamsport at its normal level range, in either late November or early December 2024, with how it appeared near its crest during the April 4–5, 2024 time frame. The rise in the river from its typical level to approximately eighteen feet caused the river to overflow its banks, spreading across the floodplain adjacent to both sides of the modern boat ramp. Bandsman Julius Lineback of the 26th North Carolina's regimental band attested to the fact that the river did just this, in the same vicinity, on July 8, 1863, when he wrote, "During the night a good deal of rain fell, and water running in under our tent, we all got very wet. The river began rising again, and the whole flat, on which the wagons are parked, was almost like a pond." He continued, "We moved our tent to the top of the hill *as the whole bottom seemed to be in danger of being overflowed*"[294] (emphasis added). One can easily envision how the river Lineback described, swollen to the level shown in the modern photographs, would have prevented attempts to ford the river.

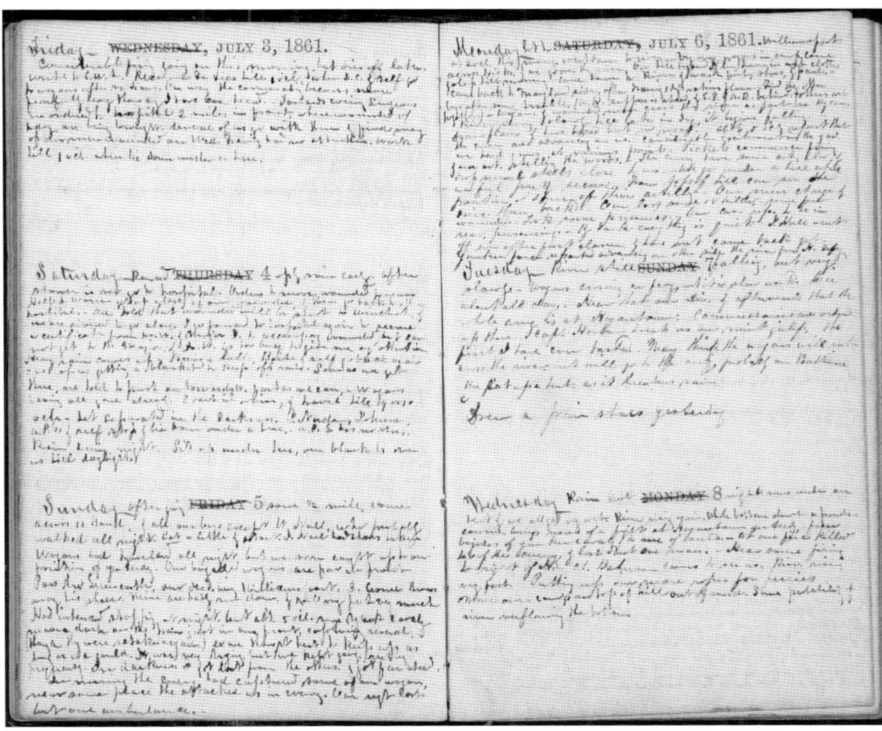

***Top*: Fig. 101** Julius Lineback's pocket diary. Note its extremely small size as compared to the pencil. *Courtesy of UNC Wilson and Ted Leinbach.*

***Bottom*: Fig. 102** Julius Lineback's diary entry for July 8, 1863. *Courtesy of UNC Wilson and Ted Leinbach.*

SCENERY OF WESTERN MARYLAND R. R.
780
Copyrighted. 18
the Potomac, Will

***Top left*: Fig. 103** The Williamsport floodplain (circa 1900–1906) as it extends downriver from the bridge over the C&O Canal. *LOC.*

***Top right*: Fig. 104** Williamsport riverfront, circa July 1862. Though this image depicts a scene from earlier in the Civil War, it shows the bluffs on both sides of the road and the bridge over the canal leading to the river. Figure 105 was likely taken from the bluff to the left roadside as shown in this image. This image was originally published in *Frank Leslie's Illustrated Newspaper*, July 5, 1862; copy shown here is from *Frank Leslie's Illustrated Famous Leaders and Battle Scenes of the Civil War*, ed. Louis Shepheard Moat (1896). The bluff to the left of the road was removed during early twentieth-century bridge construction. *Courtesy of Tim Snyder.*

***Left*: Fig. 105** W.H. Tipton image #780, 1877. This view, at times mistaken for Falling Waters, actually shows the Potomac River floodplain at Williamsport, Maryland, and the bridge over the C&O Canal. *Courtesy of Boardman Collection.*

Too much has changed along the banks of the Potomac in Williamsport for these photos to show the situation exactly as it appeared in July 1863. But these images do offer a reasonable visual representation of the river's appearance to the men of the Army of Northern Virginia while they awaited their opportunity to cross and, ultimately, their fate.

The preceding images show the Williamsport floodplain as it likely appeared in July 1863, save for the bridge over the C&O Canal, which is not the same bridge that was in place during the Gettysburg Campaign. The bridge was destroyed during the Battle of Antietam and rebuilt in March 1863 and again in subsequent years.

When Weather Mattered the Most: Let Us Cross Over the River

This chapter ends with one final "When Weather Mattered the Most." Here we close our examination of the weather during the Gettysburg Campaign with the reflections of the soldiers. After all, they shouldered the burden of coping with the elements, enduring some of the worst weather Mother Nature could send their way. Ironically, July 13, 1863, would be no different, as the Army of Northern Virginia suffered through a final cruel night of weather-related agony. Indeed, it seems that night served as the Weather Gods' exclamation point, trying the spirits of the soldiers of Lee's army one last time.

Fig. 106 *Retreat from Gettysburg*, by William L. Sheppard, shows the precarious pontoon bridge crossing at Falling Waters. *Longstreet,* From Manassas to Appomattox.

INVASION OF MARYLAND—LEE RETREATING ACROSS THE POTOMAC TO VIRGINIA, ABOVE WILLIAMSPORT, JULY 13.—FROM A SKETCH BY OUR SPECIAL ARTIST, C. E. H. BONWILL.

Fig. 107 Confederate retreat across the Potomac River at Williamsport, July 13, 1863, viewed from downriver, by C.E. H. Bonwill, *Frank Leslie's Illustrated Newspaper*, August 1, 1863. *Courtesy of Tim Snyder.*

As the Potomac River finally subsided just enough to allow the Confederate army to cross, Lee's engineers also completed a pontoon bridge at nearby Falling Waters. With this, it seemed the Army of Northern Virginia might finally escape Williamsport for the friendly confines of Virginia. But then, heavy rain returned. Regardless, Longstreet's and Hill's soldiers, who crossed via the reconstructed pontoon bridge, and Ewell's Corps, who crossed by the river fords, all faced one final "battle" with the elements. Just marching in the rain and mud to the pontoon bridge and the river fords proved hazardous and arduous enough. But the respective crossings left an indelible mark on the memory all those men who lived through the life-threatening experience. Although the luminous glow of riverside torches on the Virginia shore lit the way, to some it surely seemed as though they might never make it "home." Here, those brave men tell you their story (see color section, Figures 16A and 16B).

> General Robert E. Lee: *The enemy did not capture any organized body of men on that occasion, but only stragglers, and such as were left asleep on the road, exhausted by the fatigue and exposure of one of the most inclement nights I have ever known at this season of the year. It rained without cessation, rendering the road by which our troops marched to the bridge at Falling Waters very difficult to pass, and causing so much delay that the last of the troops did not cross the river at the bridge until 1 p.m. on the 14th.*[295]

Fig. 108 Colonel Edward Porter Alexander. *LOC.*

Colonel Edward Porter Alexander, Battalion Commander (Artillery Reserve, Longstreet's Corps): *But, oh, it was another awful night. I was now back with my battalion, & we were marching all night in awful roads, in mud & dark, & hard rain, & though we had only three miles to go, we were some distance from the bridge at sunrise. The rain was now over and the sun rose clear.... The whole night had been spent in groping & pulling through the mud, a few feet at a time, & then waiting for the vehicle in front of you to move again. And men would go to sleep on their horses, or leaning in fence corners, or standing in the mud.*[296]

Private Louis Leon, 53rd North Carolina Infantry (Daniel's Brigade, Rodes's Division): *The river was up to my chin, and very swift. We crossed in fours, for protection, as otherwise we could not have crossed. Our cartridge boxes we carried around our necks to keep the powder dry. On the south bank tar was poured so that we would not slip back in the river, as the mud was very slick. J. Engle, of our company, was stuck in until some of the boys pulled him out. We went six miles further, and I honestly believe more of us were asleep on our night's march than awake.*[297]

Private Samuel Pickens, 5th Alabama Infantry (O'Neal's Brigade, Rodes's Division): *We went to a ford several hundred yards higher up the river than where we crossed before—going up the aqueduct through water that smelt very offensively. As soon as we got near the river we knew the men were wading, by the yelling & hallooing that we heard. The Potomac being swollen, was very wide & was over waist deep.... We waded two & two side by side, holding on to each other in order to resist the current better & be more steady.... Our clothes, blankets (partly) &*

haversacks all got wet, which increased our load & made it very disagreeable marching after crossing. The banks were muddy & on this side so steep & slippery that it was difficult to scuffle up it. We were very tired & confidently expected to stop directly after getting over the river, but on we went without stopping.[298]

Fig. 109 Lieutenant McHenry Howard, circa July 1862. *Courtesy of Dave Mark Collection.*

Lieutenant McHenry Howard, aide (Johnson's Division): *It rained drearily and the march was a most tedious one. At daylight we reached the Potomac at Williamsport, a distance of only five miles. Forded the river, it being almost to the shoulders of the men—a picturesque but miserable scene....* [Howard also added:] *The river had been very high, but had fallen just enough for the deep fording. It was not easy crossing on my horse.*[299]

Fig. 110 Brigadier General John Brown Gordon. *LOC.*

Brigadier General John Brown Gordon (Early's Division): *The fording of the Potomac in the dim starlight of that 13th of July night, and early morning of the 14th, was a spectacular phase of war so quaint and impressive as to leave itself lastingly daguerreotyped on the memory. To the giants in the army the passage was comparatively easy, but the short-legged soldiers were a source of anxiety to the officers and of constant amusement to their long-legged comrades. With their knapsacks high up on their shoulders, their cartridge-boxes above the knapsacks, and their guns lifted still higher to keep them dry, these little heroes of the army battled with the current from shore to shore. Borne down below the line of march by the swiftly rolling water, slipping and sliding in the mud and slime, and stumbling over the boulders at the bottom, the marvel is that none were drowned.*[300]

Major W.W. Blackford, staff officer (Army of Northern Virginia Cavalry): *The ford was very wide and still almost past fording. I witnessed the passage of Ewell's corps and it was a strange and interesting sight. On either bank fires illuminated the scene, the water reached the armpits of the men and was very swift. By the bright lurid light the long line of heads and shoulders and the dim sparkling of their musket barrels could be traced across the watery space, dwindling away almost to a thread before it reached the further shore. The passage of the wagon trains was attended with some loss, for the current in some cases swept them down past the ford into deep water....In crossing even on horseback the cavalry got almost as wet as the infantry, and they were worse off afterwards, for they had to sit in wet saddles without the warming exercise which walking gives. Having been greatly exposed to the weather during the ten days of rain following the Battle of Gettysburg and then having to take this cold bath in the middle of the night, I felt the next morning very badly.*[301]

Perhaps Dr. Lafayette Guild, medical director of the Army of Northern Virginia, summed it up best when he said of the crossings that night:

> *The sufferings of the wounded were distressing. Indeed, the healthiest and most robust suffered extremely in crossing the river. The head of our column commenced its passage at dark on the 13th instant, and, in the afternoon of the 14th, the rear guard reached the south bank.*[302]

Fig. 111 Dr. Lafayette Guild. *From the* Encyclopedia Virginia.

In retrospect, Guild might have just as well been describing the suffering experienced by both armies throughout the entire Gettysburg Campaign. Whether the source of that suffering was the searing heat or torrents of rain, the Weather Gods had undeniably damned the Gettysburg Campaign.

10

CONCLUSIONS

A Weather Recipe for Disaster

We began our research for this book with the intention of providing the first-ever complete account of the weather during the entire Gettysburg Campaign. We started with volumes of previously overlooked data. This detailed data allowed for not only a more complete picture of the weather during this time frame but also an estimation of crucial quantities such as dewpoint and heat index. These variables had never been calculated for this purpose. We also endeavored to offer a fresh look at the story of the soldiers' experiences during the campaign as viewed through the lens of these newly defined meteorological circumstances. Our objective was to weave our new findings with the soldiers' firsthand accounts of suffering, frustration and perseverance. Then and only then could their collective courage, Yankee and Rebel alike, in the face of unfathomable weather-related suffering, truly be understood. In turn, our goal was to convey these stories in our "Situation Reports," "When Weather Mattered the Most" and "People, Stories and Matters to Remember" features. Interestingly, along the way, we uncovered details about the weather and its effects on the campaign and battle that we never expected to find. Moreover, these remarkable discoveries shed new light on overarching weather-related aspects of the campaign that, to our knowledge, no one has ever realized.

Regarding our methodology, our forensic analysis of the weather during June and July 1863 relied on four key tools. First, we used extant data from numerous government weather observers who were active during 1863. Second, we employed a recently developed NOAA reanalysis system that allowed for the reconstruction of weather conditions as far back as the mid-nineteenth century. Third, we applied over 1,500 firsthand accounts to the equation. Lastly, modern weather data for the area covered during the campaign, including the Potomac River basin, provided context to the historical observations. The application of this approach not only provided a thorough account of the weather during the Gettysburg Campaign but also unveiled the following:

> *The mid-June heatwave that haunted both armies represented a historically intense period of heat and humidity for the month of June in the mid-Atlantic region.* Our initial research revealed how much hotter this heatwave felt than historians previously understood, with the combination of heat and humidity resulting in an estimated maximum heat index just shy of 120 degrees F on June 17, itself a shade measurement. But the fact that this heatwave marked an extremely rare occurrence for the month of June in this region first came to light during our most recent research.
>
> *Heat-related circumstances during the battle, especially on July 2 and July 3, were much worse than previously understood.* Prior to our research, historians used Jacobs's 2:00 p.m. reading of 81 degrees F to represent the maximum temperature in Gettysburg and nearby areas on July 2. But the heat index in Gettysburg likely reached at least 90 degrees F that afternoon, and including sunshine in the calculation may push the "feels like" temperature to an estimated 105 degrees F. Also prior to our research, historians used Jacobs's afternoon reading of 87 degrees F on July 3 to represent that day's heat. But our findings suggest that the heat index that afternoon may have peaked in the 100–105 degrees F range during Pickett's Charge. Here again, direct sunlight may have added up to 15 degrees F, making it feel as hot as 120 degrees F to the soldiers of both armies who saw action during the charge. And soldiers lying on the ground would have felt even hotter.
>
> *The rise on the Potomac River at Williamsport, Maryland, that trapped the Confederate army for several days represented an extraordinary event for the month of July in any year for which records exist.* Prior to our research, the only estimate of the amount of rainfall that

> fell on the armies during the retreat phase of the campaign, largely taking place in the Cumberland Valley, stemmed from Professor Jacobs's records in Gettysburg. However, our analysis of modern crests on the Potomac River at Williamsport similar to the crest that trapped Lee's army in July 1863 also allowed for a reasonable estimate of how much rain fell in the period July 4–8, 1863, in the vicinity of Williamsport and the Potomac River basin. Additionally, photos obtained during a recent river crest in Williamsport demonstrate what the river may have looked like during those fateful days of 1863 when Lee's army remained trapped.

In considering these points, we recognize these highly unusual weather factors preyed upon both armies. *Moreover, regarding the weather, we believe our analysis demonstrates the cruel irony that the Gettysburg Campaign occurred during one of the most ill-fated, weather-related time frames possible.* And while the men of both armies suffered similarly due to the extreme heat, the Confederate army shouldered the burden of Mother Nature's closing wrath.

In the final analysis, we trust that historians, those with a meteorological bent, as well as anyone interested in history at large, stand to benefit greatly from this analysis of the weather during this momentous time in United States history. And in the end, we trust you now understand how *The Weather Gods Cursed the Gettysburg Campaign*.

AFTERWORD

Jon Nese and Jeffrey Harding have made a wonderful contribution to the scholarly literature about the Gettysburg Campaign. Hundreds have written about the campaign, the battles, tactics and implications for the outcome of the war. But this book has added an analysis of an underexplored factor, describing in greater depth than ever before the weather during the Gettysburg Campaign and its impact on the troops, the outcome of the battle and the Confederate southward retreat. Specifically, they combined temperature and humidity to compute the heat index during the Gettysburg Campaign, quantifying for the first time the muggy heat and severe discomfort the soldiers would have felt, such as in the 100–105 F range during Pickett's Charge on July 3, 1863—often with health risks.

Many of us have a fascination with the Civil War and the Battle of Gettysburg for a variety of reasons, not the least of which is its importance—generally considered to be the beginning of the end for the Confederate cause. Some of us, like myself, had relatives who fought in the Civil War or even at Gettysburg. Many of us have visited the Gettysburg Battlefield to obtain a firsthand feel for the terrain and topography. But Nese and Harding make us keenly aware of another factor—the sweltering heat and humidity.

I hike daily in hilly areas near Marietta, Georgia, where soldiers also fought during the Civil War. I've been thrilled at walking on such historic grounds but also amazed that weary infantry could take long marches in this type of terrain day after day, particularly in very high heat index conditions similar to that of the Gettysburg Campaign. My hikes are usually less than four miles, whereas theirs were sometimes up to thirty miles. And these men were carrying knapsacks and large, heavy muzzle-loader rifles. Some soldiers even lacked shoes. I cannot imagine marching under these hardships during the sweltering heat of the Gettysburg Campaign.

Can you imagine how awful the battle must have been? Fear of injury and death, sweltering heat, deafening noise, wails of wounded soldiers during any lulls between cannon fire and the smoke from all the cannons and gunfire. A letter written after the battle by one of my relatives, a member of the 11th Pennsylvania Volunteer Infantry, says the ground shook from all the cannonading. It must have seemed like Hell!

The heat of the last day of the battle was broken by thunderstorms with torrential rain. There were reports of Confederate soldiers drowning from flooding. Retreating Confederate troops had a long trek (nearly fifty miles) pulling wagons filled with wounded soldiers, slowed by mud from the storms. It's hard to imagine a more miserable journey, then blocked from crossing the swollen Potomac River. Nese and Harding's book has helped us understand the weather hardships encountered by the soldiers and should help us appreciate the sacrifices they made.

Gregory S. Forbes
Former Penn State Meteorology faculty member and
severe weather expert on The Weather Channel

APPENDIX

The temperatures and descriptions in the following chart are intended to broadly represent weather conditions across the areas occupied by the armies, not the weather at one specific point. The sky cover and weather descriptions are culled from the nearest official reports and soldier accounts. The temperature ranges are estimated from nearby official reports and are shade values. Being in sunlight for a prolonged period can potentially add up to 15 degrees F to these values.

	High Temp	**Low Temp**	**Max Heat Index**		
Date	**(deg F)**	**(deg F)**	**(deg F)**	**Sky Cover**	**Weather**
June 3	79–83	50–54	80–83	Mostly cloudy	Showers
June 4	76–81	52–56		Mostly sunny	Dry, cooler, comfortable

	High Temp	Low Temp	Max Heat Index		
Date	(deg F)	(deg F)	(deg F)	Sky Cover	Weather
June 5	80–84	56–60	80–84	Partly Cloudy	Warmer, late-day sprinkles
June 6	83–87	59–63	81–85	Partly to mostly cloudy	Late-day & nighttime rain & thunderstorms
June 7	74–78	51–55		Partly cloudy	Cooler, breezy, pleasant
June 8	70–74	46–50		Partly cloudy	Chilly morning, windy, comfortable
June 9	83–87	49–54	82–87	Sunny	Warm, more humid
June 10	87–91	51–56	88–93	Mostly sunny	Warmer, humid, dusty
June 11	79–84	59–65	82–86	Partly to mostly cloudy	Humid, isolated showers
June 12	82–88	62–68	86–92	Partly cloudy	Warm, windy, humid, dusty
June 13	82–87	56–61	85–91	Partly to mostly cloudy	Humid, evening and night rain
June 14	76–81	56–61		Partly cloudy	Warm, light winds

	High Temp	Low Temp	Max Heat Index		
Date	(deg F)	(deg F)	(deg F)	Sky Cover	Weather
June 15	92–98	55–60	95–100	Hazy sun	Hot, humid
June 16	90–95	66–70	92–96	Hazy sun	Hot, breezy, dusty
June 17	95–100	57–61	114–119	Hazy sun	Very hot, oppressive
June 18	93–99	65–68	104–109	Sunshine, then clouds	Very hot & humid, aftn. thunderstorms
June 19	80–85	63–67	84–89	Cloudy	Not as warm, humid, late-day heavy rain
June 20	69–73	55–60		Cloudy	Cool, scattered showers
June 21	76–80	58–63		Mostly cloudy	Scattered showers and thunderstorms
June 22	76–80	50–60		Mostly sunny	Cool morning, windy, low humidity
June 23	76–80	54–60		Mostly sunny	Breezy, low humidity

	High Temp	Low Temp	Max Heat Index		
Date	**(deg F)**	**(deg F)**	**(deg F)**	**Sky Cover**	**Weather**
June 24	75–79	52–57		Partly cloudy	Bit more humid, late-day showers
June 25	75–80	52–57		Increasing clouds	Rain late afternoon into night
June 26	68–73	58–63		Cloudy	Rain, some heavy
June 27	67–74	58–63		Cloudy	Isolated showers
June 28	73–78	58–63		Mostly cloudy	Isolated showers, more humid
June 29	75–80	61–65	82–87	Mostly cloudy	Scattered showers, humid
June 30	78–81	63–67	83–88	Clouds, some sun	Scattered showers, humid
July 1	77–80	68–71		Partly to mostly cloudy	Humid, scattered showers
July 2	82–84	69–73	85–90	Partly cloudy	Humid
July 3	88–90	68–72	97–105	Partly cloudy	Hot, humid, late-day thunderstorm

Date	High Temp (deg F)	Low Temp (deg F)	Max Heat Index (deg F)	Sky Cover	Weather
July 4	77–79	69–73		Cloudy	Humid, rain much of time
July 5	72–75	65–68		Cloudy	Rain at times
July 6	76–78	65–68		Cloudy	Rain at times
July 7	74–76	65–68		Mostly cloudy	Isolated showers
July 8	72–75	63–66		Cloudy	Rain, heavy at times
July 9	82–85	65–68	84–88	Mostly cloudy	Drying out
July 10	79–82	67–70	81–85	Partly cloudy	Humid
July 11	84–87	69–73	90–95	Partly cloudy	Humid
July 12	84–87	70–74	90–95	Mostly cloudy	Warm, late-day rain
July 13	72–75	64–68		Cloudy	Rain, heavy at times
July 14	80–83	63–67	84–87	Clouds, then sun	Overnight rain, then drying out

NOTES

Preface

1. David M. Ludlum, "The Weather at Gettysburg," *Weatherwise*, June 1960, 101–105, 130.
2. Thomas L. Elmore, "A Meteorological and Astronomical Chronology of the Gettysburg Campaign," *Gettysburg Magazine*, July 1995, 7–21.
3. Robert K. Krick, *Civil War Weather in Virginia* (The University of Alabama Press, 2007).
4. Kenneth W. Noe, *The Howling Storm: Weather, Climate, and the American Civil War* (Louisiana State Press, 2020).
5. Douglas Southall Freeman, "An Address," 10–11, https://archive.org/, text of a speech given before the Civil War Round Tables in Richmond, May 7, 1953; Krick, *Civil War Weather*, 1; Noe, *Howling Storm*, 5.
6. National Oceanic and Atmospheric Administration [hereafter NOAA] FORTS, Professor Jacobs's July 1863 report.
7. For overall background, see Jeffrey J. Harding and Jon Nese, "Pickett's Charge—'A Perfect Storm of Heat,'" *Gettysburg Magazine*, July 2022, 35–46.

Introduction

8. Goodreads, https://www.goodreads.com/author/quotes/6989.Rudyard_Kipling.

Chapter 1

9. NOAA Solar Calculator, https://gml.noaa.gov/grad/solcalc/.
10. Via Applied Climate Information System (ACIS) from NOAA/NRCC, a querying mechanism for weather and climate observation statistics, available online at https://xmacis.rcc-acis.org/.
11. See J. Chen and C. Chen, "Uncertainty Analysis in Humidity Measurements by the Psychrometer Method," *Sensors* 17, no. 2 (2017): 368.
12. R.G. Steadman, "The Assessment of Sultriness. Part I: A Temperature-Humidity Index Based on Human Physiology and Clothing Science," *Journal of Applied Meteorology* 18, no. 7 (1979): 861–73.
13. "What Is the Heat Index?" National Weather Service [hereafter NWS], https://www.weather.gov/ama/heatindex.
14. Lans P. Rothfusz, "The Heat Index 'Equation' (or, More Than You Ever Wanted to Know About Heat Index)," https://www.weather.gov/media/ffc/ta_htindx.PDF; "The Heat Index Equation," NWS, https://www.wpc.ncep.noaa.gov/html/heatindex_equation.shtml.
15. "Heat Cramps, Exhaustion, Stroke," NWS, https://www.weather.gov/safety/heat-illness; "Heat-Related Illnesses (Heat Cramps, Heat Exhaustion, Heat Stroke)," Johns Hopkins Medicine, https://www.hopkinsmedicine.org.
16. "Heat Index," NOAA, https://www.noaa.gov/jetstream/synoptic/heat-index. This estimate of sun versus shade temperature appears in many NWS publications, though without citation. The impact of direct sunshine on how the body feels is nuanced and depends on the angle of the sun above the horizon and the length of exposure, among other factors. The NWS estimate is likely a generalized, but useful, amalgam of research on the subject. For example, see Sofia Thorsson et al., "Mean Radiant Temperature—A Predictor of Heat Related Mortality," *Urban Climate* 10, part 2 (2014): 332–45, and Grahame M. Budd, "Wet-Bulb Globe Temperature (WBGT)—Its History and Its Limitations," *Journal of Science and Medicine in Sport* 11, no. 1 (2008): 20–32.
17. "Wet Bulb Globe Temperature," NWS, https://www.weather.gov/mpx/wbgt.
18. A review of several methods can be found in Bruno Lemke and Tord Kjellstrom, "Calculating Workplace WBGT from Meteorological Data: A Tool for Climate Change Assessment," *Industrial Health* 50, no. 4 (2012): 267–78.

19. "OSHA Outdoor WBGT Calculator," U.S. Department of Labor, https://www.osha.gov/heat-exposure/wbgt-calculator.
20. NOAA-CIRES-DOE 20th Century Reanalysis, https://psl.noaa.gov/data/gridded/data.20thC_ReanV3.html.

Chapter 2

21. James R. Fleming, *Meteorology in America, 1800–1870* (Johns Hopkins University Press, 1990), 55–93, 141–48.
22. Fleming, *Meteorology in America*, 55–93, 141–48.
23. "Pre-Weather Bureau Observation Networks," NOAA, https://www.ncei.noaa.gov/access.
24. "Military Forts and Voluntary Observers Database," MRCC, https://mrcc.purdue.edu/FORTS.
25. Ludlum, "Weather at Gettysburg," 101–5, 130. Ludlum made brief reference to the Naval Observatory data. To our knowledge, no other authors have used the data to analyze the weather during the campaign.
26. Gary K. Grice, "History of Weather Observing at the Naval Observatory, Washington, D.C., 1838–1913," NOAA, https://repository.library.noaa.gov/view/noaa/1219.
27. The Smithsonian form includes a column for "Dew Point," but the number there is not the dewpoint. Instead, the "Pier" and "Dew Point" columns appear to contain another pressure measurement. We will compute the dewpoint from the temperature and wet-bulb temperature.
28. Grice, "History of Weather Observing."
29. Email correspondence with Dr. Ariane Middel, associate professor, director of SHaDE Lab, Arizona State University, June 27, 2024.
30. Horace Stuart Cummings, *Dartmouth College: Sketches of the Class of 1862* (G.E. Howard Press, 1909), 137–39; Janice Brown, "He Looked to the Stars: Andover New Hampshire's Premier Astronomer and Author, Prof. John Robie Eastman, A.M. Ph.D., Rear Admiral, USN (Ret.) (1836–1913)," *Cow Hampshire*, November 4, 2014, https://www.cowhampshireblog.com.
31. William B. Cogar, *Dictionary of Admirals of the U.S. Navy*, vol. 2, *1901–1918* (Naval Institute Press, 1989), 80.
32. NOAA FORTS database.
33. Cummings, *Dartmouth College*, 137–39; Cogar, *Dictionary of Admirals*, 80.
34. Cogar, *Dictionary of Admirals*, 80.

35. Cogar, *Dictionary of Admirals*, 80.
36. Cogar, *Dictionary of Admirals*, 80; Cummings, *Dartmouth College*.
37. "John Robie Eastman," Find a Grave, https://www.findagrave.com.

Chapter 3

38. Jedediah Hotchkiss, *Make Me a Map of the Valley: The Civil War Journal of Stonewall Jackson's Topographer*, ed. Archie P. McDonald (Southern Methodist University Press, 1973), 146–47.
39. Jeffrey D. McCausland and Tom Vossler, *Battle Tested! Leadership Lessons for 21st Century Leaders* (Post Hill Press, 2020), 157.
40. ACIS, https://xmacis.rcc-acis.org/; Keith L. Eggleston, *The xmACIS User's Guide* (Northeast Regional Climate Center, 2008), http://xmacis.nrcc.cornell.edu/static/xmACIS_Users_Guide.pdf
41. Richard E. Matthews, *The 149th Pennsylvania Volunteer Infantry Unit in the Civil War* (McFarland & Company, Inc., 1994), 67.
42. Dr. Charles Edward Lippitt Diary, Southern Historical Collection, Wilson Special Collections Library, The University of North Carolina at Chapel Hill, Collection #03109-z. Lippitt was a surgeon with the 57th Virginia Infantry.
43. "'It Does Appear as if Our Soldiers Were Made Altogether of Patriotism': The Civil War Diary of Mary Gray Caldwell, Part 1," ed. Russell P. Smith, *Fredericksburg History and Biography*, vol. 11 (2012): 31–92 [hereafter Caldwell Diary].
44. Samuel Pickens Diary, Gettysburg National Military Park [hereafter, GNMP], park library, file number V7-AL5; Bradley Gottfried, *Roads to Gettysburg: Lee's Invasion of the North, 1863* (White Mane Books, 2001), 9; Wilbur Fisk, *Anti-Rebel: The Civil War Letters of Wilbur Fisk*, ed. E. Rosenblatt (E. Rosenblatt, 1983), 99.
45. William P. Wilkin Diary, Appalachian State University, Special Collections Research Center, AC.454, 15; Marcus Buck Diary, "Belmont," Volume 2, Warren Heritage Society, Warren County, VA, Front Royal.
46. Calvin S. Heller Diary, GNMP, V6-PA, 153; Thomas Ware Diary, 1861–1863, Southern Historical Collection, Wilson Special Collections Library, The University of North Carolina Library at Chapel Hill, Collection #1796-z [hereafter Thomas Ware Diary].
47. *Baltimore Sun*, June 8, 1863 (weather column details June 6 weather).
48. Henry Herbert Harris Diary, GNMP, V7; Theodore Ayrault Dodge, *On Campaign with the Army of the Potomac, The Civil War Journal of Theodore Ayrault*

Dodge, ed. Stephen W. Sears (Cooper Square Press, 2001), 274; Robert A. Moore, *A Life for the Confederacy, As Recorded in the Pocket Diaries of Pvt. Robert A. Moore*, ed. James W. Silver (McCowat-Mercer Press, Inc., 1959), 149.

49. John Camden West, *A Texan in Search of a Fight: Being the Diary and Letters of a Private Soldier in Hood's Texas Brigade* (J.S. Hill & Co., 1901), 73.

50. Ira S. Pettit and J.P. Ray, *The Diary of a Dead Man, Letters and Diary of Private Ira S. Pettit* (Eastern National, 1999), 138–39.

51. Alanson A. Haines, *History of the Fifteenth Regiment New Jersey Volunteers* (Jenkins & Thomas, 1883), 69.

52. Caldwell Diary, 50.

53. John T. Mark Diary, courtesy Boardman Collection.

54. John Dooley, *John Dooley's Civil War, An Irish American's Journey in the First Virginia Infantry Regiment*, ed. Robert E Curran (University of Tennessee Press, 2012), 151.

55. Bell Irvin Wiley, *The Life of Johnny Reb, The Common Soldier of the Confederacy* (Louisiana State University Press, 1980), 108–11; Bell Irvin Wiley, *The Life of Billy Yank, The Common Soldier of the Union* (Louisiana State University Press, 1978), 21–22.

56. Don Troiani, *Don Troiani's Regiments and Uniforms of the Civil War* (Stackpole Books, 2002), 103, 106.

57. Troiani, *Don Troiani's Regiments*, 107. Troiani points out that no summer-weight trousers were issued, but the natural properties of the kersey allowed for a "certain degree of comfort, even in hot weather."

58. Email correspondence with Mike Kwolek, museum exhibition specialist, Gettysburg Foundation and Gettysburg National Military Park, November 13, 2023, and April 1, 2024; phone conversation with Tim Sheads, S&S Sutler of Gettysburg, April 25, 2024.

59. Kwolek, email, November 13, 2023.

60. Wiley, *Life of Billy Yank*, 59; email correspondence with Tracey McIntire, director of communications, National Museum of Civil War Medicine, February 23, 2024, and March 27, 2024.

61. Wiley, *Life of Johnny Reb*, 111; Mark M. Boatner III, *The Civil War Dictionary* (Vintage Books, 1991), 111. According to Wiley and Boatner, the brown tones sometimes stemmed from faded gray but were also created through a dying process using either walnut hulls or copperas solution. Per Kwolek, the gray jackets used logwood-dyed wool, which is not colorfast and would fade to the stereotypical "butternut" seen on surviving examples. Per the editors of *Echoes of Glory: Arms and Equipment of the Confederacy* (Time-Life Books, 1996), 114, "Although gray was the

regulation color of Confederate uniforms, manufacturers increasingly resorted to using a dye made of copperas and walnut hulls, which produced the color known as butternut. Identifying true butternut uniforms poses a problem since vegetable-dyed gray oxidizes over time and takes on a tan cast."

62. Troiani, *Don Troiani's Regiments*, 107.
63. The authors thank Mike Kwolek, Tracey McIntire, Tim Sheads and Joe Bordonaro for their contributions to this summary on uniforms. Joe offers a unique perspective in that he has participated in no less than five lengthy marches retracing various portions of the Union Army Sixth Corps' march from Fredericksburg to Gettysburg. Three of these covered 120 miles each, over seven days, and included an overnight march of approximately 30 miles from Manchester to Gettysburg.

Chapter 4

64. James A. Wright, *No More Gallant a Deed: A Civil War Memoir of the First Minnesota Volunteers*, ed. Steven J Keillor (Minnesota Historical Society Press, 2001), 274–75.
65. Randolph Abbott Shotwell, *The Papers of Randolph Abbott Shotwell*, 3 vols., ed. J.G. de Roulhac and Cameron Rebecca (North Carolina State Department of Archives and History, 1929), 1:478; Noe, *Howling Storm*, 280–81.
66. Edwin B. Coddington, *The Gettysburg Campaign, A Study in Command* (Charles Scribner's Sons, 1968), 75.
67. "Annual WPC Mean Absolute Errors," https://www.wpc.ncep.noaa.gov/images/hpcvrf/maemaxyr.gif.
68. As detailed in chapter 1, heat index is a derived quantity, so any estimate comes with some uncertainty. As such, any heat index value that we report should be considered the middle of a range of perhaps plus or minus two degrees Fahrenheit.
69. Norman Ball Diary, courtesy of the CN Historical Society and Robert F. O'Neill.
70. Henry Robinson Berkeley, *Four Years in the Confederate Artillery: The Diary of Private Henry Robinson Berkeley*, ed. William H Dunge (North Carolina Press, 1961), 46.
71. Edwin B. Houghton, *The Campaigns of the Seventeenth Maine* (Short & Loring, 1886), 72.

72. Henry M. Kieffer, *The Recollections of a Drummer-Boy, Late of the One Hundred and Fiftieth Regiment Pennsylvania Volunteers* (Ticknor and Company, 1889), 129; Gottfried, *Roads to Gettysburg*, 23; John W. Schildt, *Roads to Gettysburg* (McClain Printing Company, 2003), 20; Thomas Chamberlin, *History of the One Hundredth and Fiftieth Regiment Pennsylvania Volunteers* (J.B. Lippincott Company, 1895), 101. Some in the corps estimate a bit longer, upward of twenty-five miles.
73. Warren Handel Cudworth, *History of the First Regiment (Massachusetts Infantry), From the 25th of May, 1861, to the 25th of May, 1864; Including Brief References to the Operations of the Army of the Potomac* (Walker, Fuller & Co., 1866), 383–84.
74. Charles William Bardeen, *A Little Fifer's War Diary: With 17 Maps, 60 Portraits, and 246 Other Illustrations* (C.W. Bardeen, 1910), 204–5.
75. Hazel C. Wolf, ed., "Campaigning with the First Minnesota: A Civil War Diary," *Minnesota History* 25, nos. 1–4 (March–December 1944). This extract is from no. 4.
76. Pettit and Ray, *Diary of a Dead Man*, 146.
77. Thomas Ware Diary.
78. Laura Virginia Hale and Stanley S. Phillips, *History of the Forty-Ninth Virginia Infantry C.S.A. "Extra Billy Smith's Boys"* (S.S. Phillips and Assc., 1981), 69–70. Based on the unpublished memoirs of Captain Robert Daniel Funkhouser, "Warren Blues," Company D, 49th Virginia Infantry, CSA.
79. Kieffer, *Recollections*, 129.
80. John P. Nicholson, ed., *Pennsylvania at Gettysburg, Ceremonies at the Dedication of the Monuments Erected by the Commonwealth of Pennsylvania to Mark the Positions of the Pennsylvania Commands Engaged in the Battle*, vol. 1 (E.K. Meyers, state printer 1893), 182.
81. Jonathan Hager Memoirs, University of Virginia Library, MS9044, quote courtesy of historian Robert F. O'Neill.
82. On May 31, the Naval Observatory noted rain from 10:00 a.m. to 1:00 p.m., but no amount was entered. The *Georgetown Observer* noted "a fine shower at 1 P.M." but also gave no amount. Most likely, a "Trace" of rain fell, essentially too small to be measured.
83. Krick, *Civil War Weather*, 101.
84. Coddington, *Gettysburg Campaign*, 75.
85. A plethora of soldier quotes (Union and Confederate) from sundry primary source accounts (diaries, regimental histories, *OR* reports, etc.), as well as secondary sources quoting the same, attest the severe and dire weather-related circumstances surrounding these marches. Many of

these primary sources and corresponding references appear in this book. Secondary sources containing relevant quotes include Bradley Gottfried's *The Maps of Gettysburg: At Atlas of the Gettysburg Campaign, June 3–July 13, 1863* (Savas Beatie, 2010) and his *Roads to Gettysburg*, and the complete accounts of the campaign by the likes of Edwin B. Coddington, Stephen W. Sears, Noah A. Trudeau and Glenn Tucker as well as special focus works by Noe and Krick.

86. Per various soldier quotes and corresponding analysis of information presented in Gottfried's *Maps of Gettysburg* and *Roads to Gettysburg*, Coddington's *Gettysburg Campaign* and the Heiser maps (presented herein), distances covered by respective Union army corps between June 15–18 ranged from a minimum of an estimated twenty-three miles to a maximum of an estimated fifty-five miles. During the same period, variances between Confederate sources, who often moved separately by division rather than corps, ranged from an estimated low of twelve miles to a high of fifty-seven miles.

87. The highest heat index at Dulles was 118 degrees F on July 15, 1995, while the highest heat index in downtown Washington was 122 degrees F on July 16, 1980.

88. ACIS, https://xmacis.rcc-acis.org/. We note that earlier in the calendar, the periods May 18–23, 1911, and May 30–June 3, 1895 did feature consecutive days with a high of at least 93 degrees F.

89. Gottfried, *Roads to Gettysburg*, 73–78; Gottfried, *Maps of Gettysburg*, 14. The Second Corps marched twenty miles, the Third Corps marched fifteen miles and the Fifth Corps marched twelve miles before being forced to stop due to the heat. The Sixth Corps marched through the night of June 14 and until midday on June 15.

90. New York (State) Monuments Commission for the Battlefields of Gettysburg and Chattanooga, *Final Report on the Battlefield of Gettysburg*, vol. 2 (J.B. Lyon Co. Printers, 1900), 854.

91. West, *Texan in Search of a Fight*, 75 and 89. Note that later in this source West indicates a different number of men fell out (two hundred versus five hundred).

92. Wright, *No More Gallant a Deed*, 274–75.

93. Wright, *No More Gallant a Deed*, 275.

94. A.P. Smith, *History of the Seventy-Sixth Regiment New York Volunteers* (Truair, Smith and Miles, Printers, 1867), 227–28.

95. Robert G. Carter (Captain), "Reminiscences of the Campaign and Battle of Gettysburg," Maine MOLLUS, *War Papers* 2 (Broadfoot

Publishing Company, 1992), 152–53. One other prominent victim of the heat during this time frame was none other than the 20th Maine's commanding officer, Colonel Joshua Lawrence Chamberlain. See Thomas A. Desjardin, *Stand Firm Ye Boys From Maine* (Thomas Publications, 1995), 7 and 130.

96. Shotwell, *Papers of Randolph Abbott Shotwell*, 1:478–79; Noe, *Howling Storm*, 280–81.

97. General Alpheus Williams, *From the Cannon's Mouth*, ed. Milo M. Quaife (University of Nebraska Press, 1995), 214–15.

98. Dooley, *John Dooley's Civil War*, 151; Carol Reardon, *Nothing But Glory—Pickett's Division at Gettysburg* (Thomas Publications, 1993), 183.

99. Selden Connor Papers, John Hay Library, Brown University; Coddington, *Gettysburg Campaign*, 75.

100. Charles Goddard Letters, 1861–1864, Orrin F. Smith and Family Papers, Minnesota Historical Society, June 20 letter; Richard Moe, *The Last Full Measure* (Henry Holt and Company Inc., 1993), 248.

101. Charles Smart, *The Medical and Surgical History of the War of the Rebellion*, vol. 1, *Part III* (Government Printing Office, 1888), 853–60.

102. The exact number remains uncertain.

103. B.T. Arrington, *The Medal of Honor at Gettysburg* (Thomas Publications), 4–41; James Gindlesperger, *The Medal of Honor at Gettysburg* (The History Press, 2023), 35–176.

104. Charles Mattocks, *Unspoiled Heart, The Journal of Charles Mattocks of the 17th Maine*, ed. Philip N. Racine (The University of Tennessee Press, 1994), 38–39.

105. Charles H. Weygant, *History of the One Hundred and Twenty-Fourth Regiment, N.Y.S.V.* (Journal Printing House, 1877), 162.

106. National Archives, Medal of Honor Record [MoH] for Nathan M. Hallock (file number 481855); Roy Frampton, *Noble Pillars: Medal of Honor & Confederate Medal of Honor Recipients of the Gettysburg Campaign*, vol. 1, *The March into Pennsylvania & The First Day's Battle at Gettysburg* (Gettysburg Publishing, 2013), 21; Gindlesperger, *Medal of Honor*, 41.

107. MoH Hallock (file number 481855); Frampton, *Noble Pillars*, 22; Gindlesperger, *Medal of Honor*, 41. Frampton's sources include the testimony of Captain Lewis S. Wisner, 124th New York.

108. MoH Hallock (file number 481855). Per the National Archive Record, this letter, dated July 31, 1897, was signed by the Secretary of War General Russell A. Alger. Another letter informing Hallock that his MoH had been forwarded to him by registered mail was dated September 10, 1897.

Chapter 5

109. Frederick C. Winkler, *Letters of Frederick C. Winkler, 1862 to 1865* (Privately published, 1963), 63; Gottfried, *Roads to Gettysburg*, 132.
110. "The Battles of Aldie, Middleburg and Upperville, June 17–21, 1863," American Battlefield Trust, https://www.battlefields.org/learn/articles/battles-aldie-middleburg-and-upperville; Robert F. O'Neill, *Small but Important Riots—The Cavalry Battles of Aldie, Middleburg, and Upperville* (Potomac Books, 2023).
111. Several other Confederate cavalry brigades crossed the Potomac as early as June 17 and June 18, but they were not part of General Stuart's main force.
112. Asa W. Bartlett, *History of the Twelfth Regiment, New Hampshire Volunteers in the War of the Rebellion* (I.C. Evans, 1897), 115.
113. Samuel Pickens Diary, GNMP V7-AL5.
114. Nicholson, *Pennsylvania at Gettysburg*, 1:329.
115. William H. Crennell Diary, Lieutenant, Quartermaster, 140th NY Infantry, GNMP V6-NY140.
116. Thomas Ware Diary.
117. Spencer Glasgow Welch, *A Confederate Surgeon's Letters to His Wife* (Neale Publishing, 1911), 55–56; Gottfried, *Roads to Gettysburg*, 105n10.
118. William Crennell Diary.
119. Charles Lippitt Diary.
120. Shotwell, *Papers of Randolph Abbott Shotwell*, 482.
121. Dooley, *John Dooley's Civil War*, 152.
122. Charles Marshall, *An Aide-de-Camp of Lee—Charles Marshall*, chapter 10, "The Invasion of Pennsylvania," Lee Family Digital Archive, Stratford Hall.
123. David W. Aiken, letter to his wife dated June 22 (1863), South Caroliniana Library, University of South Carolina, Columbia, SC; *Gettysburg—Voices of the Civil War* (Time-Life Books, 1995), 22.
124. Desjardin, *Stand Firm*, 13; Hotchkiss, *Make Me a Map*, 154.
125. William Heyser Diary, The Kittochtinny Historical Society, Papers Read Before the Society 1971–1978, vol. 15, 76.
126. Dodge, *On Campaign*, 295; Stephen W. Sears, *Gettysburg* (Houghton Mifflin, 2003), 295.
127. Charles D. Page, *History of the Fourteenth Regiment, Connecticut Vol. Infantry* (Horton Printing, 1906), 133; William Brooke Rawle and the Regimental History Committee, *History of the Third Pennsylvania Cavalry* (Franklin Printing Company, 1905), 253; Marshall, *Aide-de-Camp*.

128. Gottfried, *Maps of Gettysburg*, 20–27; Gottfried, *Roads to Gettysburg*, 96–139; Heiser maps; Williams, *From The Cannon's Mouth*, 214–15.
129. Winkler, *Letters of Frederick C. Winkler*, 63; Gottfried, *Roads to Gettysburg*, 132.
130. Fisk, *Anti-Rebel*, 111.
131. Gottfried, *Maps of Gettysburg*, 28–39; Gottfried, *Roads to Gettysburg*, 140–210; Heiser maps.
132. Gottfried, *Maps of Gettysburg*, 20–27; Gottfried, *Roads to Gettysburg*, 96–139; Heiser maps.
133. Fletcher L. Elmore Jr., ed., *Diary of J.E. Whitehorne, 1st Sergt., Co. "F" 12th VA. Infantry A. P. Hills 3rd Corps A. N. VA.* (McDowell Publications, 1995), 19.
134. socratic-method.com.
135. Marcus Buck Diary, Warren Heritage Society, Warren County, Virginia.
136. "ISAT Project Uncovers Forgotten Vineyards," James Madison University, https://www.jmu.edu/news/cise/2015/03/03-09-15-belmont-vineyard-nash-story.shtml.

Chapter 6

137. Rufus R. Dawes, *Service with the Sixth Wisconsin Volunteers* (E.R. Alderman & Sons, 1890), 157.
138. Gottfried, *Maps of Gettysburg*, 20–27; Gottfried, *Roads to Gettysburg*, 96–139; Heiser maps.
139. The song was Jerry Reed's "East Bound and Down." Each corps was composed of infantry and an artillery brigade (the Army of the Potomac also had a separate artillery reserve and the army's cavalry had its own horse artillery). Mile estimates herein are derived from multiple sources, including but not limited to Schildt, *Roads to Gettysburg*; Gottfried, *Roads to Gettysburg*; Gottfried, *Maps of Gettysburg*; *The War of the Rebellion, A Compilation of the Official Records of the Union and Confederate Armies*, 128 vols. (Government Printing Office, 1880–1901), series 1, vol. 27, parts 1–3 (hereafter cited as *OR*, all references to series 1, vol. 27, unless otherwise noted); Heiser maps; and numerous firsthand soldier accounts contained in the unpublished "Quotes Document" assembled by authors to include over 1,500 accounts of soldiers' experiences on the march during the Gettysburg Campaign.
140. The Antietam Campaign in September 1862 was the first.

141. A third bridge spanned Goose Creek, which was located between both Potomac River bridges.
142. Reynolds oversaw this effort as the army's left-wing commander, in overall charge of the Eleventh and Third Corps as well as his own (First Corps). Interestingly, in early June, President Lincoln had offered Reynolds command of the entire army. Shrewd enough to know his actions in the field might be stymied by meddlesome superiors in the nation's capital, Reynolds declined the offer. Tragically for Reynolds, this seemingly wise decision ultimately placed him squarely in harm's way on July 1, 1863.
143. FORTS.
144. Cudworth, *History of the First Regiment*, 386.
145. Smith, *History of the Seventy-Sixth*, 228–29.
146. FORTS; Quynn's Hardware Store, Frederick, Maryland, weather observation records for June 1863, Maryland Room, Frederick County Library, Frederick, Maryland [hereafter Quynn's].
147. Lippitt Diary. Here he described the night of the twenty-fifth into the morning of the twenty-sixth.
148. FORTS; Lippitt Diary.
149. Wright, *No More Gallant a Deed*, 280–82.
150. Dooley, *John Dooley's Civil War*, 153.
151. FORTS; John Koogle Diary, Myersville, Maryland resident, Western Maryland Room, Hagerstown-Washington County Library.
152. Charles S. Wainwright, *A Diary of Battle: The Personal Journals of Colonel Charles S. Wainwright, 1861–1865*, ed. Allan Nevins (Harcourt, Brace & World, 1962), 225.
153. R.W. McKee Diary, GNMP, V6-PA139.
154. William H. Crennell Diary, GNMP V6-NY140.
155. Dawes, *Service with the Sixth*, 156–57.
156. Worthy of special note were those of Early's Division (Ewell's Corps), Pickett's Division and Law's Brigade (Longstreet's Corps).
157. Robert Underwood Johnson and Clarence Cough Buel, *Battles and Leaders of the Civil War*, vol. 3, *The Tide Shifts* (Castle Books, 1994), 242–43.
158. Gottfried, *Maps of Gettysburg*, 34.
159. Johnson and Buel, *Battles and Leaders*, 3:242–43.
160. Taking into account Antietam, or Sharpsburg, as a drawn contest.
161. FORTS.
162. Dawes, *Service with the Sixth*, 157.
163. Wright, *No More Gallant a Deed*, 283.
164. McKee Diary, GNMP, V6-PA139.

165. FORTS; Quynn's.
166. C. Tevis, *History of the Fighting Fourteenth, Published in Commemoration of the Fiftieth Anniversary of the Muster of the Regiment into the United States Service, May 23, 1861* (Brooklyn Eagle Press, 1911), 80.
167. New York (State) Monuments Commission for the Battlefields of Gettysburg and Chattanooga, *Final Report on the Battlefield of Gettysburg*, vol. 1 (J.B. Lyon Co. Printers, 1902), 418–19.
168. Nicholson, *Pennsylvania at Gettysburg*, 2:623.
169. Wright, *No More Gallant a Deed*, 283–84, 286. Accounts vary—Wright claimed thirty-three miles.
170. FORTS.
171. Nicholson, *Pennsylvania at Gettysburg*, 1:238. Remarks of Sergeant-Major A.P. Morrison, 38th Regiment Infantry (Ninth Reserves), September 11, 1889.
172. James L. Bowen, *History of the Thirty-Seventh Regiment, Mass. Volunteers, in the Civil War of 1861–1865* (Clark W. Bryan & Company, 1884), 170–71.
173. George W. Bicknell, *History of the Fifth Regiment Maine Volunteers* (H.L. Davis, 1871), 241.
174. Mattocks, *Unspoiled Heart*, 46.
175. Gottfried, *Maps of Gettysburg*, 38–39.
176. Samuel Toombs, *Reminiscences of the War, Comprising a Detailed Account of the Experiences of the Thirteenth Regiment New Jersey Volunteers in Camp, on the March, and in Battle* (Journal Office, 1876), 71; Schildt, *Roads to Gettysburg*, 419.
177. Chris Haugh, "Caution: Baers in the Cemetery!" *Stories in Stone*, May 8, 2021, http://www.mountolivethistory.com/stories-in-stone-blog/caution-baers-in-the-cemetery.
178. *Baltimore Sun*, June 14, 1866, 2, obituary, Professor Baer.
179. 1840, 1850 and 1860 U.S. Censuses.
180. *Meteorological Stations and Observers of the Smithsonian Institution in North America and Adjacent Islands, from the Year 1849 up to the Year 1869* (Smithsonian Institute, 1869).
181. FORTS; *Maryland Weather Service*, 3 vols. (Johns Hopkins Press, 1899–1910), 1:388. Per the Maryland Weather Book, Harriet served as the Frederick, Maryland observer during 1865–66. Extant FORTS records confirm she was the Frederick observer during December 1865 and January–September 1866.
182. *Baltimore Sun*, June 14, 1866, 2, obituary, Professor Baer.
183. *Catoctin Clarion*, September 2, 1871, 3, obituary, Harriet Baer.

Chapter 7

184. FORTS. Jacobs's succinct but poignant remark appears on the "Casual Phenomena" page of his two-page July 1863 Smithsonian weather observation report for Gettysburg, Pennsylvania.

185. Thomas A. Desjardin, *These Honored Dead, How the Story of Gettysburg Shaped American Memory* (Da Capo Press, 2003), 7.

186. The three observing sites are Capital City Airport, Harrisburg International Airport and a cooperative observation site known as Harrisburg 1 NE. Harrisburg is slightly warmer, likely due to urbanization, which would not have been an issue in 1863.

187. Gettysburg is about six hundred feet above sea level and Harrisburg about four hundred feet above sea level.

188. Jeffrey J. Harding and Jon Nese, "Pickett's Charge—'A Perfect Storm of Heat,'" *Gettysburg Magazine*, Issue 67, July 2022, 35–46, University of Nebraska Press, Lincoln, NE.

189. Ludlum, "Weather at Gettysburg," 103.

190. Harding and Nese, "Pickett's Charge," 40–43.

191. Harding and Nese, "Pickett's Charge," 40–43.

192. Harding and Nese, "Pickett's Charge," 40–43.

193. Weygant, *History of the One Hundred and Twenty-Fourth*, 171.

194. Dawes, *Service with the Sixth*, 178.

195. Dodge, *On Campaign*, 303.

196. Samuel Pickens Diary, GNMP V7-AL5; Brooks D. Simpson, ed., *The Civil War: The Third Year Told By Those Who Lived It* (Literary Classics of the United States, 2013), 308.

197. David Craft, *History of the One Hundred Forty-First Regiment Pennsylvania Volunteers* (Reporter Journal Printing Company, 1885), 115–17.

198. Robert McAllister, *The Civil War Letters of General Robert McAllister*, ed. James I. Robertson Jr. (Rutgers University Press, 1965), 332.

199. Nicholson, *Pennsylvania at Gettysburg*, 2:751.

200. George K. Collins, *Memories of the 149th Regt. N.Y. Vol. Infantry* (Published by the author, 1891), 284.

201. A.H. Souri, H. Wang, G.G. Abad, X. Liu and K. Chance, "Quantifying the Impact of Excess Moisture From Transpiration From Crops on an Extreme Heat Wave Event in the Midwestern U.S.: A Top-Down Constraint From Moderate Resolution Imaging Spectroradiometer Water Vapor Retrieval," *Journal of Geophysical Research Atmospheres* 125, no. 7 (2020).

202. *Histories of the Several Regiments and Battalions form North Carolina in the Great War 1861–65*, 5 vols., ed. Walter Clark (E.M. Uzzel, Printer and Binder, 1901), 2:136.
203. Colonel A.B. Johnson, "Union Army on Way to Gettysburg," Fact Sheet, 1963, copy of study provided by historian Robert F. O'Neill; Coddington, *Gettysburg Campaign*, 224; *OR*, series 1, vol. 27, part 3, 212–13; Thomas Elmore, "Wagon Trian of the Army of the Potomac—Length and Comparison," Civil War Talk, August 29, 2024, civilwartalk.com; J.C.M. Hamilton (captain, Company C, 110th Pennsylvania Infantry), "Marching to Battle," *National Tribune*, October 7, 1909, 2.
204. Wright, *No More Gallant a Deed*, 291.
205. McAllister, *Civil War Letters*, 332.
206. Michael Jacobs, *Notes on the Rebel Invasion of Maryland and Pennsylvania: And the Battle of Gettysburg, July 1st, 2d and 3d, 1863* (J.B. Lippincott & Co., 1864), 16.
207. Tevis, *History of the Fighting Fourteenth*, 90.
208. Hotchkiss, *Make Me a Map*, 157–58.
209. Shotwell, *Papers of Randolph Abbott Shotwell*, 1:498–99; Richard Rollins, *Pickett's Charge: Eyewitness Accounts* (Rank and File, 1994), 54. Pickett's Division also endured an arduous and lengthy march this day. Fortunately for those men, they would not see battle on July 2.
210. "The Army Goes Rolling Along," Library of Congress, https://www.loc.gov. First titled "The Caissons Go Rolling Along," this tune, with the lyrics somewhat modified, became the official song of the U.S. Army in 1956 under the new title "The Army Goes Rolling Along." See LOC post for more details.
211. Nicholson, *Pennsylvania at Gettysburg*, 1:506.
212. W.C. Ward, "Incidents and Personal Experiences on the Battlefield at Gettysburg," *Confederate Veteran* 8 (1900): 346; Jay Luvaas and Harold W. Nelson, eds., *The U.S. Army War College Guide to the Battle of Gettysburg* (South Mountain Press, 1987), 56–69.
213. John W. Busey and David G. Martin, *Regimental Strengths and Losses at Gettysburg* (Longstreet House, 1994), 16, 207, 239, 250.
214. Penrose G. Mark, *Red: White and Blue Badge* (The Aughinbaugh Press, 1911), 213.
215. *OR*, series 1, vol. 27, part 3, 469, 11:00 p.m. dispatch from Army Chief of Staff Daniel Butterfield to Sedgwick.
216. *OR*, series 1, vol. 27, part 1; Reports of Brigadier General Alfred T. A. Torbert, U. S. Army, Commanding First Brigade, 668; David A. Ward,

"'Sedgwick's Foot Cavalry': The March of the Sixth Corps to Gettysburg," *Gettysburg Magazine*, July 2000, 42–65.

217. The exact distance of the march remains a matter of debate. Primary and secondary sources vary. Twenty miles seems to be a fair estimate based on numerous sources reviewed by the authors.

218. George T. Stevens, *Three Years in the Sixth Corps* (D. Van Nostrand, 1870), 240.

219. Nicholson, *Pennsylvania at Gettysburg*, 1:377; 61st PA Inf. Monument dedication, addresses of Robert Orr and Sergeant A.T. Brewer.

220. Bowen, *History of the Thirty-Seventh*, 174; Gottfried, *Roads to Gettysburg*, 222; Gottfried, *Maps of Gettysburg*, 42.

221. The maximum temperature at the Naval Observatory on July 2 was 88.5, and the estimated maximum dewpoint at the time of the high temperature for the day was 75.5.

222. Harding and Nese, "Pickett's Charge," 35–46; FORTS, Gettysburg and Harrisburg, PA reports, July 1863.

223. NOAA, Heat Forecast Tools, Heat Index, https://www.weather.gov/safety/heat-index.

224. FORTS, Gettysburg, Pennsylvania, July 1863.

225. William C. Oates, *The War Between the Union and the Confederacy* (Neale Publishing, 1905), 211; Harry W. Pfanz, *Gettysburg, The Second Day* (University of North Carolina Press, 1987), 217.

226. Oates fainted during the retreat back up BRT. At least three of the five regimental commanders in Law's Brigade fainted during the actions of July 2, 1863, see Oates, *War Between the Union*, 220–21; Pfanz, *Gettysburg*, 236; R.T. Coles, *From Huntsville to Appomattox: RT Coles History of the 4th Alabama Volunteer Infantry, C.S.A., Army of Northern Virginia* (University of Tennessee Press, 1996), 103–4.

227. A complete discussion of these episodes of the battle is far beyond the scope of this work and is not its intent. Rather, the discussion of Sedgwick and Law serves as a prime example of when weather mattered the most on day two of the battle.

228. David L. Ladd and Audrey J. Ladd, eds., *The Bachelder Papers: Gettysburg in Their Own Words* [hereafter *Bachelder Papers*], 3 vols (Morningside House, 1994), 3:1,409.

229. James A. Hessler and Wayne E. Motts, *Pickett's Charge at Gettysburg, A Guide to the Most Famous Attack in American History* (Savas Beatie, 2015), 52–53. Per Hessler and Motts, this number excludes the division's artillery brigade (Dearing's). Hessler and Mott provide a thorough discussion of the numerical strength of Pickett's Brigade at Gettysburg.

230. The Confederate and Union cavalry also saw heavy action on July 3. This occurred as the Confederate horseman moved around the Union fishhook line of defense to disrupt the rear of Meade's army, attempting to position themselves to capitalize on any breakthrough in Meade's fishhook by Lee's army. Here the Union cavalry rose to the occasion and stymied Jeb Stuart's cavalry.

231. Save for our recently published articles, presentations, podcast interviews, etc. on this subject to include but not limited to Harding and Nese, "Pickett's Charge"; Jeffrey J. Harding, "Death by Dew Point," *Civil War Times*, Autumn 2022, 52–59.

232. Ludlum, "Weather at Gettysburg," 104.

233. Frank Aretas Haskell, *The Battle of Gettysburg* (Wisconsin History Commission Democrat Printing, 1908), 88; Rollins, *Pickett's Charge*, 76.

234. Dooley, *John Dooley's Civil War*, 157.

235. Thomas D. Houston, "Storming Cemetery Hill," *Philadelphia Times*, 1882, accessible via the Gettysburg Discussion Group, http://www.gdg.org; *Philadelphia Weekly Times*, October 21, 1882.

236. William Nathaniel Wood, *Reminiscences of Big I*, ed. Bell Irvin Wiley (McCowat-Mercer Press, 1956), 43–44; Rollins, *Pickett's Charge*, 180–82.

237. *Bachelder Papers*, 3:1,409.

238. *OR*, series 1, vol. 27, part 1, 393.

239. *Bachelder Papers*, 1:57.

240. Henry E. Jacobs, "How An Eye Witness Watched the Great Battle," *Baltimore American*, June 29, 1913. We note that since ancient times, speculation has abounded regarding a connection between large artillery battles and the rain that sometimes fell afterward. However, the processes that produce rain occur at a much higher altitude than the smoke and concussion produced by even the largest battle, so any connection lacks firm scientific footing. For more on the subject, see James R. Fleming, *Fixing the Sky: The Checkered History of Weather and Climate Control* (Columbia University Press, 2010), 61–64.

241. *Bachelder Papers*, 1:467, letter of Colonel William C. Oates, Abbeville, Alabama, March 29, 1876.

242. Ezra de Freest Simons, *A Regimental History: The One Hundred and Twenty-Fifth New York State Volunteers* (E.D. Simons, 1888), 145; Elmore, "Meteorological and Astronomical Chronology," 14.

243. W.A. Popkins, "Imboden's Brigade at Gettysburg," *Confederate Veteran* 22 (1914): 552; Kent Masterson Brown, *Retreat from Gettysburg: Lee, Logistics, & the Pennsylvania Campaign* (University of North Carolina Press, 2005), 150.

244. Jacob L. Carter Diary, Company C, 148th Pennsylvania Infantry, GNMP, V6-PA148.
245. Bartlett, *History of the Twelfth Regiment*, 135; There is also the possibility that some soldiers may have drowned because of the heavy rains that set in after the battle. This would have been due to the rise in creeks and streams either on or adjacent to the battlefield where wounded soldiers were closely located, most notably the Army of the Potomac's Second Corps hospital along Rock Creek. For more, see Roland R. Maust, *Grappling with Death* (Morningside, 2001), 879–94.
246. John Imboden, "Lee at Gettysburg," *The Galaxy* 11 (1871): 510.
247. Norval Baker, "Isaac Norval Baker Civil War Memoirs," VMI Archives Digital Collections, Diary of I. Norval Baker, Private in Company F, 18th Virginia Cavalry, 2, https://vmi.contentdm.oclc.org; Brown, *Retreat from Gettysburg*, 150.
248. Willard W. Glazier, *Three Years in the Federal Cavalry* (R.H. Ferguson & Co., 1872), 268; Brown, *Retreat from Gettysburg*, 132–33; National Archives VSR and CSR files, VS File—11010vs1885, courtesy historian Robert F. O'Neill. Glazier's service record provides somewhat ambiguous data regarding his rank at the time; he was either a sergeant or second lieutenant.
249. Brown, *Retreat from Gettysburg*, 168.
250. Ludlum, "Weather at Gettysburg," 105; Samuel G. Hefelbower, *The History of Gettysburg College, 1832–1932* (Gettysburg College, 1932), 109; biographical sketch of Professor Michael Jacobs, https://www.gettysburg.edu; Jeff Harding, "Dr. Michael Jacobs: Gettysburg's Weatherman," *The Gettysburg Experience*, July 2018, 45–54.
251. Ludlum, "Weather at Gettysburg," 130.
252. Gettysburg College Archives, Michael Jacobs Collection, Folder MS-107, Memoirs of H.E. Jacobs, 63.
253. Gettysburg College Archives, Michael Jacobs Collection, Folder MS-107; Abraham Lincoln papers, series 1, General Correspondence 1833–1916, Library of Congress, loc.gov, Michael Jacobs to Abraham Lincoln, Saturday, October 24, 1863.
254. Hefelbower, *History of Gettysburg College*, 135–37; E.S. Breidenbaugh, *The Pennsylvania College Book, 1832–1882* (Lutheran Publication Society, 1882), 160; Henry Eyster Jacobs, *Memoirs of Henry Eyster Jacobs, Notes on a Life of a Churchman*, vols. 1–3 (Church Management Service, Inc., 1974), 1:12–13.
255. Henry Jacobs, "How an Eyewitness Watched the Great Battle," *Baltimore American*, June 29, 1913.

256. Jacobs, *Memoirs*, 1:6–7; wayside sign, Michael Jacobs house, Gettysburg, PA; *Gettysburg Star and Sentinel*, October 31, 1859, 2; *Gettysburg Compiler*, August 20, 1860, 3. See also "Innovative Curiosity," Gettysburg College, https://www.gettysburg.edu.
257. Ludlum, "Weather at Gettysburg," 105; "Portrait of Michael Jacobs," Gettysburg College, https://www.gettysburg.edu.
258. Ludlum, "Weather at Gettysburg," 101; Ben Gelber, *The Pennsylvania Weather Book* (Rutgers University Press, 2002), 22–25; Jon Nese and Glenn Schwartz, *The Philadelphia Area Weather Book* (Temple University Press, 2002), 6–11.
259. Ludlum, "Weather at Gettysburg," 101; "Meteorological Observations Made for the Franklin Institute, 1839–1865," American Philosophical Society Library & Museum, https://as.amphilsoc.org/repositories/2/resources/485; Nese and Schwartz, *Philadelphia Area Weather Book*, 8–10; Jacobs, *Memoirs*, 1:12.
260. Ludlum, "Weather at Gettysburg," 101; Nese and Schwartz, *Philadelphia Area Weather Book*, 8; Gelber, *Pennsylvania Weather*, 23. The Pennsylvania legislature appropriated $4,000 (in 1837 dollars) to support The Franklin Institute's program.
261. Nese and Schwartz, *Philadelphia Area Weather Book*, 10.
262. "Joseph Henry: The Father of Weather Forecasting (And the First Smithsonian Secretary)," Smithsonian, ssec.si.edu.
263. FORTS report February 1865. Evidence seems to suggest that the Gettysburg weather observation station went unoccupied between March 1865 and July 1889; see United States Department of Commerce Substation History, Musselman Library Archives VFM-386.
264. M. Jacobs, *Notes on the Rebel Invasion*, 24–25; Jacobs, *Memoirs*, 1:56–57.
265. Nese and Schwartz, *Philadelphia Area Weather Book*, 8–9. Not all weather observers had proven reliable; some had been flat-out unreliable. And this was apparently under normal circumstances. All of this speaks volumes about Jacobs, who unfailingly kept up his duties as an observer, even rising to the occasion when circumstances were the most difficult.
266. Ludlum, "Weather at Gettysburg," 105. Note that Jacobs's son, Henry Eyster Jacobs, assisted his father in his weather observation duties.
267. *Biographical Encyclopedia of Dauphin County* (1896), 526–27; Gerald G. Eggert, *Harrisburg Industrializes: The Coming of Factories to an American Community* (Pennsylvania State University Press, 1993), 66–69; email from Historical Society of Dauphin County, November 8, 2019.
268. "Death of an Old Citizen," *Harrisburg Telegraph*, September 20, 1869.

Chapter 8

269. Johnson and Buel, *Battles and Leaders*, 3:429.
270. Heiser Map; Brown, *Retreat from Gettysburg*; "Gettysburg Campaign | July 4–14, 1863," American Battlefield Trust, https://www.battlefields.org.
271. John D. Imboden, "The Confederate Retreat from Gettysburg," in *Battles and Leaders*, 3:425; various sources indicate that at times at least two additional makeshift ferries or flats were also used.
272. Imboden, "Confederate Retreat from Gettysburg," in *Battles and Leaders*, 3:426–27.
273. FORTS.
274. Johnson and Buel, *Battles and Leaders*, 3:429.
275. Computed via https://xmacis.rcc-acis.org/, using two inches or more of rain in a day as a definition of "heavy rain" and the recent fifty-year period 1975–2024.
276. J.F.J. Caldwell, *The History of a Brigade of South Carolinians, Known First as "Gregg's" and Subsequently as "McGowan's Brigade"* (Continental Book Co., 1886), 104.
277. Toombs, *Reminiscences of the War*, 85–87; Schildt, *Roads to Gettysburg*, 48.
278. William Alexander Gordon Memoirs, Gordon Papers, Leyburn Library of Washington and Lee University, 144; GNMP, V7 ANV ENG.
279. Abner Hard, *History of the Eighth Cavalry Regiment, Illinois Volunteers, During the Great Rebellion* (Aurora, Illinois, 1868), 264; Thomas J. Ryan and Richard R. Schaus, *"Lee Is Trapped and Must Be Taken"* (Savas Beatie, 2019), 191.
280. The reasons for Hanshew's apparent lack of reporting after June remain uncertain. He may have filed reports that were never received by the Smithsonian. Or he may have been overwhelmed by circumstances surrounding the aftermath of the battle, given that Frederick shouldered a tremendous burden caring for the wounded. Regardless, the NOAA FORTS database contains no records from Hanshew beyond June 1863.
281. Interestingly, Jacob Bell was related, by marriage, to Professor Michael Jacobs, the Smithsonian observer for Gettysburg. Bell married Jacobs's sister Anna Maria Jacobs Bell. Find a Grave, https://www.findagrave.com/.
282. Searches of every conceivable location turned up no official observations. However, Heyser kept a diary with generalized comments on the weather. Evidence indicates Bell continued keeping records during the war. This, per a *Hagerstown Mail* newspaper article published on January 5, 1865, that

quoted his annual rainfall figures for 1863 (only a yearly total) and 1864 figures (by month). Nothing could be found pertaining to any records, official or unofficial, for Marvin.

Chapter 9

283. John Brown Gordon, *Reminiscences of the Civil War* (Charles Scribner's Sons, 1904), 172–73.
284. *OR*, series 1, vol. 27, part 2, 303. Report of R.E. Lee to General S. Cooper, Adjt. and Inspector General, C.S. Army, Richmond, VA., sent July 21, 1863, from HQ, Army of Northern VA, regarding the night of July 13 into the morning of July 14.
285. James Longstreet, *From Manassas to Appomattox* (1896), 429–30.
286. Email correspondence with Alaina MacFarlane, senior hydrologist, NWS, Mid-Atlantic River Forecast Office, State College, Pennsylvania, April 6, 2024.
287. Email correspondence with Alaina MacFarlane, July 11, 2024.
288. Email correspondence with Jeremy Geiger, senior service hydrologist, NWS, Baltimore/Washington, D.C., September 26, 2024.
289. Via Applied Climate Information System (ACIS) from NOAA/NRCC, available online at https://xmacis.rcc-acis.org/.
290. ACIS.
291. ACIS.
292. Email correspondence with Alaina MacFarlane, September 19, 2024.
293. We would like to express our sincere appreciation to historian Tim Snyder for alerting us to the April 2024 river rise and for placing us in touch with Tom Freeman, who graciously shared images he recorded of the river near its peak. Tim, Tom and historian Sandy Izer, of the Williamsport History Museum, were also kind enough to share post–river rise images.
294. Julius Lineback Diary, #04547, Southern Historical Collection, Wilson Special Collections Library, University of North Carolina at Chapel Hill. Quote included here from Lineback's post-1900 diary rewrite, see Figure 178 for original diary page and corresponding quote.
295. *OR*, series 1, vol. 27, part 2, 303.
296. Edward Porter Alexander, *Fighting for the Confederacy: The Personal Recollections of General Edward Porter Alexander*, ed. Gary W. Gallagher (University of North Carolina Press, 1989), 272.

297. Louis Leon, *Diary of a Tar Heel Confederate Soldier* (Stone Publishing, 1913), 40.
298. Samuel Pickens Diary, GNMP V7-AL5; Simpson, *Civil War*, 380–81; Brown, *Retreat from Gettysburg*, 330.
299. McHenry Howard, *Recollections of a Maryland Confederate Soldier* (Williams & Wilkins Company, 1914), 216–17.
300. Gordon, *Reminiscences of the Civil War*, 172–73; Schildt, *Roads to Gettysburg*, 103–4.
301. W.W. Blackford, *War Years with Jeb Stuart* (Charles Scribner's Sons, 1945), 234–35; Schildt, *Roads to Gettysburg*, 107.
302. *OR*, series 1, vol. 27, part 2, 327.

ABOUT THE AUTHORS

Author's collection.

Jon M. Nese, PhD, is a teaching professor in the Department of Meteorology and Atmospheric Science at Penn State, where he also oversees the undergraduate program. He teaches a variety of courses ranging from *Introduction to Weather Analysis* to *Weather Risk and Financial Markets*. He also leads the department's Weather and Climate Communications Group, which is responsible for *Weather World*, Penn State's long-running weekday weather magazine show. Prior to joining Penn State, Dr. Nese was chief meteorologist at the Franklin Institute in Philadelphia from 1998 to 2002 and an on-air storm analyst at The Weather Channel from 2002 to 2005. He is the coauthor of *The Philadelphia Area Weather Book*, which was awarded the 2005 Louis J. Battan Author's Award from the American Meteorological Society, and a college-level introductory textbook, *A World of Weather: Fundamentals of Meteorology*, now in its sixth edition.

Jeffrey J. Harding currently works as a Licensed Battlefield Guide at Gettysburg National Military Park, an independent historian and a leadership consultant. Previously, he served thirty-three years as an intelligence analyst and professional development specialist with the

Courtesy of FCCS and Doug Huber.

Office of Naval Intelligence. A recipient of the Department of the Navy's Meritorious Civilian Service Medal, Jeffrey was also inducted into the Nimitz Operational Intelligence Center Hall of Fame. He is the author of the highly acclaimed *Gettysburg's Lost Love Story: The Ill-Fated Romance of General John Reynolds and Kate Hewitt*, and numerous major publications have chronicled his historical sleuthing efforts. He has spoken at many notable events, including a ceremony honoring the sixty-eighth anniversary of the end of World War II held on the Battleship Missouri Memorial, Gettysburg College's Civil War Institute and the Gettysburg Foundation's Sacred Trust. He has also appeared on numerous television broadcasts and media podcasts.